Questions to
Think

ALSO AVAILABLE FROM BLOOMSBURY

Using Questions to Think

How to Develop Skills in Critical Understanding and Reasoning

Nathan Eric Dickman

BLOOMSBURY ACADEMIC

LONDON • NEW YORK • OXFORD • NEW DELHI • SYDNEY

BLOOMSBURY ACADEMIC
Bloomsbury Publishing Inc
50 Bedford Square, London, WC1B 3DP, UK
1385 Broadway, New York, NY 10018, USA
29 Earlsfort Terrace, Dublin 2, Ireland

BLOOMSBURY, BLOOMSBURY ACADEMIC and the Diana logo are
trademarks of Bloomsbury Publishing Plc

First published in Great Britain 2021

Cover design and illustration by Rebecca Heselton

A catalogue record for this book is available from the British Library.

Library of Congress Cataloging-in-Publication Data

Names: Dickman, Nathan Eric, author.
Title: Using questions to think : how to develop skills in critical
understanding and reasoning / Nathan Eric Dickman.
Description: London; New York: Bloomsbury Academic, 2021. | Includes
bibliographical references and index. |
Identifiers: LCCN 2020055573 (print) | LCCN 2020055574 (ebook) | ISBN
9781350177727 (hb) | ISBN 9781350177710 (pb) | ISBN 9781350177703
(ebook) | ISBN 9781350177697 (epdf)
Subjects: LCSH: Thought and thinking. | Critical thinking. | Reasoning. | Questioning.
Classification: LCC B105.T54 D53 2021 (print) | LCC B105.T54 (ebook) | DDC 160–dc23
LC record available at https://lccn.loc.gov/2020055573
LC ebook record available at https://lccn.loc.gov/2020055574

ISBN: HB: 978-1-3501-7772-7
PB: 978-1-3501-7771-0
ePDF: 978-1-3501-7769-7
eBook: 978-1-3501-7770-3

Typeset by Deanta Global Publishing Services, Chennai, India
Printed and bound by CPI Group (UK) Ltd, Croydon, CR0 4YY

To find out more about our authors and books visit www.bloomsbury.com and
sign up for our newsletters.

Contents

Part III Make Questions Explicit in Dialogue

Preface

For nearly twenty years, I have been engaged in philosophical dialogues. As an undergrad in philosophy club, with my fellow classmates during graduate school, and throughout my professional career with life-long friends and colleagues. Along with teaching, social justice activism, travel, family relationships, and more, these dialogues have ranked among the most fulfilling experiences of my life. In a way, it is through dialogue that I've come to appreciate and savor many of these other elements of my experience.

As a professional scholar working in philosophy and the academic study of religions, I have noticed a peculiarly dissatisfying pattern in theory and writing about basic reasoning and critical thinking. Every textbook feels essentially the same, however innovative they may be in design. Have you noticed the ever-intensifying cleverness of titles? Who would buy *How to be a Good Pain in the Ass*? Every popular article on employers wanting "critical thinking" from their undergraduate employees feels eerily vacuous. What seems to underlie all this is an instrumentalization of logic and reasoning. My wager is that an alternative approach is available, one that emphasizes questioning. I take my lead from the following by hermeneutic philosopher Hans-Georg Gadamer:

> In spite of its formal generality, [philosophical hermeneutics] is not legitimately classified within logic. In a certain sense like logic, it is universal, yet in a certain sense it surpasses logic even in its universality. Certainly every context of connections in an assertion can be looked at in terms of its logical structure—the rules of grammar, syntax, and finally the laws of consequential logic; all of these can be applied at every moment to connections in speaking and thought. The strict demands of a logic of assertions, however, are seldom adequate to the real context of lived speaking. Speech and conversation are not statements in the sense that they consist of logical judgments whose univocity and meaning is confirmable and repeatable; rather, they have their [side as an occasion]. Assertions occur in a communication process, and in this process the monologue of scientific speaking or demonstrating something scientifically constitutes only a special case. In normal language use, language fulfills its mission in dialogue; this conversation may also be the dialogue of the soul with itself, as Plato characterized thinking. Philosophical hermeneutics as a

> theory of understanding and of reaching an understanding is of the greatest possible generality and universality. It understands every statement not merely in its logical valence but as the answer to a question, and this means that whoever understands must understand what the question is, and since understanding must gain the meaning of an utterance from the history of its motivations, it must necessarily move beyond the logically graspable content of any statement. (Gadamer 2007, 63)

While Gadamer's point is that hermeneutics—the art and science of interpretation—is more universal than logic, I believe our uptake should be that it is essential to have reasoning and hermeneutics work together. As the logician Jakko Hintikka urges, the challenge of developing an explicit logic of questions is not met by the best known erotetic logics (the relations of question and answer), unless they have "reached a satisfactory analysis of the all-important notions of presuppositions and of question-answer relationship" (Hintikka 2000, 496). This is, he believes, one of the most important opportunities of cooperation between different philosophical traditions "and perhaps even synthesizing them" (Hintikka 2000, 496). What basic reasoning textbooks lack is making questioning explicit as they relate to definitions of proposition, premise, conclusion, validity, and more. Identifying a proposition is not the same as understanding the proposition, and understanding is related intrinsically to asking the question to which the proposition answers.

Years of teaching logic, reasoning, and critical thinking have led me to believe that the most effective pedagogy is to position students to ask questions rather than be trained merely to answer them. My book is an effort to put this in words in its excruciating detail. I wrote this text for college sophomores, with specific former students in mind, where I believe it works well as a secondary reading in a basic reasoning or rhetoric and composition course. At the same time, this text is for people looking to bridge divides in philosophy—such as between the analytic and continental traditions. Three of the chapters are based roughly on previous research articles and anthology chapters. The current basic reasoning industry shows a marked absence of hermeneutics, perhaps due to the latter's often inaccessible terminology or its localization in legal and biblical studies. I address this gap with my text: a solid grounding of thought, reason, and dialogue in a developed theory of the hermeneutic priority of questions. In doing so, my text sheds a much-needed critical new light on the basic reasoning industry and advances knowledge about critical thinking.

The topics in this book would not be as thought out without extensive dialogue in the Student Inquiry Group for Humanist Thought (SIGHT) at Young Harris College. During my time there, SIGHT held weekly hour-long free-floating dialogues, like a church for questioners where—instead of praying together—the members question together. As a SIGHT exec explained every week: this gathering is for dialogue; it is not a debate club. It was like a laboratory for the study of dialogue. How do conversations move? What happens when new visitors contribute as if it is a debate? I want to give a shout-out to all the student leaders over the years: Tad Foster, Ember Foster, Alyssa Lowery, Britney Bennett, D.J. Bohannon, Arin Satterfield, Taylor Davis, Zachary Champion, Thomas Johnson, Anderson Moss, Andie Weaver, Alejandro Lemus-Gomez, Courtney Huskins, Joseph DeFrank, Astheris Miller, Xavier Jacobs, Elizah Huff, Kate Greene, Ashley Sweeney, Lillie Morris, Guerin Brown, Kristen Brown, Trey Lapine, and Jacob Perry.

Acknowledgments

I would not have been able to write this book without the help and support of Christoffer Lammer-Heindel. Thank you for your friendship and all our philosophical dialogues.

Introduction

An Age of Answers

Where do people with questions go to gather with like-minded people? Are there masjids, temples, zendos, or churches for those who question? Can the question mark itself serve a community of questioners as their symbol of ultimate concern, like a yin-yang or crucifix works for other groups? For the time it takes to work through this book together, let's commit to be evangelists for questions. I hope this text might serve as a sort of foundational scripture for what we might irreverently—yet affectionately—call "the temple of questioning."

Maybe schools were supposed to be just these sorts of churches? Did you know that the English word "school" comes from the Greek word *skole*, which means "leisure" (see Bourdieu 2000, 13–18)? Consider it. At some point, enough people secured all the necessities of life, which resulted in the privilege of free time. They had shelter to protect themselves from the elements. They had enough food to store and distribute. They had relative peace between competing or warring communities. They reproduced enough children to carry on their genes. They were not subject to slavery by a foreign or domestic oppressor. (It should probably dawn on us here that we are talking mainly about men.) It's impossible to do literally nothing, right? These people would do *something* to preoccupy themselves in their free time. They made marks on a wall, and voilà, they invented art! They combined words from business contracts into new arrangements, and voilà, they invented poetry! They dissected an animal—not to prepare it for eating but just to see what parts it had—and voilà, they invented biology! That is, these people with the rare privilege of leisure and free time on their hands created what most colleges and universities call the liberal arts and sciences. The liberal arts are not about turning college students into political liberals. The liberal arts are, literally, the crafts of free people. I want to say more about this before we get back to questions and questioning, so stick with me here.

There are two big implications or results, among many others, due to thinking about the creation of schools this way. Didn't we just set up an unfair hierarchy between people, those with the privilege of free time and those without such privilege? Isn't this unfair? One goal of social justice calls for accessible education in tandem with good and just governance is the increased distribution of this privilege. Democratic calls for affordable access to education is an effort to stretch the domain of freedom farther, to help more people access it. Most people see education as a "good" that people should be able to have if they want it. This is not solely because a college (or even a high school) education will get you a higher-paying job, although this is normally the case. While few people say it, the deeper reason that education is good for you is because through it you become freer. If you know about history, you are less likely to repeat it. If you know how to question and argue, you are less likely to be pushed around by people trying to control you. If you know about nutrition, you are more likely to be healthy—which is necessary for doing things in our free time. You can probably come up with more examples. My point is that, ideally, schools should help reduce unfair distribution of privileges. I hope recognizing this unfairness inspires efforts to make it fairer for all.

The second important implication I want to discuss has to do with an analogy with agriculture. I grew up near cornfields in Iowa, and I helped corn seed companies that were trying to improve their crops. We would prune and often detassel cornstalks (remove their pollen-producing parts) to both help them grow and cross-pollinate different varieties of corn. That is, we cultivated the corn into ideals we had for it. The same thing happens when people prune bonsai trees or tend their garden—they cultivate the plants to help the plants reach their ideal states, sometimes for stronger harvests but other times for our aesthetic enjoyment of their beauty. Schools are "cultivating" students, too. Teaching and learning things is like pruning and watering to help students grow, to grow into a specific sort of human being: a free one. Many ancient Greeks used the word *eudaimonia* to name this ideal (see Aristotle 1999). The word used to be translated into English as "happiness." Today, though, many people assume happiness is a feeling, so we have started to translate it as "flourishing." Feelings are things that happen to you; you can be passive to them. Flourishing includes *doing something* in addition to feeling things while doing it. In other words, flourishing and happiness are not things you feel, but things you do. Flourishing names this maximal exercise of our capacities. Thus, schools, in the agricultural metaphor, grow students into flourishing human beings. Schools ideally help students develop skills, knowledge, and dispositions needed for flourishing. People can really only practice and obtain these skills and exercise their capacities in their free time. Practicing these make people cultured (see Gadamer 2013, 7–16).

In a way, then, schools were and are supposed to be the ultimate *recreation* activity. Pay attention to that word. It has two important parts: the prefix "re-" and the root word "-create." Through learning, students were to try on what it is like to be a different kind of person, to experiment with exercising their freedom and to receive feedback to help them maximize their freedom. We get the English word "essay" from the French *essai*, which just means "to try." In schools, as safe places for experimenting with our capacities for thinking, writing, acting, and more, we are constantly giving things a try. This is very different from how we use "recreational" today. Consider how some people talk about "recreational drug use," where people use drugs to escape their lives, escape their freedom, rather than live it more fully. Think of how many people will brag about getting wasted and "blacking out." It is as if the use of free time, when people finally get a break from work, is to escape even experiencing time. How can you experience time if you are unconscious?

I'm confident that if you are a student, you don't feel like school is what you do with your free, leisure time. Instead, homework just feels like labor, work from which you hope to have a break. Many students express themselves like many people in the labor force, those who we can describe as "living for the weekend." Many students I've met live for the weekend, too. Moreover, perhaps you've heard all the criticisms of standardized education, where the quality of schools and teachers is measured by student performance on standardized tests—maybe you've repeated these criticisms yourself in expressing your feelings about what seem like pointless courses and coursework. Students are treated like containers, and teachers need to fill those containers with information. Students memorize the information, perhaps cramming it in, to pass the tests. In fact, we know this results in many teachers "teaching to the test." Teachers use class time to prepare students to take the exam, perhaps by simply going over all the likely answers. Students memorize the answers, and then recall them for the test.

In addition to the criticism of schools as conforming to standardized tests, perhaps you have heard about different learning styles or advocacy for experiential learning, where students learn not by memorizing things in a classroom but by having real-world experiences. I have had both students and colleagues say they cannot learn through merely reading, but need experiences and applications of content to learn it. My impression of these sorts of statements is that these people are trying to avoid the homework! In a technical sense, reading a book and sitting in a classroom discussing it is literally an experience. But my objection is beside the point. The point is that many of us recognize there is some problem with standardized or institutionalized education whether in primary school or in higher education.

I want us to approach the problem this way: we live in an age of answers, to such an extent that we have neglected questioning. Questions are eclipsed by all the answers. Consider it. Students are evaluated on their ability to answer questions, not asking questions. In essays, students are supposed to have a thesis statement, not a thesis question. On exams, students are supposed to answer the questions for a grade, not ask questions for a grade. This is despite calls from educators that they want students to learn to question everything. That is, schools give lip service to valuing questions, but do not embody this value in practice. Even in the classroom, we know that teachers ask far more questions per class period than students do, and that the majority of these questions are either procedural ("What date is the essay due?") or checking student retention ("Who won the battle of Waterloo?") (see Dickman 2009). Such a system—to return to our agriculture metaphor—cultivates students into answerers, not questioners. Schools train students to be answerers, and if they do not have answers, then they often are graded as low performing. This is, again, as true of higher education as it is of primary school.

It is not merely academic institutions that suppress questions, though. A lot of social factors converge to suppress questions. Surely you have heard people talk about how a lot of religious institutions perceive questions as a sign of doubt, or—what's probably worse from their perspective—disloyalty to their community. It is not just religious communities that purport to have all the answers that matter. Political parties, popular science outlets, news media, advertisements, and more bombard us with claims to have this or that answer. The Industrial Age has given way to the Information Age. Technological advances such as smartphones have made getting the answers or information we need nearly immediate. What is the quickest way to get from here to Fayetteville, Arkansas? We can just ask Alexa or Siri, and they will provide us with route options as well as historical information about Fayetteville or links and websites some algorithm determines to be helpful.

If you don't already have the information you want, you can just use a search engine such as Google to find it. What is more, we seem to correlate authority with having all the answers. Imagine a leader—whether a corporate CEO or a prime minister or president—asking questions. And not just rhetorical or dismissive questions, but genuinely curious ones. Picture a press briefing with either the president's press secretary or the president themself asking the press corps questions rather than the other way around. Imagine the president asking the press, "What do you think we should do about impeachment?" Being awash in answers and information has come to be called "data rich, information poor" (DRIP), a phrase to point out that while institutions might collect a ton of data about itself, they often do not have a meaningful way to interpret that data to use it for their improvement. From the perspective I want us to take throughout this book, we should approach this phenomenon of being "data rich" as having a lot of answers to questions no one is actually asking or cares to ask. Without questions to which that data is useful, then it will not become relevant information. On a broader level, we are awash in information and answers because we have access to all sorts of answers to questions no one is asking.

I believe there is a deeper reason this happens, a vulnerability intrinsic to the structures and processes of thinking itself. I will discuss this phenomenon throughout the book as "the propositionalist ideology." Thought itself, in this perspective, occurs in propositions or complete thoughts, which are expressed in sentences of a particular language. We can distinguish a proposition from sentences by comparing the "same" thought as it is expressed in multiple languages. For example, the Spanish sentence "La nieve es blanca" and the German sentence "Der Schnee ist weiß" both express the proposition that is expressed in English as "The snow is white." The only point that I want to make for now is that this approach to how language works—that there are abstract propositions behind expressed sentences—also contributes to the eclipse of questioning. Consider what happens when we ask, "Who is asking whether the snow is white, and why would they even ask such a question?" My point is that while looking at language in an abstract or laboratory condition we seem to be able to isolate these things called "propositions," but language does not really occur in abstract conditions outside of conversations and interactions with others. We do not simply come across sentences just sitting in the middle of nowhere waiting for us to grasp the proposition they express. Sentences happen in a broader process of linguistic exchanges that include questions to which the sentences respond.

Instead of perpetuating and placating our contemporary culture of answerers and its implicit propositionalist ideology, I want us to promote and nurture a culture of questioning. As critical pedagogy theorist Paulo Freire puts it:

> Curiosity as restless questioning, as movement toward the revelation of something hidden, as a question verbalized or not, as search for clarity, as a moment of attention, suggestion, and vigilance, constitutes an integral part of the phenomenon of being alive. There could be no creativity without the curiosity that moves us and sets us patiently impatient before a world that we did not make, to add to it something of our own making. (Freire 2001, 37–8)

Yes, schools are not always successful at creating this sort of culture, even if it is one of their main ideals. I want this book to help school us in questioning, where we can achieve more refined detail about what questions are and how they work. My hope is that by practicing more technical skills and precision in questioning, where—through such cultivation—we become freer questioners, we are able to flourish in even more freedom of thought than we have had the privilege of so far.

We would perceive it as absurd if politicians running for office were asked a question, and they answered, "That is a good question. I don't know. Let's dwell with the question for a bit." Every leader—perhaps to be perceived as a leader—is *supposed* to have answers, indeed, have *all* the answers. Instead of a leader, imagine if Google pondered questions with you! If you were to type in a question, and instead of leading you to resources to answer your question, Google responds with saying "That's a good question!" and tried to dwell with you with your question. Instead of Google, imagine a monk or imam delivering a speech in which they pose open-ended questions, without indicating ways their sacred sutras or hadiths might be resources for answering those questions. Furthermore, imagine if teachers only asked students questions to which the teachers themselves did not know the answer. Perhaps we are fortunate to have search engines, information resources, teachers, priests, and even some informed leaders. Some of our questions and needs are so pressing that dwelling with the questions would not only be silly, it may even be life-threatening.

I am concerned here with thinking, not answering, though. What is it to think? Has our "information age" saturated us so much with answers that our capacity to think has been inhibited? Information and knowledge are so easily accessible, and so easily manipulable, that we have shifted into a disinformation age or a post-truth age of alternative facts. For me, a resultant problem is not merely the rise both of anti-intellectualism and of nationalist protectionism despite global connectivity. My problem is that our situation of being awash in information has piled on answers to questions no one is even asking. Our needs are created artificially so that we buy surplus supplies. Answers are accessible everywhere, and so their questions seem artificial. We live in a technocratic society where means and ends are coordinated instrumentally.

The approach I develop opens space for resisting a technocratic approach to thought, reason, and dialogue. Questions and answers are reduced often to a rote technology reproducible in approximations of AI. Consider the "20Q" phenomenon, where game consoles are characterized as ambassadors for the online version—whose founder claims this 20Q is a living AI, who learns and responds and adapts (see Dickman 2009). This model of "questioning" structures the mainstream liberal approach to dialogue, too. The technocratic paradigm is one in which there are allegedly technical solutions to every problem. The answers are out there, we just need to get the smartest people in a room and figure them out. We can find them if we just ask the "right" questions. The goal is to do away with questions, as if questions are really just problems to be solved. As hermeneutic philosopher Hans-Georg Gadamer writes, "Problems are not real questions that arise of themselves. . . . It is interesting that in the nineteenth century . . . the concept of the [problem] acquires a universal validity—a sign of the fact that an immediate relation to the questions of philosophy no longer exists" (Gadamer 2013, 385). In prioritizing questions and hermeneutics in this book, and through our interrogation of the prevailing opposite trend—namely, the reduction and elimination of authentic questions—I seek to perform an *apocalypsis* of sorts. I seek to reveal the conditions for the possibility of authentic openness, of indeterminate, creative responsiveness to topics, the world, other people, and other perspectives.

Overview of the Book

I work through these themes in three parts, where I scaffold thinking, reasoning, and dialogue. I place these three domains of cognitive activity into a system of raised frameworks, where the former supports and informs that latter, but also where the latter place the former in a better light. In each domain, I provide a preliminary sketch of our cognitive capacity and then develop ways in which questions are operative in it. The sketch remains incomplete until we clarify how questions work within the cognitive activity, and each activity remains incomplete until we ascend to the next level of the scaffold. In my sketch of thinking, I stipulate that thinking is the process of combining and separating subjects and predicates into complete thoughts. In my sketch of reasoning, I then stipulate that reasoning is the process of combining and separating multiple complete thoughts, as premises and conclusions, into arguments. In my sketch of dialogue, I also stipulate that dialogue is the process of combining and separating multiple arguments, as theses and antitheses, into ever-unfolding expansions of horizons. In each domain of activity, they move and are possible only via questions.

By defining thinking first, we provide primitive terms or building blocks from which I construct both a theory of reason and a theory of dialogue. However, only once we grasp this theory of dialogue do we really understand both thinking and reasoning. That is, later chapters shed new light on what came before, in such a way that a reader might engage this book in alternative sequences than how the chapters are laid out in the table of contents. For example, maybe you want to start with the brief descriptions of thinking, reasoning, and dialogue, and so will read Chapters 1, 4, and 6 first. And then you can turn to look at questions in each domain with Chapters 2, 5, and 7. Or maybe you want to start from the end with Chapter 9 and work your way back to the beginning to Chapter 1. I want to provide a map for my book here in the introduction so that wherever you start or wherever you find yourself, you can know what other directions you can go. I will develop this map according to the order provided in the table of contents. Let me briefly summarize the chapters of the book.

Part I focuses on the topic of thinking with questions. We should use questions to think. Perhaps this is a trivial cliché in today's world that purports to care about critical thinking, but I do not believe this has been sufficiently developed to speak well to today's world. In Chapter 1, I define thinking through breaking down complete thoughts into subjects and predicates. Subjects identify particular things; predicates put those things into an intelligible context. In Chapter 2, I explain how questions relate to complete thoughts, providing in particular a phenomenology of what it is like to ask a genuine question rather than express a command or an imperative. In Chapter 3, I develop a logic of the relations between questions and answers, pointing out numerous ways that questions pull complete thoughts apart while simultaneously suggesting ways subjects and predicates can be combined.

In Part II of the book, I focus on the topic of reasoning with questions. We *should* use questions to reason. In Chapter 4, I stipulate that reasoning happens in arguments, and arguments consist of *relevantly* related complete thoughts. On the one hand, premises are supportive complete thoughts. On the other hand, conclusions are supported complete thoughts. In Chapter 5, I clarify that relevance in reasoning is logical inference, and distinguish between validity and strength. I explain how rules of inference set thinking free and provide a phenomenology of what it is like to reason with questions. In Chapter 6, I develop a rationality of questioning's reciprocity with reasoning, pointing out numerous ways that questions pull arguments apart while simultaneously suggesting ways premises and conclusions can be combined.

In Part III of the book, I focus on the topic of dialogue with questions. We should use questions to have dialogues. In Chapter 7, I distinguish dialogue from mere pleasant conversations, where dialectics names the relevant interaction of multiple arguments in dialogue. Despite their limitations for explaining dialectics, I employ the use of theses, antitheses, and syntheses as defining moments of dialectical dialogue, where they initiate, move, and conclude dialogues. In Chapter 8, I clarify that questioning is a way we listen to others, both isolating the fact that we share questions to transfer complete thoughts to one another and providing a phenomenology of what it is like to experience a fusion of horizons or reaching an understanding with others through questions. In Chapter 9, I develop the culmination of all this work on questioning in thinking, reasoning, and dialogue—that it concerns our very subjection as people with the capability of response. Questions constitute us as responsible, and so are a fundamental embodiment of human freedom. I point out numerous ways that questions pull dialogues apart while simultaneously suggesting ways theses and antitheses can be combined or ways "self" and "other" can reach understanding.

By way of my Conclusion, I meditate on the joy of questioning, a joy that comes with flourishing as questioners. Let us turn to look at thinking, and ways questions work to stimulate thinking.

Part I

Make Questions Explicit for Thinking

Part I: Make Questions Explicit for Thinking

Let's work through two topics in this first part: thinking and questioning. What even *is* thinking? How might questioning relate to thinking? You have probably considered questions like these before. Many people have given me advice like, "Don't overthink it." Is "overthinking" possible? Other people have told me to "think before you speak." Is it possible to speak without thinking, or think without speaking—at least in an inner voice (see Dolcos and Albarracin 2014, and Alderson-Day and Fernyhough 2015)? I heard someone say recently, "I finally relaxed and stopped thinking." In whose interest is it to get us to believe that relaxing involves putting a pause on thought?

Our primary topics for Part I are no small task to explain, of course. Yet we do not have to start from scratch because numerous writers, researchers, and—if I may—*thinkers* have already formulated theories of thinking. Consider the following philosophers from across global history. The ancient Greek philosopher, Aristotle, developed thinking as identifying what particular substances are included in distinctive categories, categories that highlight what is shared across multiple particular things. The medieval Buddhist philosophers, Dignaga and Dharmakirti, alternatively, developed thinking as the exclusion of all other phenomena from that which someone is attempting to indicate with a name or concept. The European enlightenment philosopher, Immanuel Kant, developed thinking as the combination or synthesis of possible particular sensations with general concepts and categories. The late continental feminist philosopher, Pamela Sue Anderson, developed thinking as, in part, a process of conceptually explaining and interpreting metaphorical and mythic images.

There are many more theories of thinking, from many more angles than just philosophy. We can, for example, identify differences between the ways neuroscientists and meditation specialists approach and define thinking. For neuroscientists, thinking is an electrochemical process of synaptic networks. Buddhist meditation specialists, however, approach thinking as one among our many temptations to cling to things, where we increase our own suffering by not being able to let go of them.

Let us take the time to dwell with thinking and what calls for it. In this part, I will look closely at fundamental elements of complete thoughts: subjects and predicates. I will then turn to examine ways questioning facilitates the separation and combination of subjects and predicates in complete thoughts, emphasizing in particular what it feels like to question. I will also formulate a schema for at least four orientations of questioning in relation to complete thoughts. I will close this part by reflecting on what happens to "thinking" when we repress or forget its intrinsic interplay with questioning.

1

Thinking Only Happens in Complete Thoughts

Because words often are used in many ways, it is helpful to stipulate a definition to focus our attention on a shared topic. The approach to thinking I want us to take throughout this book will be based on what a "complete thought" consists of. Let's reflect back all the way to our grammar textbooks in elementary schools. You might recall that a complete thought consists of both a subject and a predicate, or a noun and a verb. These are the fundamental particles of thinking. A sentential subject isolates that about which we have something to say; a predicate is what we say about that subject. The famous *Schoolhouse Rock* song puts it this way: "Mr. Morton is the subject of our sentence, and what the predicate says, he does." Inasmuch as complete thoughts are combinations of subjects and predicates, then—on this elementary level—thinking is the activity of combining (or separating, as the case may be) subjects and predicates. Let's break this down in more detail.

In this chapter, I will examine both subjects and predicates, and then turn my attention to the processes of combining and separating subjects and predicates. I will end the chapter with some discussion of the agency of thinking (i.e., the thinker), as well as what we can mean by "critical" thinking in this framework. Upon completing this preliminary discussion of thinking itself, we will be positioned well to turn our attention to relations between thinking and questioning.

Sentential Subjects Pick Out Particular Things

What is a sentential subject? Examples of subjects are things like proper names, pronouns, definite descriptions, indexicals, and more. On the whole, subjects pick some singular thing out as the topic about which one has something to say. They answer the question, "What is being talked about?" I visualize it this way: in the midst of fluctuating sensations, we lift up some sliver of experience to do something with it. Because we have particular experiences that stand out to us, we have something to say about them. This is something we're all familiar with: sometimes an experience strikes us in such a way that "it" stands out from a background, or what we can call a horizon of experience. Once it stands out, it is available to us as something about which we can speak. We objectify—or make into an object—this element of our experience, so that we can use a name or pronoun to point to it and speak about it.

This process takes on a special, and negative, significance when it is applied inappropriately to persons—that is, when a person is "objectified." Our propensity to do this to other people is unfortunately very common, even though most of us know it should not happen. It is wrong to objectify people into mere things, because people are not things or tools to use and discard. Nevertheless, to be able to speak about people, we must "subjectify" them in this sense of isolating a topic—not just as agents of their actions, but also as sentential subjects standing out from broader horizons of our experience. Because of our tendency to objectify others, though, we should be careful about our ways of subjectifying others, perhaps by being careful about what it really is to "subjectify" as such. We know, for instance, that when we talk about "love"—such as in the complete thought "Love is blind"—that love really is not a mere object or thing even though we have to treat it that way to talk about it. The process of treating something abstract like love as a concrete or specific object is called "reification." Reification happens all the time, and it is okay, unless we forget about it or we misrecognize we are doing it (see Bell 2009). When we forget or misrecognize we are doing it, we are likely to take our heuristic as if it were how things really are, we take our way of representing things as how things must be.

My approach to sentential subjects matters because it *inverts* some traditions of linguistic philosophy that lead into what has been called "the problem of reference" (see Nye 1998). The problem of reference comes up because we ordinarily believe there is a rigid division between, on the one hand, *lived experience* of reality or even some reality outside our minds, and, on the other hand, *thought about* our experience or *statements about* reality. In frameworks that assume this division, a worry emerges: How can we be sure our words—words that often appear to be mere arbitrary conventions or social constructs—cross that chasm between our minds and reality out there as such? We can diagnose such approaches to language as being centered on names and sentential subjects. Names seem to be used to refer to particular individuals. Are words just names, though, like nametags or Post-It note labels, placed on objects out there in the real world? Such approaches to language and reality start from an assumption that thought and language are merely in our minds or merely in our social conventions, and then move to ask (surely accompanied by a puzzled look!) about how we reach from here (inside the mind, or within our system of symbols) to things in themselves as they "truly" are independent of our distorted languages. One might ask, "Do our mental representations accurately correspond to things 'out there'?" For us here, though, it is not that we need to figure out how our thoughts and language correspond to reality. We are not assuming this representational model of language as the central feature for how language works. Instead, experiences, especially those worthy of the name, stand out and *compel* us to speak up about them.

Note that an interesting limitation to complete thoughts emerges in this development of sentential subjects. There are some things that can never really be subjects of sentences or topics. That is, even if we can place them in the subject position in a complete thought, it does not mean we are *actually* thinking that which we are saying. Even if we try to reify these things, as we do with abstract notions like love, we will be unsuccessful. Take, for example, the sentence: "Everything just increased by ten times its size." This seems to be a complete thought with a subject ("everything") and a predicate ("just increased by ten times its size"). However, can "everything" really work as a sentential subject? Recall that, by our definition, subjects pick out some *single* thing from the midst of everything else or our broader horizon of experience. So, since "everything" is not one single thing but the totality including all broader horizons, it cannot work as a sentential subject successfully. There needs to be a contrast between what is set off by the sentential subject for predication, a contrast between this and something else. However, a sentence with two subjects still can work: "Mandy and Xavier just increased by ten times their size." Unlike the names of particular individuals, the word "everything" has no contrast. This example sentence might strike us as a "deep thought," something we might see on a shower thoughts blog. It might even lead some philosophers into metaphysical investigations, where they attempt to clarify the nature of reality to solve how everything cannot indeed increase by ten times its size all of a sudden. For us, though, this apparently deep puzzle can be dissolved by pointing out the surface grammatical issue that "everything" cannot be a subject of a complete thought. Notice that *this* complete thought ("'everything' cannot be a sentential subject") is about sentential subjects, where we are saying something about a concept ("everything") and not saying something about some one thing out there or reality as a whole. We could surely come up with other examples similar to this. How about "nothing"? Could that work as a subject of a complete thought? Why not? What about "being itself"? What about "the universe"? Pointing out such a grammatical restriction for these sorts of terms does not mean we should never *try* to think about these things. In fact, trying to think about them has proven to be excellent exercises for improving thinking (see, for example, Nagarjuna 1995). We also might have other interests in using them to expose limitations of thought, or—as the ancient Buddhist philosopher, Nagarjuna, uses them—to facilitate someone's realization of nirvana.

Predicates Situate Sentential Subjects

Let's turn our attention to predicates now. What is a predicate? Predicates are what we say about a subject. Thought and language—we will return to ways these are related later—really get started with predication. Predicates are the distinctive trait of complete thoughts. We might think language starts with individual signs or labels like names. Individual signs are elements of language. While we find signs or single words with definitions in dictionaries, these lexical entries are only virtual or potential instances of language. It is in the predicative use of words, in predications we actually make about subjects in specific moments, that language gets traction between us in dialogue; it is in the predicative use of words that language has actuality. I want us to approach it all this way: there are no "words" in dictionaries, but merely abstract signs. Words transform—or decompose, really—into signs when they are placed in dictionaries. As hermeneutic philosopher Paul Ricoeur puts this:

> Are not words lying quietly in our dictionaries? Certainly not. There are not yet (or there are no longer) words in our dictionaries; there are only available signs delimited by other signs within the same system by the common code. These signs become words charged with expression and meaning when they come to fruition in a sentence, when they are used and take on a use value. Of course they come from, and after usage fall back into, the lexicon; but they have real meaning only in that passing instance of discourse we call a sentence. (Ricoeur 1998, 34–5)

Signs only transform into real or actual words through their usage in complete thoughts. This distinction between signs and words is pretty apparent when we try to learn other languages. As long as we have to take terms from the new language and translate them into our more familiar language, we are not yet to a point of using that new language's words *as words*. You may have heard some people say that you do not really have fluency in a new language until you have a complete dream in that language. When we have fluency, we are capable of predicating of subjects without term by term, or sign by sign, translation.

Predicates answer the question, "What is being said about the subject being talked about?" On a primal level, something strikes us so vibrantly that we just cannot help but have something to say about it. Whereas sentential subjects tempt us to picture the world as piles of discrete things or objects, predicates show us relations and processes. Put another way, predicates place subjects in a *predicament*. Subjects are predicable. Subjects are that of which one is able to predicate. Predicates are relevant predicaments of subjects as predicables (see Kant 2007, 106).

Consider this example: "Your keys are on the kitchen counter." Being on the kitchen counter is the predicament your keys are in. Of course, the fact that they are on the counter may not be the most relevant aspect of the situation. Perhaps what's missing from the complete thought is an emphasis on "kitchen," where your keys are still inside the house on the other side of the locked door. Sometimes thoughts dawn on us that show us we locked ourselves out of our house. Predicates situate subjects in an articulate and intelligible context. And insofar as they succeed at this, they also show us something about our own situation. I will return to this when I speak about the agency of thinking and subjectivity.

We need to be careful in defining predicates so that they do not come off as just bigger or more general names. We should not confuse predicates with subjects. Names indicate subjects, and to take predicates or even complete thoughts as just bigger names is to reduce the predicative function of thought to the identificatory function of names. To assume naming is the paradigm of all language, the essence of how language works, is "a leftover from sorcery, the residue of 'the magical theory of words'" (Ricoeur 2003, 89). This tendency is more prevalent than it may at first seem. Consider that predication is the Latin transcription of the Greek word for category. Predicates are categories, and categories are predicates. Reflect on how resistant people are to being placed in any category whatsoever. Some of us might even believe it is wrong to categorize people. The Christian ethicist Robert Spaemann has noted that persons are nonidentical with their predicates, or the categories in which they belong (see Spaemann 2007). Yet we also know that, in many cases, categories seem absolutely crucial, such as in zoology where living organisms are divided up and organized according to notions of genus and speciation, or such as in movie genres where we want to know what kind of movie we are about to watch. Many people I know love horror flicks, but do not want to be stuck at a rom-com. Such taxonomies treat concepts as more general names for more general or ideal things. This tempts us into what has come to be called "Platonism," where abstract or generic phrases are seen as referring to ideal entities that exist in some realm independent of our minds or independent of our social constructs. It is as if there is some dimension in which "love itself" exists as a thing, but in an ideal or virtual realm. Some people take love as it is represented in romantic comedies as what true love actually is. These "entities," though, are odd. Can we point at "human being" as such, apart from a particular one? Can we touch, taste, smell, hear, and/or see "treeness" as such, independent of a specific tree? Yet we have come to think about categories as just bigger or more generic names for specific—however abstract or ideal—things.

Instead of assimilating the notion of "predicate" to our contemporary use of terms like category or label, let us assimilate our contemporary use of category and label to a renewed understanding of predicate. Predication is not about merely labeling something or placing something in a class with other similar things. Fundamentally, predication is about showing and revealing relational networks about a subject by placing the subject in a relevant context. In this way, predicates *supersede* subjects (see Gadamer 2013, 482; and Dickman 2016). Predicates play an elucidatory function, raising subjects into an intelligible or meaningful order. For example, of the many directions we face and orientations we can take, one might stand out in a given moment. We might ask what direction we are facing. That is, this specific direction stands out as a sentential subject in preparation for predication. And, in one intelligible order, we might predicate of the direction that we are "facing North." Yet in a different order of meaning, we might predicate of the direction that we are "facing toward Mecca." The predicate "facing toward Mecca" reveals a relevant aspect of and context for the direction isolated as the topic.

A number of upward metaphors suggest themselves when we think about the nature of predication. Predications "lift" subjects into a "higher" order. Predications "raise" subjects into the "light" of complete thoughts. Thus, instead of picturing thought and language running parallel to the world, we can imagine thought and language running *perpendicular* to the world. This should strike us as counterintuitive, though. We have inherited a model of complete thoughts as pictures of the world, where facts in the world are captured in mental pictures (see Wittgenstein 1922). Our pictures purportedly run parallel to facts. We can diagnose this tendency as giving privilege to the subject side of complete thoughts, where complete thoughts are taken just as bigger sentential subjects, or just bigger names. When such labels correspond to facts, they run parallel to or correspond with the facts. On the one side, we have thought and language; on the other side, reality. Hence the problem of reference we discussed earlier.

With predication as we have developed it here, however, there is no redundant layer. We have also inherited—even if we're not always attentive to it—a model according to which thought and language *animate* the world, transforming what was chaos into intelligibility. Consider the creative divine word in *Bereshit* or *Genesis*. The divine being gives order to the world through discourse when the god says, "Let there be light." Thus instead, predicates lift subjects into fields of intelligibility. These fields of meaning are constituted by forms of life, communities of practice, narrative traditions, and more. Because of predication, we live in a *world* and do not merely survive in an *environment*. Through predication, we transform our environments into meaningful worlds (see Ricoeur 1976). Perhaps another example will help solidify this.

Siddhartha Gautama is the personal name of the purported historical Buddha. That is, "buddha" is not his name, but his title. Buddhahood is something speakers and writers say of or about Gautama. Around Gautama's lifetime, there was a community of people looking for an "awakened one" (the Sanskrit root "bodh" means "awake"). In a way they were asking, "Who will be my Buddha?" And in Gautama, they found their answer. Now, we can note here that not all people have a language or worldview with the predicate "buddha." It is only operative in those forms of life and communities of practice where awakening is a particularly relevant spiritual capacity. We can apply this similarly to the Prophet Muhammad for Muslims and to Jesus the Christ for Christians. Neither "prophet" nor "christ" are proper names. Instead, they are operators within fields of intelligibility local to specific communities and forms of life, and those communities lift particular subjects into those fields of meaning through their predicative practices. Not all communities of practice have a concept like "prophet" or "christ"; not all communities of practice who have those concepts apply them to Muhammad or Jesus, respectively (Dickman 2017). Because I am interested especially in how this theory of thinking applies in comparative study of religions, many of my examples and illustrations come from there. However, we can imagine other contexts and applications for this clarification in areas of life with which you might be more familiar. We can think of roles people play in sports, in choirs or symphonies, in businesses, and more. Let's predicate of the person with the number twenty-three printed on her jersey that she "is the forward." For those familiar with both soccer and basketball, we know that the word "forward" has applications in both games. Each game has its distinctive field of intelligibility, and so we need further context to make use of that title as an appropriate predicate for the player. Nevertheless, the word "forward" plays a distinctive role in specific forms of life, and when we predicate it of a player, we lift that subject into an elucidatory field of intelligibility.

We should now have some preliminary grasp on two fundamental particles of complete thoughts: subjects and predicates. Yet since thinking is the process of combining and separating subjects and predicates, let us look more closely at what it is to combine and separate these particles of thought.

The Copula Is More Than the Sum of its Parts

The word "copula" names the fundamental layer of unity or connection whereby predicates link with subjects. The copula usually consists of varying conjugations of the verb "to be." It is implicit in complete thoughts that do not directly use conjugations of "being." This is because being is implied in every act of thought. It is impossible, as I have suggested in our close study of "everything," to think nonbeing or nothing as a sentential subject. There is nothing to isolate with the word, to subjectify it for predication. Being, on the other hand, makes every thought possible or includes the possibility of every thought. "Being" is not a name for some mind-independent reality, though, as if it were a label running parallel to a reality. Presumably, minds and social constructs are just as much a part of being, and even the word "being" is in being (if the preposition "in" even works there! Are we "inside" some container called "being"?). Instead, for us here, in our effort to explain the combination of subjects and predicates into complete thoughts, "being" is that semantic or intelligible linking between subjects and predicates. Of course, intelligibility is real, and so "being" is still a fundamental dimension of reality—but in this counterintuitive way. For us, "being" captures that synthetic aspect holding a complete thought together. The relation between semantics and being is practically coextensive. When we try to combine a subject with a predicate that does not go with it, we can see there is no being there. Consider the forced combination, "A bachelor is a married man." It is false, in part, because they do not successfully combine into a being, a meaning.

What is the nature of combination of subject and predicate? The synthesis of a subject and a predicate produces a new entity, a new being: a complete thought. Complete thoughts belong to an entirely different species from the signs of which they are composed. Complete thoughts are not simply bigger signs or names. Thus, the combination is productive, in that the combination produces something new. The subject and predicate come together into one body, a complete thought. Predicates subsume or absorb subjects, and in so doing create complete thoughts. The word "copula" captures that generative aspect of the created combination. The archaic meaning of "copulation," as well as its recent sexual connotations, are not without some illuminating metaphorical value here. *Subjects and predicates copulate to give birth to complete thoughts or meanings.* Complete thoughts cannot be reduced to merely the sum of the elements of which they are composed. They are not just a pile of signs.

Moreover, there are no species greater than complete thoughts where their combination leads to the birth of completely new entities. Complete thoughts can be added together only through concatenation and interpolation, but cannot be synthesized with other complete thoughts

(Dickman 2014). Concatenation is the process of collecting complete thoughts into a series, such as an argument, or essay, or narrative. These are not syntheses of complete thoughts, but only interactive relations among them. We can compose stories and arguments with complete thoughts, and these compositions can be produced through conventions of genres. We can decompose complete thoughts into their constituent elements or signs. But complete thoughts are peculiar and distinctive. Indeed, they can be identified as the fundamental unit of language and thought. If predication is where thought and language really get traction, then complete thoughts are paradigmatic or even essential for our models of language. Signs and symbols are, insofar as they are only elements of sentences, derivable only from their proper mode of being in complete thoughts. We will return at times to this issue with signs and symbols throughout the rest of the book.

An Intersection of Language and Thought

I seem no longer to be able to avoid addressing relation(s) between thought and language. As you've probably noticed, I've used these words almost interchangeably up until now. The relation between language and thought is among the most mysterious topics. Can we think without language? If all languages are arbitrary, and if language is crucial for thought, then does that imply all thought is arbitrary? Yet language and thought cannot be identical completely because, as I pointed out earlier, we can say something and not be able to think it (e.g., "Everything just increased by ten times its size"). Language seems to extend further than complete thoughts in that we can combine words to invent new expressions, yet our understanding is limited to a smaller number of complete thoughts than the number of those new expressions. We seem to be able to construct sentences that seem, or are, nonsensical (that is, not thinkable). Nevertheless, with poetry and metaphor and creative inventiveness within discourse, we do seem to push the frontier of what is thinkable further and further. Metaphors bring to light new resemblances that previous classifications prevented us from seeing. They break old categorizations and, as Ricoeur says, "establish new logical frontiers on the ruins of their forerunners" (Ricoeur 2003, 233).

We need not solve this mystery about language and thought once and for all. However, what I would like to add as a crucial framework here is one consideration that ought to open a different avenue for addressing the relation(s) between thought and language. I want us to conceive of written, signed, and spoken sentences as our *perception* or *sensation* of complete thoughts. Written and signed sentences are things that we can see and touch, and are potentially complete thoughts we can understand. Sentences are complete thoughts as they are perceived by our senses. Spoken sentences, for instance, are complete thoughts that we can hear. Complete thoughts, alternatively, are sentences understood. I am sure many of us have had the experience of looking at a page of sentences, seeming to read the page yet only to get to the end of the page and wonder what it was we just read. We can see the sentences and even recognize the language as one of our own, and yet not understand what we see. What we understand when we both see and comprehend sentences are complete thoughts. Complete thoughts and sentences are two sides of the same coin. Sentences are complete thoughts in their dimension of sensibility; complete thoughts are sentences in their dimension of intelligibility. In those moments when we have *seen*, but not *understood*, we do not find ourselves in the presence of a complete thought but only in the presence of a sentence. I will return to this issue in Chapter 2.

I have not solved the problem of thought and language in any comprehensive way, of course. Yet this starting point allows us to say that thinking—at least thinking as we have developed it here—is intrinsically verbal. And, we can always say more than we understand. Complete thoughts require both nouns and verbs, subjects and predicates. Moreover, words—whether names and sentential subjects or predicates and categories—have their proper place in sentences, and are no longer really words when abstracted from complete thoughts into discrete signs. Again, there are no words in dictionaries, but signs. We can learn to manipulate and process signs without understanding their meanings. This is why we can distinguish semiotics—the study of signs—from semantics—the study of meanings. A further key in the avenue opened here for addressing the relation(s) between language and thought is that complete thoughts are not representational. That is, complete thoughts are not pictures of facts in worded form. Rather, predicates render intelligible those elements of experience set in relief by sentential subjects.

Orientations for Critical Thinking

Before turning to roles questioning can play in thinking, there are two further elements of thought that should be addressed in preliminary ways. Who or what is the agent of thinking? What is the "thinker"? Additionally, where or when does an individual thought take place? What are the conditions or contexts for thought, and are there structures that inhibit or even oppress it?

The word "subject" is ambiguous, which is why I have often clarified that I am talking about *sentential* subjects. Yet we also know about subjectivity, that aspect of ourselves that we indicate with the word "I." It is not just that we can picture things, but we can think about them, and combine and separate complete thoughts with reference to them. For the father of modern philosophy René Descartes, subjectivity is bound up with thinking. The "I" is, for Descartes, a thinking thing. Is thinking, though, something the I does, or something that happens to the I? On the one hand, it seems that we choose what to think about and how to think about it. On the other hand, it seems that we often come across phrases like such and such a thought "strikes me" a certain way or that such and such idea "occurred to me." These suggest thinking is not something we do, but something that happens to us. Some skilled Buddhist meditators call thinking the "monkey mind," where thinking jumps from thought to thought like a monkey swinging around in trees (see Suzuki 1995, 101). They do not encourage trying to control your thoughts from leaping around, but encourage stepping back and simply observing the thinking and the leaping from thought to thought. Who is it that does the stepping back? Who is it doing the leaping? Who ought we identify with more—the leaper or the watcher? Are these models really fitting for what seems to be going on in the so-called theaters of consciousness in our brains? These seem like particularly pressing questions in an era concerned about freethinking and freedom of speech. If there is no agent of thinking, then who is it that is even free?

Rather than attempt to address these questions, I want to de-emphasize this typical worry about being original, about being the originating cause of particular thoughts. Instead, I want to emphasize that we take responsibility for thinking—the processes of combining and separating subjects and predicates—*as if* it was our own even if we are not the originator of thoughts. My concern here is less with making sure we think our own thoughts and more with making sure we are careful with the thoughts we do think regardless of whether we are their originators or not. This resistance to positioning the thinker as the generator of complete thoughts will become even more significant once we move into analyzing questions in relation(s) to complete thoughts.

A challenge going on here in the background is to the conceit of the "ego" or the I as self-sufficient (Ricoeur 1975, 95). The individual ego seems to try to establish itself as an ultimate origin. Our egos, though, are actually transcendent to consciousness when you think about it (see Sartre 1960). The ego is a reification or objectification of ourselves when we try to think about ourselves in reflection. It is as if we cannot help but force whatever we think about into the box of sentential subjects. To talk about "love" is to make "love" the subject of a sentence. If we are not careful, we will likely take love to be a thing, even though we know it is not. The same applies to ourselves. Subjectivity is literally not an object or a thing, and thus is systematically elusive to consciousness. This is because consciousness is always conscious of some specific thing. We construct a model of ourselves, or an ideal person as that of which we are conscious when we are *self*-conscious. Consider how self-conscious people are embarrassed to give a speech. It is, in part, because they have constructed a peculiar model of themselves as "bad public speakers." Are we doing something similar in constructing a peculiar model of ourselves as "thinking things"? It seems that "thinking," in the very moment when we are thinking something, cannot work as either a subject or a predicate of complete thoughts!

We often identify with our ego, and thereby believe that thinking belongs to us—belongs to us in the sense of belonging to our egos. Complete thoughts do not belong to us as egos, though; we belong to them. Before we construct a model of ourselves as an ego through reflective introspection and self-examination, we participate in the world in our families, societies, and states. As Gadamer writes, "The focus on [egos] is a distorting mirror. The self-awareness of the individual is only a flickering in the closed circuits of historical life" (Gadamer 2013, 289). This can get even weirder. In their distinct ways, Aristotle, the medieval Islamic philosopher Ibn Sina, and the modern philosopher Benedict Spinoza described thinking less as something we choose to start doing or something we can control and more as something in which we participate. That is, for Aristotle, Ibn Sina, and Spinoza, thinking is already happening in what they refer to as the "divine mind," and when humans think they are tapping into that stream already going on—a stream of thought originating long before us and continuing long after us (see Aristotle 1983, 1072b24; Ibn Sina 2005, 32; and Spinoza 1992, 91). The god thinks, and we just happen to embody aspects of that god's thought.

I want to neither argue for nor against this. Instead, I want to slightly modify it away from a divine intentional agent or divine ego whose thoughts we reflect or refract, and toward a feature of subject matters themselves. I want to change the topic from a god radiating thoughts we can access to subject matters themselves radiating thoughts we can access. Whereas mere objects or things seem to sit there inertly, I want us to see subject matters as radiating predicative possibilities, a horizon of possible meanings. This radiation is constantly in flux, and makes possible any particular thoughts we might have (see Dickman 2016). When a predicate works, when it appears so fitting, we find it hard to imagine never having thought it before, it is as if the predicate was always there available to us for that sentential subject. The power of metaphorical predication helps bring this out. To think that "Paul is a lion," the literal predication implodes so that the metaphorical predication can emerge from those ruins. If the predicate is revelatory of Paul's essence and vitality, then we might be surprised to have never actually thought that thought before. Thus, the stream of thinking in which we participate radiates from subject matters themselves. We do not need to posit a divine mind as the ultimate origin of thinking. Who is it that thinks? Is it us or the subject matters themselves? I want to leave these questions suspended here.

One further dimension of thinking I want to flesh out in some detail, before turning to questioning, is what makes a thought "critical." If thinking is the combining and separating of subjects and predicates, then what makes thinking critical (or not)? There does not seem to be anything intrinsically critical about combining or separating subjects and predicates. We might be inclined to see *separating* subjects and predicates as critical because separating them would seem to include a sort of negation. We might, for example, illustrate separation by means of adding a "not" within an otherwise positive predication. With regard to the earlier illustration about keys, this would yield the sentence "Your keys are *not* on the kitchen counter." Some of us are tempted to object and say that this too is a combination, not a separation, of a subject and a (negative) predicate. That temptation is, however, a result of correlating language and thought. The sentence including the "not" expresses the separation. The example sentence asserts that the predicate "on the kitchen counter" does not apply to the subject at issue, "your keys."

For thinking to cross the threshold into criticism or for thinking to become genuinely critical, we need to be reflexive or metacognitive—where we simultaneously think a thought *and* think about the thinking of that thought. All criticism puts specific thoughts and the thinking of them into a context, and that context reveals limitations to the thinking and the thoughts. Some feminists refer to this as one's epistemological "standpoint" (see Collins 1990, and Lugones and Spelman 1983). Instead of purporting to have a neutral or universal perspective in one's thinking and thoughts, standpoints or points of view indicate that someone's thinking and thoughts are but one perspective and embodied location among many others. Any number of avenues can be taken to think reflexively like this besides standpoint feminism. We could think about the psychological motivations for a specific thought. We could think about the economic conditions under which that specific thought is possible. We could elucidate racist presuppositions in the thought (see DiAngelo 2011). We could identify the transcendental conditions that make possible any thought whatsoever (see Kant 2007). Indeed, most academic disciplines and fields form areas in which we can become critical about our thinking. In essence, critical thinking is self-criticism. It makes use of the fundamental principles of disciplines for application to a specific instance of one's thinking a thought. Of course, one might be more knowledgeable or skilled in the application of some fields over others. We might, for example, know more about neurological predispositions and propensities toward biases. In such cases one can reach levels of subtlety and nuance in criticism otherwise unavailable, albeit in a way that is different than if one had been knowledgeable or skilled in a different field. Yet even rudimentary knowledge and skill in a discipline can open up thoughts to criticisms. The mark of excellence in critical thinking would be and is comprehensiveness in interdisciplinarity.

Why think critically at all, though? For our approach to thinking laid out here, critical thinking helps sharpen thoughts to a surgical degree. In a sense, each field of criticism tests and examines thoughts, and if thoughts survive such trials either unscathed or through adaptation and qualification, then we can more confidently rely on such thoughts. If they do not survive, if we end up needing to reject the thoughts in light of all the criticism, then we come out more awake to our previous limitations and opened for new thoughts.

In this chapter, I have developed a preliminary notion of thinking, identifying the primary particles of thinking: subjects and predicates. We have seen how thinking involves combining and separating subjects and predicates. We have also looked into reflexive or metacognitive aspects of thinking. On the one hand, we need to be conscious of the ambiguity of the I. On the other hand, we are empowered by academic disciplines for rigorous and comprehensive criticism. Let us now turn to look at relation(s) between questioning and thinking.

What Do Questions Do to Complete Thoughts?

It probably strikes some readers as pretty odd to ask, "What is a question?" To ask this question requires that someone already knows what a question is, at least intuitively. How could we ask the question if we didn't already know what a question is? But that's just it. I want to make explicit what is implicit in acts of genuine questioning, especially as questioning pertains to thinking complete thoughts. Complete thoughts do not just happen in ontological (or semantic) outer space. Recall that *complete thoughts are sentences as they are understood*, and sentences are complete thoughts as they are perceived. What does it take to convert a sentence perceived into a complete thought understood? My fundamental axiom here is that to understand a complete thought is to understand it as an answer to a question (see Dickman 2018). Without asking the question to which a sentence answers, the sentence does not really "make sense" as a complete thought. We might sense—as in have a literal sensation of—a sentence, but the complete thought gets buried by it without asking its proper question. Asking the question to which the sentence answers, though, positions us not just to see or hear the sentence but to understand the complete thought the sentence expresses.

However, does that mean, then, that we do not understand questions? Questions facilitate understanding complete thoughts, and so are distinct from complete thoughts. Thus, in a way, no, we do not understand questions. In our technical framework for understanding complete thoughts, the combination or separation of a subject and a predicate, questions are not complete thoughts. We do not understand questions; we *ask* them. In another way, I do not want to say that we never have moments where we don't understand questions. If someone speaking Mandarin asks me a question, I will not understand it since I am not fluent in Mandarin. Yet if a fellow English speaker asks me a question with a conjunction of words I have difficulty putting together, perhaps due to unfamiliarity, I also will not understand it. As I will explain in more thorough detail throughout this chapter, the point is simply that when I *do* understand a question, I simultaneously ask it. Asking it *is* the understanding of it. In this chapter, I will examine both the grammar and the phenomenology of questioning. I will first look at the primary grammatical types of questions— open and closed questions—and turn to isolate those kinds of questions that are not reducible to other grammatical moods such as imperatives or declaratives. We will see that many questions can be translated into commands, such as how "What is your name?" can be put as "Tell me your name." Some questions cannot be translated into commands, though. These we will call genuine questions. Then I will turn to look at the noetic and noematic (explained below) dimensions of questioning in a phenomenology of questions. What is it that we are conscious of when we hold a question in mind? This should prepare us well to move into the logic of question and answer in Chapter 3.

We do not simply "make statements," however much protestors or performance artists might object to that. Statements are motivated. That is, they answer questions. In grasping and asking the question to which a statement responds, we can understand the statements. Perhaps some performance artists seek to make incomprehensible "statements" in order to avoid taking responsibility for thinking or saying anything at all! Under interrogations, such as on a witness stand where we are asked questions by a lawyer, we are unclear as to the motivation for statements we are forced to make or are unclear to which use our statements may be put. While lawyers or law enforcement officers might have motives for their interrogations, witnesses knowing their motivations may distort the statements made by witnesses. What is crucial here is that without the questions to which the statements answer, those statements are lost on us. We might perceive the sentences, but we do not understand the complete thoughts.

Closed and Open Questions Can Be Neutral or Loaded

We all seem to know how to ask questions. You've probably played the game "Twenty Questions," where one person selects an item and other players use yes-or-no questions to narrow options down and try to guess the selected item. In manuals for conducting interviews and polls, in scholarship about therapeutic clinical practice with clients, and even in advice about getting to know people on first dates, we are told to ask open-ended questions (see, for example, Aron et al. 1997). Such questions, advice-givers tell us, invite respondents to share more and, thus, invest more in the moment and connection with another person. In all these ways and more, advice is ubiquitous throughout culture about how questions work or how they should be used.

In education, teachers are encouraged to have students answer the so-called "higher-order" questions rather than "lower-order" ones for increased learning (Dickman 2009, 5). Numerous teaching guides claim that getting students to perform cognitive tasks like synthesis or evaluation—purportedly higher-order thinking skills—takes asking them correspondingly higher-order questions. Teachers are encouraged to employ Benjamin Bloom's taxonomy of cognitive learning objectives (or some version of it) and to try to correlate kinds of questions with kinds of learning outcomes. It is as if a student needs to be prompted to evaluate or synthesize information by evaluative or synthesis questions. These higher-order questions are said to "demand" more from answerers, where an answerer cannot get by with just single word answers or rote information.

In this sense, higher-order questions are sometimes (con)fused with open-ended questions. Many education specialists are tempted to equate open or open-ended questions with higher-order thinking skills and increased student motivation, and to equate closed questions with lower-order thinking skills and lower levels of investment. With an abundance of manuals of question kinds in all sorts of fields, almost all of which emphasize this distinction between open and closed questions, it should prove helpful to get at some rudimentary grammatical aspects of questions to help keep us focused. Indeed, we will see that this belief in open questions to provoke higher-order thinking is, at least on the grammatical level, mere myth. Be warned—this may get boring for readers who assume, like advice columnists and others, that we already know everything we need to know about questioning. It will prove useful, though, for isolating questions that do not load or bias answering in a particular direction.

English interrogative sentences—questions—are marked by one of three things: an operator (or verb) preceding the sentential subject, an interrogative word at the beginning of the sentence, or a rising intonation. Open questions are "wh-questions," formed with any interrogative word, such as who, whom, whose, what, which, when, where, how, or why—either by themselves or in more complex constructions. Both "if" and "whether" can function to ask questions when they are used in an interrogative subclause of a larger sentence. The interrogative element comes first in the sentence, and the question word takes the first position in interrogative clauses. One exception is in formal English, to avoid ending a question with a preposition. For example, "What did you do that for?" is rendered formally as "For what did you do that?" Interrogative operators function like algebraic variables (see Harrah 1961, 42). This is what makes them "open," because in each case there is an unlimited number of potential answers satisfying the interrogative clause. For example, asking someone "What is your name?" opens to any possible name.

There are two kinds of closed questions: yes-no ones and alternative ones. Yes-no questions only admit of affirmative or negative answers, and are typically formed by placing interrogative operators before the sentential subject and using a rising intonation. The interrogative form of the declarative statement "The ice cream will melt" is "Will the ice cream melt?" One peculiar version of the yes-no kind of closed question is the tag-question, which adds either "right" or a repetition of the verb operator with a pronoun (often in a negative form), such as with, "The boat has left, hasn't it?" Alternative questions specify a disjunctive set of two or more options. Some alternative questions are like yes-no questions, concluding with a falling intonation, such as, "Would you rather be invisible or fly?" Other alternative questions are like wh-questions, by combining a wh-question with an elliptical alternative question, such as, "Which soft drink would you like? Coke, Pepsi, or Sprite?" What makes yes-no and alternative questions "closed" is that they limit the set size of possible answers. Wh-questions, on the other hand, are in principle unlimited in their set size of possible answers, and so are called "open." We can model this difference this way: grammatically closed questions are reducible to "true/false" or "multiple choice" problems, whereas grammatically open questions are reducible to "fill in the blank" or "short answer" problems. That open questions call for higher-order thinking seems to be mere myth—at least, speaking grammatically. Open or closed, an answerer can get away with brief answers. Consider how un-talkative kids are when guardians ask them the open question, "How was your day at school today?"

Whether open or closed, all questions are intrinsically neutral because, like many negatives, they are *nonassertions* (Quirk and Greenbaum 1973, 24 and 193). This is crucial to get down. Questions are not assertions; questions are not answers. What distinguishes interrogatives and negation statements from assertions is that they do not readily admit of using "some-words"—such as something, someone, and so on—but only "any-words" (see Leech and Svartvik 1975, 289). In the positive assertion "She offered her friend some chocolates," the word "some" fits but could not be replaced with "any." However, "some" is ambiguous in the negative version of the sentence: "She did not offer her friend some chocolates." Did she offer none or all of them? The proper form is, alternatively, "She did not offer her friend any chocolates." The word "any" makes the complete thought or sense determinate.

With questions, some-words get used to bias answers in a particular direction or to load the question (see Piazza 2002). A question encourages a positive answer if it uses assertive words rather than nonassertive ones. Such a construction transforms questions into assertions. For example, the question "Has the bus left already?" indicates that the questioner presumes the answer is yes and so is basically requesting confirmation. Instead, "Has the bus left yet?" is relatively neutral with regard to questioner bias. Negative bias in questions also loads them in an assertive direction, typically to express disappointment or annoyance. For example, "Aren't you ashamed of yourself?" indicates the questioner believes the respondent ought to be ashamed and ought to act accordingly. Moreover, declarative questions have assertive characteristics, indicated by the inadmissibility of nonassertive constructions, such as "The guests have had anything to eat?!?" Instead, it should be said as "The guests have had nothing to eat?!?"

For us, it matters less whether a question is open or closed in the grammatical sense of the terms and matters more whether a question is neutral or loaded. It depends on if the questioner is trying to assert something by means of the question asked or even bias the respondent to answer in a preferred way. A neutral question seems to respect respondents in such a way that respondents themselves might determine answers for and from themselves rather than be prompted by the questioner. Indeed, for us, it is more the *neutrality* of the question than the *scope* of the set of possible answers that makes a question "open." Rather than grammatical openness, we are more concerned with openness in the sense of hospitality. An open question, for us, is hospitable to a genuine answer or complete thought without distorting it or prompting it with bias. Of course, as we will see soon, all questions have presuppositions—even unbiased questions. Loaded questions, though, display preference for a specific answer or attempt to entrap the answerer. The presuppositions of questions, alternatively, constitute the context for any answer whatsoever, biased or not. For example, in asking someone, "What did you do today?" we presuppose that the respondent did indeed do something today, but the question displays no preference for one answer over another.

Despite these grammatical facts, beliefs persist in the purported evocative power of questions. Grammatically open questions are believed to have greater potential in creating learning conversations (Dickman 2009, 6). They are seen as a way to stimulate student interest and motivation, to cultivate critical thinking skills, to inspire independent pursuit of knowledge, and more. It seems that something as simple as a question is capable of doing amazing things! Yet it does seem intuitive that some questions create moments of responsible and thoughtful engagement. My point is merely that isolating the kind of questions which do this cannot be done by means of the "lower-" and "higher-"order binary corresponding to the grammatical distinctions of "closed" and "open" questions. Neutrality, alternatively, leads us to a different yet important distinction within kinds of questions. Let us turn to isolate what I want us to call "genuine" questions.

Genuine Questions Are Not Epistemic Imperatives

One predominant way questions are analyzed in philosophy of language is through erotetic logic, or the so-called logic of question and answer. Many consider erotetic logic to have enormous potential in automating search engines and other information transmission systems (i.e., libraries). Isolating the logical structure of questions through formalization creates a path for defining the truth and falsity of answers as they pertain to propositions presupposed in the questions. The formal logical character of questions is not about syntactical or other grammatical conventions since the "same" question can be asked in different ways and in different languages. All questions, in this framework, contain presuppositions or presupposed propositions, and the only way a question can have a true answer is if the presuppositions are true. For example, the question "Is it raining?" presupposes the proposition that "Either it is raining or it is not raining." This proposition must be true for either answer to be true (Bell 1975, 198). Questions with false or narrow presuppositions can be corrected by either rejecting the presuppositions or fleshing the question out to incorporate more potential answers. For example, "Have you stopped beating your dog?" might be rejected by simply pointing out you have never had a dog. The point is, nevertheless, questions—from the approach of erotetic logic—just are (disjunctive) sets of propositions from which answerers must select or answerers must change the topic in some way. So the question of whether it is raining could be rephrased in the following way. "Select one: It is raining. It is not raining."

This overlooks the performative force with which questions are given and taken. Questions also make requests about selection from the presupposed propositions (see Bell 1975, 196). They could be expressed with urgency or indifference to how fast the answerer provides their answer. The question "Did you earn a Bachelor of Arts or Bachelor of Science degree?" requests that selection be made between two alternatives, and the request disallows "neither" as an answer—though of course that could be used to reject the question. This has led many theorists to locate interrogatives as a species of imperatives. The theory labels questions as "epistemic imperatives" (see Aqvist 1965). The illustrative cases of questions used here as paradigmatic for all questions in general are those instances in which: (a) the questioner does not know the answer and, in asking the question, (b) expresses the knowledge the questioner *does* have about the subject matter. For such standard cases, we are to transform questions into the form "Make it the case that I know X." For example, take the question "Which US presidents were generals?" This is to be transposed into "For each X where X is a President and a general, 'make me know' that X was a President and a general" (Harrah 1982, 26–7). The response to the question only counts as an answer if the request is satisfied, in that the questioner comes to know which presupposition is true. We can extend the so-called standard cases like this to, say, classroom contexts where teachers already know the answer. Instead, the formal structure can be modified to something like, "Make me know that you know X." This is just what exams do, because presumably teachers are not going to ask students questions to which the teachers do not know the answer!

Beyond the construal of questions as imperatives in terms of their formal or logical content, questions are also regularly classed as "directives" or commands in terms of their illocutionary or performative force. Not only do questions appear to *state* imperatives, they also seem to *perform* like imperatives. Questions are requests for the performance of speech acts in which the form of proper response is already prescribed by the question (Searle 1992, 8). The point of a question, what questions *do*, is to prompt another person to speak within the constraints set out by the question. This is in part due to the flexibility of the verb "to ask." Asking someone to tell you where they are from ("Where are you from?") is a polite form of the imperative mood, but an imperative nonetheless ("Tell me where you are from."). For example, we can render the question "What is your name?" into the explicit command "Tell me your name." or even the more rigorously discrete "Select one from the following: Your name is Muhammad. Your name is Ruth. Your name is . . . [ad infinitum]." Simply because a question can be rendered into a command does not mean it is insincere, though. In this Speech Act approach to questions, there are key "felicity" or sincerity conditions that must be met: the questioner does not know the answer, the questioner wants to know it, and the questioner uses the utterance to attempt to get the answer (Searle 1969, 60). Thus, this command counts as a *sincere* question. My point here is that most questions in our day-to-day lives are sincere questions, whether they are expressed in the interrogative mood as a question or in the imperative mood as a command.

At this point, though, I think we should be getting a little worried. Are there any questions that cannot be reduced to commands? Why do we have questions at all when we can get by with soft imperatives like asking for or requesting things? An even more significant worry is whether acts of questioning, as disguised commands, are mere tools in the hands of oppressors. As continental philosopher Rebecca Comay writes:

> Perhaps one day a history will be written of the institutionalized violence lurking behind the apparent guilelessness of the question—its juridical force (the investigation, the interrogation, the cross-examination), its pedagogical power (the disputatio, the quiz, the exam), its religious authority (the inquisition, the catechism), its medical prerogative (the examination, the inquest), its prestige as an instrument of surveillance (the interview, the questionnaire). (Comay 1991, 149)

If questions just are tools for oppression, then perhaps there are no questions that cannot be reduced to or translated into commands. Slavoj Žižek, the pop culture philosophical provocateur, illustrates this in the mouths of totalitarians, "It is *we* who will ask the questions here!" (Žižek 1989, 178–82;

see also Fiumara 1990). If all questions, or the paradigmatic versions of questions that purportedly elucidate their logical and illocutionary character, are merely disguised commands, then perhaps we might agree with Comay, Žižek, and the feminist philosopher Gemma Corradi Fiumara. Perhaps we ought to give up the tactic of questioning wholesale in order to help bring about less oppressive social structures. Some clinical psychologists, following the famous therapist Carl Rogers, have taken this position and refuse to use any questions when speaking with clients and patients (see Sousa, Pinheiro, and Silva 2003).

My wager is that there is a distinctive kind of questioning that cannot be reduced to commands, and I want to promote using this kind of questioning as paradigmatic for analysis of questions in general in order to preserve their unique character. And I want to approach all thinking and reasoning in light of these questions first and foremost. I want to call these "genuine" questions in distinction from sincere questions. Of course, this is not to say that typical interrogatives are not sincere, but that a more comprehensive theory of questioning needs to not only account for genuine questions but should use *them* as paradigmatic instead of epistemic imperatives. There seems to be some questions that cannot be reduced to commands. This is the fundamental crux in uncovering or isolating questions in their own right.

Genuine questioning does not primarily aim at needed answers. This is the first crucial difference between genuine questions and epistemic imperatives. If getting answers or information was the sole function of questioning, then we should wonder—with the philosophical ethicist Emmanuel Levinas—whether we are capable of complete thoughts in which words even have meaning (Levinas 1998a, 75). Recall that there are no words in dictionaries. When we treat words as just signs or marks for processing information, then they are like the signs sitting in dictionaries. When we need answers and information like this, we make questioning a deprivation-driven and calculative exercise. Indeed, we could just as easily look at a nametag—where one is available—to get to know someone else's name. That we are deprived of their name takes over and fuels our actions. Here, a question is just a tool. Genuine questioning, alternatively, is a *surplus*-driven exercise. It is rooted in not need, but a desire of one who "lacks nothing," a desire oriented by what Levinas calls "the order of the Good" (Levinas 1969, 102). *We are capable of questioning for the joy of it,* tarrying with what questioning itself opens to us, without feeling like we have been deprived of answers. It is naïve to subordinate questions to answers, as if the purpose of all questions is just to get answers and information. Some questions elicit questions. And some questions elicit shared asking of the questions. The point of some questions is less to get an answer and more *to get another person to ask the questions with us*. Such questions are a way we bring about a state of *communitas* with others.

Let us turn to flesh out aspects of the experience and activity of genuine questioning. Phenomenology is a helpful approach to get at these aspects of it. What is it like to be struck by a genuine question?

A Phenomenology of Genuine Questions

I assume that readers are probably not that familiar with phenomenology. Don't be intimidated by the word. This approach will help us get at what it feels like to have a question occur to us. Unlike the grammar of questions, erotetic logic, or Speech Act theory, phenomenology focuses exclusively on consciousness. Its first major step is to bracket out normal and natural assumptions we make about whatever it is we are studying—in this case, questions. We normally and naturally expect that questions are for the sake of answers. It is like going to a science fiction or fantasy movie where we suspend our disbelief, where we stop saying "That's not real" or "That can't really happen." If we didn't suspend our disbelief, we wouldn't be able to enjoy the movie. A phenomenology of questions requires the same thing from us, where we suspend our assumptions about questions. Our goal is to isolate what it is like to be conscious of questioning when we are considering a question.

In phenomenologies of questioning, a relevant distinction recurs between passive and active questioning (Morgan and Saxton 2006), guiding and grounding questioning (Blok 2015), derived and originary questioning (Meyer 1995), or naïve and phenomenological questioning (Plotka 2012). Genuine questioning belongs with the latter category in each pair. To get at the experience of genuine questioning by itself, let us suspend for now the natural attitude of subordinating questions to their answers, our normal assumption that the point of questioning is to get an answer. Consider questioning as something very weird! Consider questioning as something worthy of exploration for its own sake.

Emphasis on the *experience* of genuine questioning rather than the *logic* of it may seem like a choice that favors an idealistic phenomenology of questioning, as if our target were to examine an isolated ego's self-perception. It is as if we are supposed to introspect and reflect on what it is like to ask a question. How else could we look at what it is like to have a question? Ricoeur asks, "That consciousness is outside itself, that it is towards meaning, before meaning is for it, and still more, before that consciousness is for-itself [as ego], is this not what the central discovery of phenomenology implies?" (Ricoeur 1975, 96). The individual ego does not have mastery over complete thoughts that are understood, let alone complete thoughts that are intended, because they inform self-consciousness before an ego "means" or intends anything (see Gadamer 2013, 489). It is not that we first become self-conscious as an ego, and then start to speak. Instead, we learn languages and models for thinking about ourselves, and only then do we form an idea of ourselves as a separate and intending ego. Thus, the experience of genuine questioning, its mode of intentionality, is not analogous to the ostensive subject/object duality of immediate sensation, where there is the experiencing ego on the one side and the thing we experience on the other side. Such a model is misleading when it comes to openness for complete thoughts or meanings. We often take images as weak subjective sensory substitutions for mind-independent objects, and this undermines our awareness about image-laden language enhancing meanings (Ricoeur 1979, 129). Not all images are residual sensations. Poetic images reverberate because of complete thoughts understood rather than because of things seen or felt. We "see" some things by first reading or hearing them.

I want to examine both the *noetic* (acting) and the *noematic* (content of the acting) poles of genuine questioning—which are the two key domains of phenomenological inquiry (see Dickman 2018). This difference appears in ordinary expressions such as "asking a question" and "the question asked" (Welton 1999, 99). The phenomenologist Maurice Merleau-Ponty posits questioning as the fundamental essence and origin of all noetic activity (Merleau-Ponty 1968, 121). Noematic content, however, is not intrinsic to conscious noetic activity. It is what one is conscious of in the questioning activity. Noema are actual objects under the *epoche*, or "bracketing out," of our naïve or natural attitude toward them. Bracketing brings into relief not objects in the "external" world or reified Platonic ideals in the "intelligible" world but the willed *as willed*, judged *as judged*, and questioned *as questioned*. What are the noetic and noematic dimensions of genuine questioning?

The acting pole of genuine questioning is not an introspectively directed reflection on an ego's experience, but an unreflective participation in the flow of everyday activity. Just as with music or games, we can get in the zone with questioning. We need to put this right up front because we forget this when we get caught up in questioning. Questioning is an openness, an original matter of consciousness's aiming at things. Merleau-Ponty labels questioning our "ontological organ" and the "ultimate relation to Being" (Merleau-Ponty 1968, 121). It is more than a mere sensory or perceptual "aim," because it includes a kind of contraction to consider potential answers or complete thoughts. The contraction in genuine questioning is like the dehiscence Merleau-Ponty emphasizes, which is definitive of our embodiment. Dehiscence names the splitting of our body in two directions, simultaneously as feeling and as being felt, such as when we touch our own hands in such a way as to grasp or envelop something in our bodily folds (Merleau-Ponty 1968, 117/123). We naively believe we see things in the "external" world, as if our senses receive a film of them—the ancient notion of sensory effluvia. Instead, we envelop things through our dehiscent bodies. For Merleau-Ponty, this is why we say of something we experience that it is given "in person" or "in the flesh" (Merleau-Ponty 1968, 373). Without this emphasis on embodied folds, we might be tempted to abstract questioning, in the feminist philosopher Luce Irigaray's words, "from its carnal taking root" (Irigaray 2002, 74). The body gives itself to itself in a network of potentials, which Merleau-Ponty describes as the bodily "I can" (Merleau-Ponty 1968, liv). Our bodies are oriented by anticipatory projections, or prejudices, which are effects of conformity with inherited social norms and culture (Gadamer 2013, 289; and Ahmed 2006, 168).

Something interesting about genuine questioning can be revealed in light of all this about historically and socially conditioned dehiscence. Questioning articulates the dehiscence of understanding, such that complete thoughts *as complete thoughts* may be enveloped. How so? Because *questioning has the logical structure of suspending* complete thoughts or judgments, including prejudices, it maintains a distance from them as well as simultaneously being open to them as possible answers (Gadamer 2013, 310; and de Beauvoir 2015, 10–11). Questioning does not eradicate embodied prejudices, but puts assumed complete thoughts—whether as presuppositions or as answers—at risk by testing or considering them as possible answers. As Gadamer writes:

> What we find happening in speaking is not a mere reification of intended meaning, but an endeavor that continually modifies itself, or better: a continually recurring temptation to engage oneself in something or to become involved with someone. But this means to expose oneself and to risk oneself. Genuinely speaking one's mind has little to do with mere explication

and assertion of our prejudices; rather, it risks our prejudices—it exposes oneself to one's own doubt as well as to the rejoinder of the other. (Gadamer 1989, 26)

The dehiscence of understanding is given "in the flesh" of perceivable spoken, signed, or written interrogative sentences. Genuine questions express the locus where understanding "touches" itself, where questioning is the skin of understanding and answering is the flesh of meaning.

A sincere need to know something seems to be an additional noetic element of questioning, and this is emphasized across philosophical loyalties. The early twentieth-century philosopher Martin Heidegger says every questioning is a seeking (Heidegger 1996, 3). Searle says wanting to know is a necessary sincerity condition for questioning (Bell 1975, 207). Levinas, however, urges that questioning embodies a completely different intentionality and aim. If information is all we need, then we do not need to ask a question at all. Does questioning *have* to involve consciousness seeking fulfillment in knowledge (Levinas 1998a, 71)? Levinas writes, "Must we not admit, on the contrary, that the request and the prayer that cannot be dissimulated in the question attest to a relation to the other person . . . ? A relation delineated in the question, not just as any modality, but as in its originary one" (Levinas 1998a, 72). Anxious grasps for information distort exploration and dwelling with others in questioning itself. A want for knowledge might motivate questioning, but need not accompany it. In genuine questioning, we do not know ahead of time where we might end up, as if there should be some "final solution" (Meyer 1995, 204–5). We must, as Socrates describes it, follow thought wherever it, like the wind, blows (Plato 1991, 394d). Unlike individual anxious need, genuine questioning—as a surplus-driven shared desire—is an opportune responsibility, a letting go or expropriation to the subject matter (Irigaray 2002, 36). It is how we get in the zone.

The content pole, or noemata, of questioning is *not* the possible answers. This is a substantive contrast to erotetic logic, and the focus on presupposed propositions. It is the question asked within the questioning. Most theories of questioning start here. A useful distinction in semantic content is between "reference," the *what* ostensibly indicated by the question's sentential subject, and the "sense," the articulated interrogative sentence itself including both a subject and a proposed predicate (Ricoeur 1976, 12–13). Complete thoughts are the "sense" of sentences, if the sentences answer a question you are actually asking. Answers are complete thoughts, syntheses of sentential subjects, that enact the identifying function of language, and predicates, that enact the elucidatory function (Ricoeur 1976, 19). We have a tendency to reduce questions about "the meaning" of something to the referential dimension of discourse, where we tend to look for what the sentential subject indicates. That is, reference dominates as the "true" or normative definition of meaning (see the translation of *Bedeutung* in Wittgenstein 2009). Irigaray criticizes this hegemony toward reference as freezing the flow of lived experience, forcing moments into submission to our needs (Irigaray 2002, 40). It makes it seem as if questioning is primarily about some "thing" in the external world beyond mere language. We believe questioning gets us answers not just about mere words but about "real" things. However, reference is not a meaning in our restriction that meanings or complete thoughts are answers to questions. References are not answers to questions because they are not complete sentences. As the theorist of rhetoric Michel Meyer explains, the sentential subject of the answer refers back not to an object in the external world but to the interrogative pronoun in the question (Meyer 1995, 217). Answers "refer" us to their questions, not to objects "out there."

Sense displaces the seemingly immediate character of reference. Sense, as complete thoughts, displaces direct experience to where we can instead interpret that experience and speak about it. To discuss experience is to dignify it by raising it to the light of understanding. Making sense of things is what questioning envelops. In constructing a complete thought, we lift the subject in light of the predicate. But that does not entail that we understand the meaning of what we are saying. Recall that we can see or hear a sentence without understanding the complete thought it expresses. Genuine questioning makes it possible to receive sense, makes it possible for sentences to appear *as* complete thoughts for understanding (Ricoeur 1975, 97). As Gadamer writes, "Being that can be understood is language" (Gadamer 2013, 490). Not merely sentences perceived, but sentences understood as complete thoughts are language.

Moreover, only sentences have the potential to be understood. This might feel like I am atrophying our understanding because in our natural attitude we believe we ought to understand everything, not "merely" language. We express despair and disappointment when we do not understand some things. The scholar of religion Talal Asad writes the following toward our experience of death and horror about suicide bombings: "Breaking into this paranoid [frenzy] may be the sudden realization that in any death there is nothing to understand—that there's no role for the meaning-making subject.

The thought that makes chance deaths more horrible is that they cannot be redeemed by a comforting story" (Asad 2007/2008, 129). If only sentential answers to asked questions can be understood, then this despair is not a problem of understanding proper, but *a problem of our inflated expectations for understanding* where we try to smear it across all things. We act as if we are entitled to know everything, or shrug off quests for knowledge with statements of indifference like "Some things are a mystery." My point is, alternatively, we cannot understand such things because they are not sentences or complete thoughts that answer to questions. We participate in events, undergo experiences, meet others, and make something of ourselves, and all these generate in us a desire to speak up or make us poetically productive. We understand discourse—no more, no less. Unlike Asad, moreover, we are discussing not the meaning-making subject, but instead the meaning-receiving subject, the one who can understand whatever meanings are made by asking questions where we open our bodies, we open our consciousness, to receive meanings.

Consider this further example. When people tell us about their experience, do we understand *them* or what they *say*? We often hear people say "I get you" or "I don't understand you." As Gadamer writes:

> It belongs to every true [dialogue] that each person opens himself to the other . . . to such an extent that he understands not the particular individual but what he says . . . Where a person is concerned with the other as individuality—e.g., in a therapeutic conversation or the interrogation of a man accused of a crime—this is not really a situation in which [different] people are trying to come to an understanding. (Gadamer 2013, 403)

We do not understand the other person, but what the other person says. We might empathize with others, but that is not the same thing as understanding meanings or complete thoughts.

This has an interesting application. Some people protect others from assimilation by saying things such as, "You will never understand someone else's experience." This seems like a profound metaphysical thought, that we are in some way trapped in our own subjective experience or trapped in our own separate egos. It may even be a reaction to the wish for something like telepathy, a purportedly direct access to the content of others' minds. While that may be, the content of such as statement is for us here more a grammatical rule, similar to the problem with "everything" as a sentential subject. Such statements give off a rhetorical veneer of standing up for people and trying to prevent assimilation, the reduction of others' experience to mere modifications of the "same," of normative perceptions. *We do not understand people, though. People are not complete thoughts.* So, it is redundant to say we cannot understand another person's experience. This is not disappointing, though, because we ought to never have expected to understand other people. It is not truly redundant, but instead is a category mistake. The trouble is with our expectations, with what we think "must" be the case (see Thich 2010; and Wittgenstein 2009). These grammatical distinctions between the order of understanding and the order of empathetic experience ought to help us protect others from naïve assimilation and protect understanding from pretentious inflation. It is not that I understand *you*, but rather what you have to *say in response* to questions that are actually being asked.

If complete thoughts understood are the sense of sentences perceived, what is the *sense* of genuine questioning? So far, we have only negated potential options for addressing this question: not reference, not events, not other people, and so on. Let us turn now to positive proposal(s) for addressing this by moving into what we can call a different logic of question and answer.

3

A Different Logic of Question and Answer

The "logic" at issue here is not formal symbolic logic, where logicians might teach us to mind our "p's and q's" with regard to propositional inferences from premise to conclusion. (This is not completely irrelevant, though. I will turn to address propositional rationality and symbolic logic more closely in Part II on reasoning with questions.) I am focused primarily on logic as structure or order. What order does the dynamic of questions and answers have? What is the nature of their arrangement and movement? In what follows, I will first address in discrete detail the sense of genuine questioning, or that of which we are conscious when we find ourselves caught up in questioning. I will also examine relation(s) between presuppositions in questions and the answers that appropriately respond to them, looking in particular at the historical character of presuppositions as inherited biases and background assumptions rooted in our cultures.

How to Question Complete Thoughts from at Least Four Directions

For our purposes, sense is articulated in sentences that answer questions. Sense is not an abbreviation for physical sensations. By bracketing out our natural concern about reference to external objects, we exhibit a new dimension of being, that of meaning—or "sense" in its broadest sense, like a sense of direction, a sense of humor, a sense of ritual, or common sense. Sense displaces a purportedly immediate character of sensory perception of particular objects, but displaces this so that we might speak of and thus interpret experience in response to our dehiscent questionings. This sort of sense is not rooted in sensations. Genuine questioning makes it possible to receive sense, makes it possible for sentences to appear as complete thoughts or meanings for understanding. Because the noematic or content pole of thinking is the complete thought or the unity of subject and predicate, it might seem reasonable that the noematic content of questioning is the separation of subject and predicate. This is not so (see Schumann and Smith 1987, 365).

Let us examine the sense of sentences in more detail first. Phenomenologically, the unity captured by the copula in a complete thought is not merely an ascription of a property to the fixed base of an object referenced by a sentential subject. Our natural attitude biases us to conceive of propositions this way. We point at something with our sentential subjects, some "this" out there, and then we ascribe a property to that subject, such as "is tall." Such a reified proposition as "this is tall," a seeming complete thought, is abstracted from the irrigation and fertilization in genuine questioning (Gadamer 2013, 482). Abstract sentential sense is merely representational, where one picture is laid on top of another. Perhaps we are looking at a tall tree, and you say to me "This [tree] is tall!" The proposition supposedly accurately or inaccurately represents the tree we see. Instead for us, the unity of meaning is where a predicate successfully discloses a subject's essence. Sentential subjects are superseded by predicates by "passing into" them. The complete thought does not state something (a predicate) about something (an underlying substance). A complete thought presents a unity by disclosing aspects of a subject's essence. Gadamer illustrates this as follows: "'God is one' does not mean that it is a property of God's to be one, but that it is God's nature to be [unified]" (Gadamer 2013, 482). With our example of the tree: "This tree is tall" does not mean that tallness is a mere property of the tree, but that we experience the tree in its tallness, as when someone says, "That tree sure is tall!"

Consider another example in terms of metaphors. Metaphors do not just replace a conventional name with an unconventional one. That is to construe metaphors in terms of representation. Instead, metaphors are sentential—complete thoughts—where literal unity implodes so metaphorical unity emerges. To say "Anderson is a lion" is to state nonsense if taken solely literally, but this opens a metaphorical dimension where the conceptual connotations of lions reveal aspects of the essence of the subject, Anderson. Similarly, to say, "This year is 1442 AH" discloses this moment as what it truly is, that the essential aspect of time is made intelligible through coordination with a moment of ultimate significance, when the Prophet Muhammad founded the *Ummah* (community) in Medina. Sentential subjects set elements of experience into relief so we might think about them (Schumann and Smith 1987, 367). Any element might be set off from background horizons so we might make a determination about them with a predicate. This subtle disclosive relation between subject and predicate is key in the conscious sense or content of complete thoughts. But then what of the content of genuine questioning?

If complete thoughts are the *actual* synthesis or unity (or separation) of subject and predicate, then questions present not the separation but the *possibilities* for unity (or separation) of subjects and predicates. As the father of phenomenology Edmund Husserl writes:

> Every possible content of judgment is thinkable as the content of a question. In the question, it is naturally not yet an actual content; rather, it is in the question only as contemplated, a merely represented (neutralized) judgment and is, as the content of the question, oriented equally toward the yes and the no. (Husserl 1975, 309)

Genuine questioning presents a neutralization of determined thoughts. Recall how neutrality is what makes a question "open" in the definition important to us here. Neutrality in questioning is the suspension of judgment, the suspension of prejudice—literally, prejudgment. Suspension is neither assertion nor negation. It precedes both in a higher order or in coordination.

There are a number of orientations of questioning coordinated by different emphases on predicates and/or subjects (see Bruin 2001, 20–4). Many questions focus in on indeterminacy of predicates. They specify a particular subject but open up predicative possibilities. In the example, "Where are my keys?" the sentential subject is explicit ("keys") but the disclosive predicate is yet to be settled. The keys may be in any number of places, and each one is a unique predicate. These are what we can call *predicament-centered questions*. This is because they concern the predicament that the subject is in. This is drawn from Kant's description of concepts as "predicaments" and fundamental categories as "predicables" (Kant 2007, 106).

Many other questions focus us in on subjects. For example, "What is for breakfast?" The predicate seems articulated ("is for breakfast"), but the subject is yet to be specified. The interrogative pronoun functions similarly to an algebraic variable. It could be "samosas," "nothing yet," and more. These are *subject-centered questions*.

The copula orients an additional focus of questioning. These questions presuppose precedent complete thoughts. For example, "Donald J. Trump is the president of the United States. But is he *really*?" In our natural attitude, we might take this as about some mind-independent object, because it seems answerable simply by looking at who the current occupant of the White House is. Yet, given our phenomenological approach, we have been bracketing this normal attitude and its accompanying expectations. What is asked about is the copula, the being of the relation(s) between subject and predicate. Is the predicate *actually disclosive* of the subject, or vice versa (Husserl 1975, 294)? These are *copula-centered questions*.

Each of these three orientations involves a distinctive fluctuation or indeterminacy, like the to-and-fro play of a teeter-totter. In predicament-centered questioning, some subject stands in relief like a teeter-totter's fulcrum, but that subject lacks a settled predicate one way or another. Consider the question, "What is the distance to New York City?" The trip to New York functioning as the sentential subject is specified, though a fitting predicate is not yet determined. The possible predicates though ae not vague, namely because numerous precise measurements are available. The abeyance rests solely in *which* predicate is fittingly disclosive of the subject.

In subject-centered questioning, some predicate stands in relief from a field of intelligibility, but the subject is not settled. For example, "What gets wetter as it dries?" The predicate is clear, and numerous subjects are available as possibly fitting for the predicate—an umbrella, a clothes dryer, a towel, and so on. The abeyance is not in the possible subjects themselves, but in *which* subject is disclosed fittingly by the predicate.

In copula-centered questioning, there is presupposed a precedent complete thought where a subject is purportedly already determined by a predicate. The abeyance adheres neither to the subject nor to the predicate poles of the complete thought. For example, "Should one *really* 'treat others as you want to be treated'?" What lacks being settled here is the justification or grounds for the complete thought (see Husserl 1975, 294). Perhaps it is supported only by mere conventional wisdom. Perhaps it is divine revelation or grounded on rational principles. The abeyance here is in *which* way we might preserve reliability of our cognitive capacities (Husserl 1975, 294–313).

A further orientation of questioning is what we are doing here: *questioning-centered questioning*. At issue in questioning is not only predication of subjects or reliability of prejudgments. Just as complete thoughts require a thinker, questioning involves a questioner. We can be oriented toward ourselves in our questioning—not as the subject matter at issue in the question, but as participants in the activity of questioning itself. Questioning envelops itself because we disclose something about ourselves, an indeterminacy or abeyance within us. Merleau-Ponty calls this reflexivity or metacognition in focusing on questioning itself "questioning to the second power" (Merleau-Ponty 1968, 120). In giving ourselves over to genuine questioning, *we disclose ourselves as a negativity* "borne by an infrastructure of being" (Merleau-Ponty 1968, 120). And yet, we who question genuinely are not a mere privative nothing or a "lack." In giving ourselves over to questioning, we allow ourselves to be distanced from, yet inextricably tied to, being. We ourselves are suspended in indeterminate yet productive abeyance between distanced negativity and immediate positivity, multiplicity, and unity.

This radical *ambi*valence is, in Ricoeur's words, "the ruin of the pretension of the ego to be established as an ultimate origin" (Ricoeur 1975, 95). Being in question, we negate our enclosing need for dominance because *we are opened to what others have to say*. We will examine this in thorough detail in Part III. Questioning is, in Gadamer's words, "not merely a matter of putting oneself forward and successfully asserting one's own point of view, but being transformed into a communion in which we do not remain what we were" (Gadamer 2013, 387). As Irigaray emphasizes, questioning is an opening in all of us, starting from which it is possible to listen to others (Irigaray 2002, 36). Questioning opens us to possibilities of understanding meanings that may transform us. Of course, to ask genuine questions deliberately to try to transform yourself misses the point here. They happen to transform us, as a by-product. To make transformation your goal is to instrumentalize genuine questions into a mere tool. This openness involves a reworking of experience and interpretations of it, but even more so a reworking of ourselves (Beatty 1999, 295). This is the reflexive existential abeyance in questioning-centered questioning. What sort of person am I in my questioning—someone open to what others have to say or someone who already knows and so does not need to listen?

Before turning to reconsider presuppositions in questioning, some readers may be wondering whether we can also have "sign-centered" questioning. We made the distinction earlier between signs as elements of sentences and words as operative in complete thoughts. It seems, then, that we ought to be able to ask questions about the signs out of which complete thoughts are composed. Perhaps. If we can, it is solely in cases that are derivative from my four primary question orientations—predicate-centered, subject-centered, copula-centered, and questioning-centered. The four main orientations emerge as possible when both participants, the questioner and the answerer, are working within a shared form of life and shared language. Sign-centered questioning, however, might occur when that sharing of a language breaks down. Imagine someone says something decontextualized, such as "Thank." One might ask in reaction to that, "'Thank' what? 'Thank you'? 'Thankful'?" Such questions are attempting to situate the decontextualized sign into a relevant context, by attempting to determine if the word is working as a predicate with an implied subject or as a subject with an implied predicate. These are sincere questions. As we distinguished earlier, though, sincere questions are distinct from genuine questions. Once these sincere questions are settled, once a shared language is established, that is when genuine questioning really gets off the ground.

Presuppositions Provide Constraints in Questions

We still have not completely settled the "sense" of questioning. What is it we are conscious of in questioning in any of the four orientations? What is the intentional correlate or noema of questioning? "Intentionality" is the term phenomenologists use for the intrinsic structure of consciousness—where there are the two poles of the subjective origin point or noesis and the targeted meant point or noema. Consciousness is always conscious *of* some meaning. The feminist philosopher Simone de Beauvoir emphasizes that intentionality is our original type of attachment to being, and is not a "wanting to be," but a "wanting to disclose" (de Beauvoir 2015, 13). De Beauvoir illustrates this:

> I should like to be the landscape which I am contemplating, I should like this sky, this quiet water to think themselves within me, that it might be I whom they express in flesh and bone, and I remain at a distance. But it is also by this distance that the sky and the water exist before me. My contemplation is an excruciation only because it is also a joy. (de Beauvoir 2015, 13)

Intentionality is a way we make worlds present to us or allow meaningful worlds to present themselves to us. Questioning, then, is a way in which we make present the fluidity of subject matters radiating predicative possibilities and predicates radiating possible subjects. Our intrinsic structural negativity—that subjectivity is literally not an object—is what makes space for things to appear, and through this we make clearings for the appearance of things in their questionability. As Rod Coltman translates Gadamer, "Such bringing-into-suspension . . . is the proper and original essence of questioning. Questioning always allows the possibilities of a situation to be seen in suspension" (Coltman 1998, 109).

The intentional correlate or sense of questioning is not a "mind-independent" state of affairs, but an aspect of states of affairs, a consciousness of them, present only in questioning. Questioning unfolds varying possibilities of relations between subjects and predicates, all of which we might consider or test but none of which we have to assume in the midst of our questioning. In our natural attitude, questioning *seems* to aim at cognitive closure and determination in that we seem to need answers to our questions. Suspension, however, allows us opportunities to dwell with varying possibilities. Questioning suspends predicative possibilities, for example, but not explicitly in providing every discrete option. We would need to explore possibilities, and this takes time. Nevertheless, while both subjects and predicates may be separately determinate, their possibilities for relation are not yet settled. The fluidity of possibility is like that of numbers, the continuum to infinity, where each number is available for bringing into relief, but which recedes back into the ocean of infinity.

Questioning is a basic mode of intentionality, and thus has a unique intentional or noematic object (Bruin 2001, 17). Questioning is not merely an introspective taking notice of an inner experience of our having yet to determine something, a taking note of our own confusion or wavering between options. When we ask a question, we are not merely expressing something about our own inner experience (Schumann and Smith 1987, 364). If this were the case, we could just frown rather than ask a question. The frown expresses our inner experience as much as a question would. But this is false. The phenomenologist Johannes Daubert explains the noematic element of questioning by developing a distinction between subject matters or *Sachverhalt* (literally, "subject matter") as known or cognized— *Erkenntnisverhalt* (literally, known subject matter)—and *Sachverhalt* as in question—*Frageverhalt* (literally, questioned subject matter) (see Schumann and Smith 1987, 368–9). We can further refine aspects and modes of being of *Sachverhalt*, such as *Wunschverhalt* (literally, wished for subject matter) or states of affairs as wished, and so on. In a phenomenology of wishing, we could distinguish between the noesis or subjectivity in the mode of wishing and the noema or states of affairs as that for which we wish or hope will come. In this way, Daubert shows how questioning has an objective yet noematic correlate that is not reducible to a mere inner sensation or subjective perception. The objective correlate of questioning is an "opening up" of a certain structure about subject matters, like a pop-up book, unfolded by separating yet suspending predicates and subjects in abeyance (Schumann and Smith 1987, 369). The *intentional object in questioning is the questionability of the object*, the *Frageverhalt*. When we ask a question about something, we are, as it were, expressing its questionability, just as when we declare a judgment about something, we express its knowability. The activity of questioning can also involve—but it need not involve—an attempt to move from a relatively open and undetermined *Frageverhalt* to a relatively closed *Erkenntnisverhalt*. At issue for us, regardless, is that questioning reveals the questionability of what is in question.

Moreover, the aspect of questionability or *Frageverhalt* has logical and hermeneutical priority over answers or complete thoughts. This is crucial to get down. As Gadamer puts the priority, "To understand a question is to ask it, but to understand a meaning is to understand it as an answer to a question" (Gadamer 2013, 383). Put another way, it is only in asking a question that we can come to understand something said as an answer; *it is only in this way that a sentence perceived can be transformed into a complete thought understood.* Asking questions stands in an order different from understanding meanings because it is a necessary condition for acquiring meanings *as meanings*. Only statements can mean something, and can only be meaningful if they answer to actually asked questions.

That does not imply, though, that we have to own or "mean" an answer even if it addresses a questioning we ourselves are expressing. A complete thought is a meaning because we can *consider it* as one among many possible answers to our question. It takes appropriation, though, to "mean" a meaning. In contrast, the only way to "understand" a question—the only way to "mean" it—is to *ask* it. As Gadamer points out, there is no "tentative or potential attitude of questioning. . . . Even when a person says such and such question might arise, this is already a real questioning that simply masks itself, out of either caution or politeness" (Gadamer 2013, 383). We might decide whether to express a question publicly, but we cannot intentionally decide whether a question occurs to us. Getting caught up in questioning is less an intentional activity and more a passivity, a mode of what Levinas calls "nonintentional consciousness" (Levinas 1998b, 123–32). Questions occur to us, or sometimes "strike" us. While we might decide to use interrogative statements to command or otherwise direct others, questioning's occurrent character—as opposed to its intentional or ego-driven character—distinguishes it *as genuine questioning*. Note that I am not claiming we do not have moments where we do not understand questions. If someone asks me a question in a language I do not have fluency in, I will not understand the question. Even if someone asks me a question in my mother tongue, I might not understand it if there are conjunctions with which I lack familiarity. The point is solely that understanding a question is to simultaneously be asking it. The asking *is* the understanding. Understanding a question is embodied in asking it. Just as sentences are complete thoughts perceived and complete thoughts are sentences understood, interrogative sentences are questions perceived and asked questions are interrogative sentences understood.

An illustration might help here. Surely, we have all experienced times where, in reading a difficult book (or perhaps a boring book like this one!), we finish a page and think to ourselves "What did I just read?!?" That is, we know that we looked at text, at a series of sentences, and yet we know that we have not comprehended what was being said. Numerous factors can be brought out as relevant for explaining this. Maybe the text is boring and thus does not hold our attention. Or maybe the text is written in an unfamiliar language, or at a level of sophistication that renders it like a foreign language. We may have got caught up in listening to background noise. I want to focus on those times when we do this not because we are bored or distracted, and not because we are overwhelmed by sophisticated jargon. I want to focus solely on instances where we are sufficiently attentive and sufficiently familiar with the language, and nevertheless still find ourselves at a loss at the end of a page. The one factor I want to isolate here is that, on a fundamental level, when we read a text and do not comprehend it, *it is because we are not actively asking the questions to which the text answers.* If we do not ask the questions, then whatever statements are made are lost on us. The sentences composing the text do not stand in ontological outer space. They answer to specific questions, and are complete thoughts. Only by asking their questions can we come to think the complete thoughts that address the questions. This is the priority of questioning; that questions are necessary for understanding.

Note that such priority is different from logical presuppositions contained in questions that I discussed earlier in erotetic logic and epistemic imperatives. There we looked at how in some approaches to questioning, particularly those approaches that reduce questions to epistemic imperatives or commands, lay out presupposed propositions from which answerers must select. For example, we have seen the question "What is your name?" transliterated as "Select one from the following: My name is Muhammad. My name is Ruth . . . etc." These complete thoughts articulating one's name are described as presupposed in the question. Or consider this alternative question, "Do you want vanilla or chocolate ice cream?" Again, the transliteration would be, "Select one: I want vanilla. I want chocolate." These sorts of presuppositions do not have priority in the way at issue here, where questioning has priority in the order of understanding. Of course, they seem to precede answers, at least implicitly, inasmuch as an answer pulls an option out from the implicit list. There are even further presuppositions in questions. The first example about one's name, for instance, *assumes someone even has a name.* It's probably a safe assumption, but it's an assumption nevertheless. At issue is not whether one even has a name, but that this is taken for granted and it is solely a matter of *which* name. These assumptions risk loading questions and biasing answers in preferred directions. For instance, the question "Have you stopped beating your dog yet?" assumes you have a dog, that you have been beating it, and that you should stop. In cases of genuine questioning, though, these assumptions and presuppositions provide parameters and constraints that give direction toward sources from which answers might come. These constraints do precede answers, and in that way have some priority—in both chronology and content.

I want to get at a different kind of priority, though. It has been called "hermeneutic priority." This priority is not merely chronological and is not merely in terms of constraints on content. Both chronology and content constraints can flutter, and thus do not have necessary priority. There are some exceptions to them having priority. For instance, we can simply reject loaded assumptions and thereby dissolve constraints laid out that try to force a certain answer from us. When asked if we have stopped kicking our dog, we can reply that we do not have a dog. Constraints on answers, or logical presuppositions in questions, do not always have priority. In other cases, especially as readers, we often come to the questions *after* considering sentences we read—and when the questions dawn on us, we finally understand the text. Questions do not necessarily occur to us at an earlier time than answers occur to us. There is one kind of priority, though, that cannot be undermined, a necessary priority: *Questioning is a condition of the possibility of any answering whatsoever.* Questioning is necessary for understanding complete thoughts. If we take away questioning, we take away understanding—in every instance. Without a question to which a perceived sentence answers, the sentence cannot transform into a complete thought understood. In terms of what is required in order to understand something, questioning takes priority. Questioning is, in Kant's words, a "transcendental condition of the possibility" of understanding. Transcendental, for us, just means the conditions that make something possible. What makes questioning possible?

Prejudices Are Historically Transmitted Presuppositions

I have looked at questioning in general—that is, the abstract structure of questionability that opens up aspects of things in their fluid indeterminacy in combination with our ontological negativity of subjectivity itself. It is also interesting to consider what makes specific and particular questions possible. While transcendental conditions are universal and make understanding possible at all and in every instance, each instance of questioning and understanding meanings is particular and different. This is a feature of the human condition specifically and the nature of reality generally. While we can only think universals, we can only sense particulars. For instance, we might be able to think "red" as an abstract and universal concept; we cannot see that "red," though. Instead, we see this or that specific red thing. Plato inherited this problem from pre-Socratic philosophers like Parmenides and Heraclitus, and Western philosophers have come to call it the problem of "the One and the many." Socrates, for instance, asks others about what is Just or Fair or Beautiful, but his conversation partners give him examples they believe embody justice (see Plato 2002). Socrates rejects such answers because they are merely particular examples and not an account of the nature of the Just itself. This problem also is addressed explicitly in other intellectual traditions. Ancient Buddhists approached this issue in terms of "interdependence," or *pratitya-sammutpada*. There seems to be many discrete entities, and yet, in terms of conditions and relations, they all seem to be one (see Thich 2010). The great medieval Indian philosophers Shankara and Ramanuja debated differences between absolute monism and "qualified non-dualism" (see Harrison 2019). How do singular things stand out from an undifferentiated unity? A crucial dynamic that brings down to earth our general readiness for tapping into questionability of things, our potential to see things in their questionability, is what we can call the "effect of history." Like physical sensations, historical processes seem to have an individuating function (see Aristotle 1983, 19a25–35; and MacIntyre 1981).

We cannot ask questions about things with which we have no familiarity, for instance. Such things do not stand out for us as subjects about which we can ask questions. Some things stand out from the horizon of the lifeworld as significant, as question-worthy. As we will see in detail later on, the lifeworld is that total framework of significance in which a person acts, thinks, and feels. There are a few ways this happens. In one way, we inherit traditions of inquiry, sets of questions, topics, and subject matters that coalesce and sediment into what in academia we call "disciplines." Recall that each discipline and field helps us to be critical in our thinking, because we use them to be self-conscious about the conditions of our thinking itself. In other words, academic disciplines discipline thinking. We have reached a moment where there has been an explosion of growth of disciplines, where we study almost everything imaginable. For example, there is now an interdisciplinary master of arts program in the United Kingdom focusing exclusively on the band the Beatles. The program studies this subject through a vast number of questions. Some of the standard disciplines include biology, psychology, anthropology, history, literature, philosophy, and more.

Let's take "psychology" as an example for closer inspection. The word itself indicates the subject matter—the study of the psyche or mind. That is the topic. There are numerous questions and methods used in the study of the mind, from the theoretical to the empirical. Is the mind relevantly distinct from the brain? Are behaviors indications of mental states? There are boundaries, though, too. For example, asking about broader social structures, such as the way governance works, moves us from psychology into political science and sociology. The boundaries may be porous or even rough, because some scholars work in the area we know as social psychology. Indeed, some fields, like religious studies, African-American studies, and more, are intrinsically interdisciplinary—where scholars in the field make use of numerous disciplines to examine their subject matters. In religious studies, some scholars use historical methods, others use philosophy, others use literary criticism, and still others use mixtures of the three or more. Because it is a field, and not a discipline, no one discipline dominates as "the" method of religious studies. We can ask questions about the psychology of religious experience. We can ask sociological questions about the ways a religion is organized. And so on.

An additional aspect of traditions of inquiry is not merely disciplinary specialization, but also cultural and ethnic differentiation. Traditions involve both sedimentation and innovation, handing down cultural forms of life or lifeforms as well as possibilities for adaptation and change. These lifeforms involve sedimentation in that some practices settle and take on some continuity with past versions of similar lifeforms. They also involve innovation, because through being grounded in the sedimented aspect of traditions, we are freed to invent and create new aspects of or even entirely new forms of life (see MacIntyre 1988).

Language games or fields of intelligibility accompany all forms of life. And so these fields of intelligibility determine a horizon of relevance for any specified lifeworld. When we think of egocentric directions, like front, right, left, and so on, we might respond to the question, "Where is the restaurant?" by saying, "To the right." However, Muslims have also inherited a field of intelligibility that coordinates space (and time) quite differently. A key feature is represented by the *Qibla*, the indication of the direction facing Mecca. Notice how the intelligibility of space is coordinated differently; that is, the predicative possibilities are different. We can address this through illustrations about time, too. For example, we might participate in a form of life that uses a purportedly secularized version of the Gregorian calendar, taking the year to be 2021 CE. We know, despite secularizing the era-dating system (Common Era, as opposed to *Anno Domini*—or, the Year of One's Lord), that 2021 is that many years since the birth of Jesus of Nazareth. Every time secularists use this era-dating system, they are—at least implicitly or inadvertently—complicit with what we can call "Christian supremacy." Jews, Buddhists, Muslims, Hindus, and more, all use very different era-dating systems. For example, in the Jewish era-dating system the year is AM 5781. Which one is the "true" year? Is the question of truth out of place here? Both are "true" within their discursive conventions, forms of life, and fields of intelligibility. We will return to the topic of truth in Part II.

Another way specific questions emerge has to do with historical circumstances. Cultures hand down subject matters that stand out as particularly pressing topics. Some of these topics seem to transcend specific cultures and remain constant. For example, how ought we respect and take care of our elders? Not merely our parents, but our grandparents and the broader community of elders from whom we inherit our cultures? While different cultures might handle this issue differently, the topic seems relevantly similar. Some topics are specific to an historical era or region of the world. With the rise of modern science in Europe, for instance, some thinkers felt an urgent need to address the question of how to trust modern science in light of the dissolution of what had seemed reliable—religion. Some topics are quite local, like directions from one place to another or which restaurant serves the best pancakes. These communities define the horizons of inquiry and meaning, placing constraints on what is and is not relevantly significant.

In a way, they also shape our expectations and anticipations of where answers can even come from. This is the broader structure within which "prejudice" occurs. Stereotypes are only one negative aspect of prejudice. We are literally preloaded with anticipations of meaning in all cases of experience. As Gadamer writes:

> History does not belong to us; we belong to it. Long before we understand ourselves through the process of self-examination, we understand ourselves in a self-evident way in the family, society, and state in which we live. The focus on subjectivity is a distorting mirror. The self-awareness of the individual is only a flickering in the closed circuits of historical life. That is why the pre-judgments of the individual, far more than [one's] judgments, constitute the historical reality of [one's] being. (Gadamer 2013, 289)

These prejudices, or literally these prejudgments, are structural elements of what it is to be conditioned by history. Each of us live in a particular place and time, with particular languages and frameworks for interpreting experiences.

A further way specific questions strike us comes from particularly provoking experiences. We experience something out of the ordinary, and, in our surprise, we start to ask questions. A familiar scent leads us to ask, "What is that smell?" We hear thunder and wonder, "Is it about to rain?" Or perhaps even more worrisome—a part of our body feels different suddenly, such as a stomach ache, and we ask, "Was it something I ate?" Think of all the ways we attend to how our body feels and all the questioning we do in light of our bodies' fluctuations. It is no wonder that some people turn into hypochondriacs! Another level of our experience can become striking enough for questioning. It seems that cold weather is shifting, and even the amount of tundra is gradually wearing away. What causes this trend in climate change? Questions mediate between experience and thought in this way. When an experience strikes us in such a way that it stands in relief, that is itself the inauguration and raising of this experience in a question—like elastic man's getting shot by a bullet. We get unsettled when a piece of gravel pummels upward. By thinking, we bring experience back down to earth by trying to settle it with a complete thought in answer to our question(s).

A further interesting way questions emerge is through apparent changes in our very ability to experience and perceive. Perhaps you have heard of the Sapir-Whorf hypothesis from the mid-twentieth century where it was postulated that a culture's language determined their ability to perceive. For instance, it was claimed that the Inuit not only had numerous subtle conceptual and terminological distinctions between types of snow, but also that they actually perceived these different types of snow—unlike people in the lower forty-eight who only had terms like "snow," "sleet," and "ice." That is, it was believed that the words determined perception. What we know now is that the relations between language and perception are slightly different from that direct causality. It is not that a culture's words determine perception, but that a culture's words determine or encourage attention. For example, an indigenous people of Australia who speak Guugu Yimithirr exclusively use cardinal directions, like north, east, and so on, whereas Americans tend to use egocentric directions, like left, back, and so on. Thus, when people who speak this language are asked directions, say, to something located behind them, they seem to point "at" themselves—are seen as pointing at themselves by those who tend to use egocentric directions—but are really pointing through themselves (Deutscher 2010). We have come to understand that there was no word for the color "blue" in the ancient world. In the Hebrew Bible as in ancient Greek epic poetry, the sky and seas were described in terms of hues of black and gray, or even thick red or purple wines. Did ancient peoples not perceive blue, or was blue simply something to which they did not really pay attention? Nevertheless, there were few questions about blue in the ancient world, but a plethora of questions emerges about blue in the modern world. Through traditions, through historical events, and through such particular experiences, specific questions occur to us.

Why do we ask questions at all, though? This is asking for something different from transcendental conditions of questioning, such as the structure of questionability radiating from subject matters. This is also asking for something different from historical conditions of questioning, such as particular experiences or accumulated traditions with their fields of intelligibility. Rather, here we are asking an ontological and existential question. What is the structure of human being such that questioning is in our wheelhouse at all?

I think there are two main ontological structures of being human that make questioning possible for us: anxiety and the face of the Other. Since I will focus on questioning and dialogue in Part III, I will hold off on the latter until then and only focus on "anxiety" for now. In existential ontology, anxiety is the English translation for the German *Angst*. At issue is not the psychological state developed in the psychological *Diagnostic and Statistical Manual of Mental Disorders*, a condition for which one might take medication. There is no medication for angst, although many people try to evade it through preoccupations and "self-medication" (see Heidegger 1996). It is that negativity Merleau-Ponty and de Beauvoir discuss as intrinsic to intentionality. Let us be careful here, though. Is it a "lack" or an "opening"? Is the negativity of angst a deprivation or an opportunity?

Recall that, for us, genuine questioning does not aim at answers. Typical interrogative sentences, those that are transcribed easily into imperatives or commands, do aim at needed answers. If angst is a deprivation, then questioning is deficit driven, spurred on by a compulsive quest for answers. When we do not get our answers, we feel we have failed, that we have lost something. Many existentialist philosophers, such as Jean-Paul Sartre, approach angst in this way. I think genuine questioning is our clue to an alternative interpretation of angst. The negativity is a clearing in which we can grow, in which we can expand our horizons of understanding. For example, realizing that when we ask what direction we are facing we might receive answers indicative of vastly different forms of life shows us ever-expanding horizons, opening more and more opportunities to us. In this way, as we have said, genuine questioning is surplus driven, rooted in a desire and love for more. Again, we are capable of questioning for the joy of it, tarrying with what questioning itself opens to us, without feeling like we have been deprived of answers. The negativity is a clearing for growth, not a loss.

Let us turn to close this chapter with some brief discussion of "thought" without questioning.

Dogmatic Thought Lacks Genuine Questions

I want to indicate some peculiar consequences of what we can call "a forgetfulness of questioning." Without questions, thought and sentences dissolve into mere exchange of signs. I also want to suggest one explanation for why questioning seems easy to forget. It is in part because questioning literally does not say anything; answers do. I will end by showing how all this points to Parts II and III on reasoning and dialogue, respectively.

I want to call out two biases in contemporary reflection and develop some genealogical factors leading up to them. They are both species of what I want to call "the hegemony of the sign." One bias can be identified in terms of popular culture and social media with the prevalence of things such as "likes," emojis, and Instagram. The other can be identified in terms of the disciplines of logic and basic reasoning with the prevalence of focus on propositions and inferences. Let us start with propositions and reasoning. Recall that complete thoughts are only understood inasmuch as they are answers to questions we *actually* ask. If we are not asking the question, then the sentences we perceive are lost on us as meaningful complete thoughts. As I will cover more discretely in Part II, in logic and basic reasoning we are taught to focus our attention on propositions. And we are told that the fundamental unit of reasoning is an argument, consisting of the elements of at least one premise and a conclusion. What binds premises and conclusions together are entailment conditions and inferential commitments. Answers are not inferred from genuine questions, though, even if logicians try to infer them from epistemic imperatives. We showed this earlier when we explained erotetic logic, and its focus on presupposed propositions. What happens is that premises and conclusions dislodged from the questions they answer become contextless propositions. As Meyer explains, this focus represses questioning in a constant movement of abstraction into meaningless sentences (Meyer 1995, 216). We cannot understand a perceived sentence if we are not asking the question to which it answers. It takes asking the question to grasp the complete thought. Meyer calls this bias of overlooking questioning "propositionalism" or propositionalist ideology, and indicates ways it has distorted Western thinking and corroded what we consider to be critical logical reasoning. Propositionalist ideology enframes reasoning as tracking inferential commitments and entailments, where trigger-happy fallacy (bad arguments) identification and accusation become the marks of "critical" thinking. Indeed, beginner students are taught to analyze the validity of formal reasoning without even understanding the meaning of propositions. Since questioning animates consideration of meanings, though, then in this process of training in formal reasoning, we do not really understand what we are reading or hearing or thinking or what is being said. At the bottom of all this, sentences get treated as just bigger signs or labels in the propositionalist framework. Either the sentence is a corresponding label for a fact, and so is true, or the sentence does not correspond to the fact, and so is false (see Wittgenstein 1922).

This hegemony of the sign might be seen more clearly with examples from popular culture. Consider the growing prevalence of emoji in text communication (see Giannoulis and Wilde 2019). People do not state complete thoughts, but instead use faces, hands, and other symbols to communicate or express themselves. Indeed, each year the amount of emoji grows to allow for more and more discrete and subtle representations. We now have a smiling "poop" emoji, along with an octopus, a shrug gesture, hearts, and more. In a sense, these are images or representations, where we attempt to capture a corresponding feeling. Related to this is the plethora of image-focused social media such as Tumblr, Instagram, Snapchat, Flickr, Pinterest, and so on or even the plethora of moving picture media like YouTube, Hulu, Netflix, and so on. We seem to believe, on a global level, that pictures are worth a thousand words. We are placated in our reactions to these images as well, where—at least at first—our reactions were restricted to "liking" or "disliking" (or ignoring) posts. Now social media allow us to have slightly more nuanced emotional reactions, where in some cases we don't just "like" an image but are allowed to "love" it (see Seargeant 2019)! Note the passivity of reactions here. Those who are privileged enough to access social media are often placated in passive consumption of images. This is not to say social media is never productive. The Arab Spring popular uprisings against dictators in 2012 demonstrates that it can be productive in some ways (see Alsaleh 2015). It is to say that such communication, the incessant focus on images and representation, restrains, and constricts thinking complete thoughts. It creates habits of attention, habits about what is important to pay attention to and habits about what we don't have attention spans for. Can you imagine listening to one of Abraham Lincoln's speeches today, which were up to eight hours long?

This privilege of the image is, of course, nothing new or surprising. We have been idolatrous about images since early social formations, making icon panels and comic strips since we dwelt in caves. The god of Abraham seems to have been particularly sensitive to this, declaring that this god's people ought to never create idols to worship, even if the idol is supposed to represent the god itself. In India, alternatively, there was no such suspicion of representation but a trust that symbols are transparent to the divine as focal points for attention and not the actual objects of worship (see, for example, Courtright 1989). Is this or that specific idol being treated as a representation of the divine, or the divine itself? It is parallel to debates about violence in videogames. Can we trust people to distinguish virtual from actual reality?

In Ancient Greece, there were competing theories to explain language's relation to reality. One promoted a strictly natural correspondence between signs and things, which we can witness with onomatopoeia, like the word "buzz." Another promoted a strictly arbitrary and conventional relation between signs and things. We can explain the hegemony of signs by returning to the elements of a complete thought. Recall that thoughts consist of both a subject and a predicate. Is a sign most like a predicate or a subject? You got it. This drift toward signs and representative images is a drift toward sentential subjects. Merely laying out numerous sentential subjects, though, is not yet to think, even if we arrange them ornately and deliberately. A complete thought involves putting subjects in predicaments, in answering to questions that actually are being asked. Going to Instagram and having image after image thrown at you, what question does each image answer? Do images have to answer questions? No, images don't have to answer questions. Not everything needs to be an answer to a question. Recall our efforts earlier to protect understanding from pretentious inflation. There is no need to try to smear understanding across everything. Some things simply are not understandable. There are vast and many things that are not sentential answers to questions we actually ask. So do not get me wrong: The criticism is not of social media as such. It is a criticism of the surplus, the corrosive habits and effects social media has on thinking complete thoughts. We are trained to construe "thinking" itself in light of these biased habits. How can we think complete thoughts in the midst of bombardment by images demanding our loyalty and worship?

There are two problematic consequences of this drift in thinking toward sentential subjects. In academia, especially in the humanities and human sciences, there has now come to dominance a peculiar method of analysis, semiotics. Semiotics is the study of signs—the analysis of relations and conventions of signifiers (written, signed, or spoken signs), signifieds (purportedly mental ideas), and referents (the purportedly real objects in the external world). Coined by Saussure, developed by Pierce, and made en vogue by Derrida, semiotics has come to be among the major contenders for the place of the fundamental discourse of intelligibility in the academy, alongside Marxism, Historicism, and others (see, for example, Danesi 2016). Of course, semiotics is an important area of study. We could, for example, perform a semiotics of peacock mating rituals through a study of the signs of their feather displays. Scholars have helped us trace oppressive power dynamics through the rhetorical use of signs, such as signifiers of white supremacy. My problem is solely with its complicity with the hegemony of representation. Semiotics purports to be the first and final layer of analysis. It does not recognize its limits. It is one thing to analyze the signification of specific signs or even theorize the precise relations between conventions, signs, and symbols. It is another to treat complete thoughts as merely another sign, as if there were no remainder left out of account. That is, semiotics—in *some* people's hands—tries to *be* semantics, the study of sentences, by subordinating semantics to semiotics. Such people are, perhaps, just more sophisticated idolaters?

The other problematic consequence of privileging the sentential subject is what I call a glacial drift toward substance metaphysics. On a fundamental level, is reality constituted by discrete things (e.g., atoms), or by processes and relations (e.g., quantum swerves)? This is not the question of the chicken or the egg, even if it feels that way. It is in the interest of substance metaphysics, the privilege of the sign, an ideology, to get you disinterested in thinking this question through. We are trained to want the easy quick "answer," stockpiling sentential subjects. Most Westerners are, on the whole, inclining toward substance metaphysics, the idea that reality is box, and inside that box are piles and piles of things. There have to be "things" first for there to even be relations between the things, right?

There are some concerns with substance metaphysics. If there are substances, things that truly are one way, then—as has happened in the past—some people might hold others down by claiming that they are "naturally" inferior. It is just the way things are, they might say. They might say, "Boys will be boys." I am sure you can imagine other, perhaps even worse, political and social implications of substance metaphysics. We know that social Darwinism and theories of different races allowed people of European descent to placate their conscience as the oppressed, colonized, and brutalized other peoples. Note, though, that these social and political worries about substance metaphysics do not make it false. Just because we are motivated to promote social equity, that does not make substance metaphysics incorrect. It can, however, motivate us to ask about the alternative, a process-centered or relation-centered metaphysics (see Ronkin 2009). Just as we have been emphasizing that questioning has priority over answering in thinking, we can see a fit here with emphasizing that relations have ontological priority over things.

It is not like any of us really do this on purpose. It does not seem like we set out to invent a metaphysics to serve our political interests in social supremacy and exploitation of others. We see this everywhere, though, where ideologies serve the interests of the upper-class (see Marx 1970). For example, we know of many elites who have claimed throughout history and across diverse cultures that their rule is the will of the divine, as in the divine right of kings. It is interesting to note that there seems to have been just about as many gods as there have been rulers. If it has been so prevalent, can we really say it is this or that specific person's fault? Did they somehow do it deliberately, whereas others did it accidentally? I want to direct our attention away from individualized blame and toward something we may be overlooking in our effort to blame, such as historian and antiracist activist Ibram X. Kendi's focus on racist policies rather than racist people (Kendi 2019). But enough of this for now. Let's look at the insidious forgetfulness of questioning.

I believe the hegemony of signs and its politico-economic repercussions is in part explainable by way of what we can call the forgetfulness of questioning. We have forgotten to question. Questioning seems, on the whole, to have come to an end. We live in a so-called "information age." It is, we might say, data rich but information poor. But that is not because there is not enough information. It is because we have no idea what questions that data, that information, is supposed to answer. In fact, if our suggestions about the hegemony of signs are true, then a lot of our data and information are not really complete thoughts for understanding, but just a stockpiling of subjects. It is consistent with what we have come to know as "human resources," a reservoir of power that can be squeezed out of human organisms (see Heidegger 1977). It is like collectors acquiring toys or comics or records but never playing with them, reading them, or listening to them. What is the point of this stockpile of subjects? In whose interests is it to stockpile them rather than to use them in thinking complete thoughts?

Why is it that questioning is forgettable? For us, it is primarily because questions do not say anything. The only way to understand a question, to mean one, is to ask it. Only in light of questions can we understand a complete thought as an answer rather than merely perceive a sentence. Questioning makes consideration of meanings possible, but questioning does not "express" a meaning (Schumann and Smith 1987, 365). Questions, though, are not answers, and so they do not mean anything. We do not have to mean a sentence even if it answers our question. We can consider one complete thought among many possible answers, but it takes appropriation and ownership and responsibility to intend or mean a meaning. There is, however, no potential or tentative attitude of questioning. To consider a question is to be in fact asking it. To note that such and such question might arise is already a real questioning disguising itself, perhaps out of politeness. Questions, especially genuine ones, occur to us. And in this way, they are not really things we can intentionally decide. Questioning does not say anything about a subject matter; sentences do and are meanings or complete thoughts insofar as they answer to questions.

Genuine questions are language on the way to becoming complete thoughts, and thus they facilitate the process of thinking, of combining and separating subjects and predicates. Compelling experiences, traditions of intelligibility, and historical circumstances raise questions. Perhaps the most basic one is: "What is that?" Once a thought is formulated, there are questions we can also ask on the other side of it. There are questions on the way to thoughts and questions on the other side of thoughts, and questions about thoughts themselves. If we settle on a thought, we see the end of thinking. Thinking is, like most living processes, self-cancelling (see Nietzsche 2008). The end of thinking is belief in or commitment to a position. Hence, this is what a "pro-position" should mean. Belief can be dogmatic when all possible questioning is policed and repressed. Belief can be reopened to more thinking if further questions are allowed. Notice that the hegemony of signs and its accompanying substance metaphysics is complicit with dogmatic belief.

Because we cannot think everything we know all at once, we have to draw it out bit by bit. And in this way, thinking is like a dialogue with oneself. As Plato approached thinking, it is a dialogue of the soul with itself (see Gadamer 2013, 422; and Plato 1997). What kinds of questions are we asking ourselves in our thought processes? Are we asking ourselves (and others) genuine questions (see Dickman 2018b)? Or are we deploying epistemic imperatives in trying to control and command others and ourselves? In Parts II and III that follow, we will be looking at the nature of reasoning and the nature of dialogue, focusing in particular on the roles questioning plays in both of those.

Part II

Make Questions Explicit for Reasoning

Part II: Make Questions Explicit for Reasoning

Let's work through two topics in this second part: reasoning and questioning. What even *is* reasoning? How might questioning relate to reasoning? I addressed similar topics above with regard to thinking. Thus, our preliminary step needs to be to coordinate relations between thought and reason. Are they not the same thing, just named by different terms? Is it possible to think without reasoning, or reason without thinking?

Delving into all these topics, like those concerning thought, are no small task. Yet, again, we do not have to start from scratch because numerous others have sought to develop accounts of reasoning. There seems to have been a shift in culture—sometimes ascribed to ancient Greeks, although we can find similar patterns in ancient South Asian, East Asian, and Central American civilizations—away from appeal to supernatural authority and toward appeal to reason. Earliest appeals to authority took the form of religious or mythic dictates, an authoritarian form of discourse (see Lincoln 1996). We see elements of this in the Greek consultation of oracles, in the Chinese mandate of *Tian* or heaven, and more. Such authoritarian discourse remained prevalent throughout medieval cultures, and we still witness instances of it today when government officials appeal to biblical passages to justify policies, such as in the United States' separation of refugee families at the US-Mexican border in mid-2018. Former attorney general Jeff Sessions cited Romans 13, where Paul urges obedience to a government because it has been ordained by the god (see Gonzales 2018). With the global rise of reasoning, we see efforts to address questions like "why do we believe what we believe" or "why do we do what we do" by appeal to logical inferences, principled grounds, scientific and natural evidence, and more.

Reason comes from the Latin *reri*, which means to reckon and think, and has a significant correlate in Greek, namely, *logos*. The word *logos* is interesting because it has many connotations, ranging from discourse and language to reason and logic. It forms the suffix of many terms that name contemporary academic disciplines, where it means "the study of"—such as sociology, biology, and more.

Let us take time to dwell with reasoning and what calls for it. In Part II, I will look closely at fundamental elements of reasoning: premises and conclusions. I will then examine ways questioning facilitates separation and combination of premises and conclusions in complete reasonings or arguments. I will also formulate a schema for at least four orientations of questioning in relation to reasoning. I will close this second part with investigations about generative and creative limits of reasoning, particularly as these contribute to worldbuilding without dogmatism.

4

Reasoning Only Happens in Explicit Arguments

Chapter Outline

Let us stipulate a definition of reasoning to focus our attention on a shared topic. The approach to reasoning I want to take can be developed on the basis of what a complete argument consists of. An argument consists of, at the very least, a premise and a conclusion. That is, an argument involves relating at least two complete thoughts. One might suppose, then, that an argument is just a pile of sentences; however, a specific relation between the sentences constitute an argument and distinguish one from other differently structured collections of sentences. In moving from thought to reason, we can see that while thinking coordinates subjects and predicates via the copula, reasoning coordinates multiple thoughts in the unique relations of premises, conclusions, and principles of derivation or inferential support between the complete thoughts. Inasmuch as the fundamental particles of reasoning are the premise and the conclusion, then it seems that reasoning is the activity of combining or separating multiple complete thoughts in a specific way called "inference." Let's break this down for more detail and context. In this chapter, I will examine ambiguities in the notions of "argument" and "reason." I will develop the crucial elements of reasoning: premises and conclusions. And I will close with a discussion of "truth" in thought and reason.

One Cannot "Win" an Argument

What are we doing when we argue? When someone asks us why we are doing what we are doing, why do we supply them with reasons for it? Can someone "win" an argument? Colloquially, we often use the word "fighting" interchangeably with arguing. We all know that arguing is not the same as a fistfight or boxing match, of course. Yet we see arguing in light of fighting, where fighting is taken as the way in which people work out disagreements or even take out frustration or anger on one another, whether justified or not. As philosophers of language George Lakoff and Mark Johnson explain that this is not just a way of talking, but of modeling our experience of reality (Lakoff and Johnson 2003, 4–5). Argument *is* fighting because we experience arguments in terms of it. Consider all the connotations of battle that we associate with argument. People "defend" their positions and claims. Others "attack" an argument. People often are complimented on "bringing out their big guns" in an argument. It seems then that, just as we can win or lose a fight, so also can we win or lose an argument.

Fighting, though, is only one among many metaphors or models for the discrete analysis and experience of arguing. In fact, it is a dead metaphor because we have a difficult time even realizing it is a metaphor and a difficult time taking other metaphors for it seriously. As a metaphor, fighting helps order our values about arguing. We seem to want to win arguments—indeed, this is part of the basis of debate teams, clubs, and competitions. This structuring of arguments in terms of fights is only partial, though. It provides a systematic way of seeing arguments, but it hides other aspects of arguments. The model is so pervasive and hegemonic that it is difficult even to imagine alternatives. What would argument look like if we used "doggy-paddling in a swimming pool" as a model for it? Is it really in the nature of argumentation as such that we cannot accept use of alternative metaphors for it? Given the hegemony of this model, I think we should ask whose interests it serves to get us to see arguing exclusively in terms of fighting. Should we continue to subject ourselves to this model of argumentation? This model serves patriarchal interests and restrictive gender roles that support those interests. Let me explain.

Argument is approached primarily in terms of an adversarial structure, in a social context where masculinity is associated with aggressiveness and femininity is associated with relationality (Burrow 2010, 235). We live in a society where "you throw like a girl" is a derogatory slur—even though many of us know it shouldn't be this way. Argument is associated with aggressive terms, like "sparring," "shooting down the opponent," and more. Because it focuses on win-lose competition, the tactics used often involve testing claims against the most extreme opposition rather than collaborative efforts at helping build better arguments together. Debaters look for contradictions or exaggerated thought experiments for which positions cannot account. When a position cannot account for every such extreme thing, opponents cynically reject it whole. The pursuit of identifying contradictions is so prevalent that we do not even listen to others, but merely look for contradictions. We have become trigger-happy with contradiction accusations—just look at any characterization of political partisans, where they call each other hypocrites, saying one thing and doing another or being inconsistent over time. This sort of aggressive defense counts as a "good" argument in social media frenzies as well as in professional academic settings.

What is more, this orientation fits with gendered tendencies and sexist hierarchies, where masculinity tends to perform aggressively and adversarially (Burrow 2010, 236). Such argumentative contexts are oppressive to women and gender-nonconforming individuals. Thus, we need to be cautious about our complicity with this model for argument. It has a history of complicity with patriarchal oppression, where women have turned away from disciplines like philosophy because adversarial classrooms and conferences alienate women and others. Just think about ways women are caricatured when they participate in masculine-associated behaviors. In cases where women participate in these institutions, women are often judged as "too aggressive," and they are labeled with other negative terms. People are bullied to give up their ways of being so that they conform to adversarialism, and they are policed and punished for not doing so. The double standard makes it particularly challenging to women and gender-nonconforming individuals trying to formulate and put forward arguments or hold positions of authority. Consider all the studies of student perceptions and treatment of women and minority professors, such as in course evaluations or even in challenges to professor grading (see Mitchell and Martin 2018). People who use politeness tactics are subordinated; people who seek to win might deploy any tactics necessary to gain the upper hand. If winning is what matters, what happens to truth? Is it not subordinated to the interest of winning?

In Part III, we will turn to look at the possibilities and prospects for collaborative models of argument like dialogue, but for now let us stipulate our approach to argument in light of our approach to thinking. For us, an argument is *not* adversarial opposition, but a fundamental unit of reasoning.

An argument consists of at least two statements or complete thoughts—namely, a premise and a conclusion. An atom of reasoning is an argument, and the two particles that make up this atom are the premise and the conclusion. Recall that a complete thought consists of a predicate unified with a subject through a copula. And recall that a complete thought is a sentence understood, but a sentence is a complete thought perceived with the senses. We can clarify a parallel distinction on the level of reasoning. A unit of reasoning or an argument consists of a relevant relation between at least two complete thoughts. Below, I will elaborate on this relation of relevance as it is better known as "logical inference." For terminological parsimony, let us name a *potentially* relevantly related set of sentences a mere "exposition." An exposition is a group of sentences nearby one another that may seem, at first glance, as if they are relevantly related. It takes understanding the sentences and their relation, not merely seeing them nearby one another, to grasp the argument *as an argument*. Thus, an argument is an exposition understood; an exposition is an argument perceived.

We can see someone is trying to present an argument to us because they use a number of cues, such as concluding words like "therefore" or "thus," or premise indicator words like "because" or "since." It is possible to perceive the cues, and yet not understand their argument. We might not understand the complete thoughts forming the premises or conclusion, or we might not follow the inferential relations they are drawing among their premises and conclusions. Just as it takes questioning to understand a sentence *as* a complete thought, it takes questioning to understand an exposition *as* an argument, to follow the lines of reasoning. An exposition is only an alleged argument if we do not understand it. We might see sentences braided together, but that does not mean we understand their inferential relations. Let us keep this distinction between exposition and argument in mind as we proceed.

Notice here just how different an argument is from a "fight." Whether an argument or merely an exposition, it is foremost a list of sentences. That is it. So far, it does not matter *whose* sentences they are. That is, it makes little difference if they are "yours" or "mine," and so this approach undermines convenient identification of winners and losers. An argument is a unit of reasoning because premises are "reasons" for their conclusions.

This should help us clarify another aspect of argument and reasoning. I am not talking about motives for actions or opinions. Sometimes people will do something, and a companion will ask, "Why did you do that?" When they answer with their motive, we sometimes call that their "reason" for what they did. Just like the word "bank," the word "reason" gets used in many ways. We can keep usages straight by indicating that we are focused exclusively on argument and not psychological motivation. When someone does something on the basis of a motivation (whether intentional or unintentional), we see that there is a kind of linear causal relation between motive and action. They did this *because* of that. Indeed, we sometimes use appeal to motives to dismiss what someone says or argues. Consider how women are dismissed unfairly when accused of having premenstrual syndrome, as if that renders what women might say in that condition innocuous. Appeal to motivations provides an explanation for why people believe what they believe or do what they do, an explanation that often can be used to explain *away* their beliefs and actions. For us, an explanation is not an argument.

Reasoning in an argument is an attempt to provide an adequate justification or warrant for a specific belief or action, and can include determination of inferential relations among statements as well as elaboration on principles concerning those inferential relations. I will be detailing this throughout the rest of this chapter and throughout Part II overall. For now, though, note that this capacity requires both articulation—elaborating and defining your terms—and reflection—stepping back from the seemingly immediate pulls of a situation. It requires articulation because to state two complete thoughts involves defining and clarifying our terms. We need to spell out each idea into a complete thought with both subjects and predicates, and do this in accord with specific questions. We need to avoid buzzwords, vague words, and jargon the best that we can in most situations of argument. We can do this by stipulating definitions as needed, and by making explicit what would otherwise be merely implicit. Keep in mind, though, that the demand for definition can neglect that we often arrive at understanding through dialogue, and definitions are often results of, not necessarily conditions for, argument.

Argument also requires reflection, where we step back from the multifarious forces colliding in a situation. We do not have to be caused to engage in action and thoughts merely by the force of nonrational influences. For us, thoughts are as "real" as falling rocks. They are part of the total causal network of the universe, but we call the causal relations between thoughts "reasons" or "inferences." In fact, it may be unhelpful to model the relations between premises and conclusions in arguments on the basis of linear causality as we seem to see it in dominos and pool halls. Premises do not "cause" conclusions like one domino piece falling into another. Instead, reflection clears a space in which we can reason, draw out logical or inferential relations among and between thoughts. Reflection is our ability not only to be conscious of something happening, but *to be conscious of our consciousness*. It is, as I explained in our rudimentary phenomenology of subject matters in question, our awareness of the questionability of phenomena.

Such stepping back, however, is not merely in our power as if there were some "free will" independent of the multifarious causal network of a situation. Stepping back is a natural process of consciousness, a specifically dialectical process where—like a seesaw—experience informs consciousness and consciousness informs experience. As the modern philosopher Georg Wilhelm Friedrich Hegel elaborates, consciousness seems to seek fulfillment in what it takes as the most immediate relation to reality, but it is constantly pulled up short and frustrated by its inability to get what it thinks it wants (Hegel 1977, 58–66). For example, consciousness seems to want complete certainty, and construes this certainty as available in the immediacy of sensory experience. It seems such sensations allow for pure and undistorted access to reality as it is. When we look carefully at immediate sensory experience, though, the knowledge available there is so vacuous and indeterminate that we can hardly feel satisfied with it as "knowledge." All we are given are the vaguest of coordinates like "this," "here," and "now." In this frustration, we realize that we need mediation—concepts and predicates—for knowledge and understanding. We know that a map to scale representing every detail would be a useless map (see Baudrillard 1983). Models help us access what matters. Reflection is this capacity of consciousness to overcome dissatisfactory frustration by striving for greater understanding through the creation and application of models and concepts.

Before moving into examinations of premises and conclusions separately, let us briefly indicate those things which are *not* arguments so that we may stay focused by contrast. Explanations and accounts are not arguments, though we might use arguments to support commitment to one explanation rather than another. An explanation tries to show *why* something is the case, not prove *that* it is the case or show that it is probably the case. Is it about common knowledge? If so, then it is probably an explanation. Is it concerning a past event? If so, then it is probably an explanation. Aphorisms, or pithy "deep thoughts," are not arguments either, though we might interpret arguments out of them as we ruminate on them. Definitions are not arguments, because they are not even complete thoughts. Summaries and lists are not arguments. They merely convey information about a subject, and not necessarily in any order—especially not in the structured order of premise and conclusion. A report about an argument is not an argument or a making of that argument. We should take particular caution here, employing the "mention" and "use" distinction. Just because we mention something does not show that we endorse it or seek to use it. Illustrations and examples are not arguments either. They might provide an instance of a broader claim, perhaps to clarify it, or they might figure into an argument as a premise. On their own, however, they do not support or prove a claim. Unsupported assertions and unwarranted assumptions are also not arguments, but here again they might figure into an argument. An assumption is something we take for granted, taking it as true without evidence and reasons. Many assumptions may be motivated by experience or tradition, but things like stereotypes are where assumptions go awry. Unsupported assertions are statements a speaker might believe, like the quip, "People are not afraid of dying; they are afraid of never having lived." Conditional statements might look like arguments, but they are not. Conditional statements are "if, then" statements that involve an antecedent and a consequent—such as "If it is raining, then the picnic is canceled." The antecedent is not a premise, and the consequent is not a conclusion, even though we do sometimes use the word "then" to indicate conclusions. At times, though, such conjunctions can be shorthand for inferences or arguments.

In sum, none of these are arguments because the sentences do not stand in the supportive relevant relation we call "inference." But enough of what arguments are not. Let's turn to examine elements of what makes arguments what they are and the nature of rational support.

Conclusions Are Supported Complete Thoughts

Recall that an argument is the combination of at least two complete thoughts that stand in a relevant relation of premise and conclusion. Let us dig into conclusions, and then turn our attention to premises. Conclusions are complete thoughts, and so must consist of both a subject and a predicate. The subject of the conclusion is what the argument as a whole is about, and what is predicated of the subject in the conclusion is what the argument as a whole sets out to support. This means that a conclusion is a complete thought that allegedly *receives* support from other thoughts. That is, the conclusion is supposed to be supported by one or more premises. Premises are supporting complete thoughts; they are what allegedly *provide* support to the conclusion. Conclusions are what arguers are trying to get people to believe, to agree to, or even to do. Premises are the means by which arguers do so.

There can only be one conclusion to an argument. Of course, the conclusion may be used as a premise to any number of further arguments. But in one unit of reasoning—in one argument—there is only one conclusion. And conclusions are indicated by a select number of terms or indicator phrases, such as "therefore," "thus," "hence," "it follows that," "consequently," "this shows that," and more. Although we have come to expect conclusions to be at the bottom or end of an argument when printed on a page, there is nothing that forces such an arrangement. Indeed, thesis statements in essays, inasmuch as they form the argument's conclusion, often appear in an introduction before any premises. We expect this arrangement of conclusions coming at the end of an argument because of all the other uses to which the word "conclusion" is put. Stories and songs often conclude with a resolution. A ceremonial event concludes with a procession and exit of the main participants. Conclusions have come to be seen as synonymous with chronological endings. But the notion of "conclusion" we are after here has less to do with where the complete thought occurs in an arranged exposition and more to do with the nature of the relevance between it and its premise(s).

There are two key aspects of conclusions I want to emphasize here. The first comes from an etymology of the word "conclude." Notice that the prefix, "con-," means "together" or "with." It forms the prefix of numerous other words like "concept," "concern," "concatenation," "concierge," "concentric," and "concert." Concentric circles are those that share a center. A concierge is a fellow servant. The point is that there is a notion of togetherness and sharing or convergence connoted by the prefix. The root word, "-clude," comes from the Latin term for closing, fastening, shutting, or terminating. Thus, a conclusion brings things—namely a specified relation of subject and predicate—together in a closure. This closure is a closure of our horizon of possible commitments. It limits what is available to us to commit to or to believe. The closure is about the open-endedness of the horizons of our lifeworld. Inasmuch as a conclusion is supported, it is true (or at least *probably* true—we will clarify this difference in the following paragraphs). Inasmuch as it is true, it delimits possibilities for further understanding and knowledge.

Notice again that this has little to do with chronological finish lines. Instead, it sets a boundary for our field(s) of intelligibility and coherence of that field. The conclusion of an argument is a mental determination, determined by the process of reasoning. We might worry that such limits restrict our imaginative freedoms. This is not so. We are still free to imagine other possibilities. Indeed, such structures actually *open* possibilities for freedom. If there were no determinations, we would not have freedom to think differently but be stuck with mere chaotic scrambling. In some cases that may be all we have. Arguments, though, help us set up boundaries within which we are set free to play ever further.

A second aspect of conclusions I want to develop is the sense in which conclusions are yields, or products, of reasoning. In agriculture, we farm to produce yields of grains, fruits, and more. We till the soil to help it be fertile. We weed out other plants that compete with our crops. And, given sufficient time, we harvest what the field yields. This notion of "yielding" stands in contrast to other connotations it has, such as surrendering or capitulating. When we give way to pressures and demands, or when we stop to let other traffic by before us, this is not the crucial aspect of a conclusion at issue for us here. Conclusions are yielded by premises, like the fruit yielded from trees.

In a way, this accounts for the alternative connotations of the word. For example, when we yield to pressure, that pressure can take the form of an argument's conclusion with which we agree. We give way and cease to contest the premises of an argument when we reach its conclusion. Premises ideally provide a conclusion worthy of commitment. Conclusions are the product yielded by arguments. Conclusions are indicators of flourishing arguments. It would be interesting, and perhaps crucial, to develop a critical analysis of labor conditions and production in argumentation. Who owns the means of production of conclusions? Are the means of production in the hands of the laborers? Regardless, the nature of a supported conclusion is one of both delimitation and yield. It is nourished to grow out of premises; once it bears fruit, it delimits our lifeworld's horizon.

Turning our attention to premises ought to help us clarify further the nature of support and the nature of conclusions.

Premises Are Supportive Complete Thoughts

Again, an argument is an instance of reasoning, and the elements of which an argument is composed are two complete thoughts standing in a relevant relation, namely, of premise and conclusion. We have briefly considered aspects crucial to the nature of conclusions. Let us examine premises with more discrete detail. Premises, like conclusions, are complete thoughts, and so they must consist of both a subject and a predicate. Conclusions are supported statements; premises are supporting statements. What does it mean to support? To support is to prop up, bring forward, and even sustain. The premises make the conclusion stand out as a discrete complete thought from the backdrop or horizon of the general field of intelligibility. Without the premises, the conclusion is no longer a conclusion but merely an independent thought. We might support it with alternative premises, but to be a conclusion it needs premises of some sort or another. Inversely, premises are not really premises without a relevant conclusion. The interrelation or interdependency is one where premises "lead to" conclusions and conclusions "follow from" premises. The linearity suggested by "leading" and "following" raises again the specter of linear causality. Do premises support and yield conclusions like one domino falling on another? Is chronological and linear causality the only kind there is?

Consider what we can gain from examining the etymology of the word "premise." The prefix, "pre-," means "before." And the root word, "-mise," comes from the Latin word for sending on a mission. Premises set before us reasons to agree to a conclusion that follows from them. It was first used predominantly in late medieval logic and grammar to note previous propositions from which another follows logically, and only later on was it used in legal deeds and wills where it refers to matters stated previously in the document. Because the matters discussed in wills and deeds predominantly consisted of land and households, in Europe's early modern period we see the use of the word "premise" to refer to houses, buildings, and grounds. The connotation of the word emerged in such a way that we now think of perpetrators or criminals entering or leaving the premises.

Note the metaphor here. We can see certain aspects of premises in light of the roles "grounds" play in arguments and in our lives in general. We build structures on the premises; people are on top of, standing on, premises. Premises support the structures built on them. Just like the support for a house, premises seem to support conclusions. They are grounds for accepting or asserting conclusions; they are grounds for building arguments. Depending on the quality of the land on which a house is built, or how deep the foundations go for the house, the structure might be blown over by the elements. Conclusions can have strong or shaky foundations, depending on the quality of their premises.

It might seem that we took this notion of natural ground and extended it to argument, but it is actually the other way around. The logical relations of premise and conclusion helped us see a quality of relation between the land and our habitats built on the land, a relation other than linear causality. Yes, the grounds "cause" the house to be, but neither in the ways of the architect and construction contractor and workers nor in the ways of materials out of which a house is made. Indeed, this kind of "cause" broke out of Aristotle's classical model of four primary causes: the efficient cause (the builder), the formal cause (the house blueprint), the material cause (the wood, etc.), and the final cause (the purpose of the house sheltering people dwelling in it) (see Aristotle 1983, 194b20–35). Like conclusions resting on solid premises, houses rest on solid ground—or at least reliable ones do. Such an extension of the logical relation of premise and conclusion helps us see our landscapes and dwelling places differently, which in turn helps us see premises and conclusions differently. The relation is not a linear or chronological causality, but one of interdependency and support.

This is why it is absolutely crucial to hold rigorously to our technical distinction between reason and motive in our theory of reasoning, despite often seeing them used synonymously in casual conversation. Indeed, we might ask in whose interests it is to get us to see reasons as mere motives. It is easier to dismiss an argument if it rests on mere psychological egocentric preferences. The key here is that reasons stand in an entirely different order than chronological causality. When we identify someone's motives, we provide chronologically preceding thoughts and feelings that predictably lead to or cause actions or other thoughts. That is, we explain why someone did or thought something on the basis of psychological motives. To the degree that we can isolate predominant character traits, personality types, or even diagnose psychological disorders, human behaviors seem predictable, predictable in the strict sense of causal chains of events. Given that this person got angry, it is no surprise that they shouted and broke a window. People are given less harsh sentences for "crimes of passion" in contrast to calculated murder because it seems that people cannot help but succumb to the causal force of their passions, whereas calculative murderers somehow stand above the causal network so as to make a free choice for which they are more responsible. We live in a tension between a commitment to "free" choice, on the one hand, and a commitment to causal orders, on the other hand. Immanuel Kant provides a moderate solution to or at least a compromise to this tension, and his proposal is consistent with what we have been laying out here. Reasons stand in a completely different order to physical and psychological causality (see Kant 1993, 53–4). Whatever freedom we might have must rest uniquely on our ability to reason autonomously, despite simultaneously being bound up in physical and psychological causal networks. *Reasoning*—developing arguments where conclusions follow fittingly from reliable premises—*is what sets us free*. That does not mean, as we will see in Chapter 5, that freedom is random spontaneity. It has a pattern and order governed by a set of rules for its enactment.

There are a few further miscellaneous aspects of premises that we should note before moving to the structure of relevance needed between premises and conclusions. Just as some complete thoughts might have implied subjects, some arguments might have implied premises. When a premise is implicit, we need to make it explicit so that we might grasp and assess the argument in its entirety. Moreover, many premises—perhaps all of them—are, or can be, conclusions to different arguments. Those distinct conclusions have their own premises. And, further, even these premises may be conclusions to other arguments. Indeed, this process of uncovering premises upon premises indicates another orientation reasoning takes alongside inference in arguments. It is the quest for reliable fundamental premises or solid ground(s). Kant describes it as reason's quest for the "unconditioned" (Kant 2007, 294/311). Such grounds would ideally serve as the fundamental condition upon which to build all other arguments and support all other conclusions. Some foundational premises like these are called "axioms." Axioms are special premises assumed in specific systems or fields of intelligibility. Indeed, they define the parameters of coherence and rationality within a system—something we will look into with more detail in Chapter 5. What Kant is pointing out, though, is that there must also be some principles that make possible any system whatsoever, and so must be shared across the relativity of each and every system. Without such general principles of reasoning, a worry arises that there could be no particular relative systems of intelligibility and no coherence internal to each system (see MacIntyre 1988).

A key issue that keeps emerging is the question of truth. Let's conclude this chapter with a discussion of truth in relation to complete thoughts and arguments.

Arguments Are Neither True Nor False

Truth in thought and reason is a feature of complete thoughts, and solely a feature of complete thoughts. That is, *only a complete thought can be true or false*. This is, of course, a stipulation to clarify the kind of truth at issue for us. Like the word "bank," we use the word "true" in many ways in colloquial settings. That is okay because we know that words take on different meanings in their different uses and contexts—what early twentieth-century philosopher of language Ludwig Wittgenstein described as "language games" (see Wittgenstein 2009). There are three predominant uses of the word, though, and I think we can identify a heart to the phenomenological experience of truth despite apparent differences in the uses (see Scharlemann 1981).

The first use is the one I believe most people think of when they think about the truth or falsity of sentences. Let's call it "truth as correspondence" or correspondence truth. This is where we have a sentence, like a picture, that either matches a state of affairs—and so is true—or does not match a state of affairs—and so is false. This way of framing "truth" presumes there are objective facts about our world, and our words either describe them accurately or do not describe them accurately. When we suppose or have evidence that words successfully represent the world, we say that there is correspondence between our words and the world (see Wittgenstein 1922). When we see purported debates between religious believers and proponents of scientific theories, one thing both sides assume is this correspondence model of truth. The topic of "creationism," for instance, involves the assumption that a religious narrative accurately (or inaccurately) describes the coming to be of the universe as whole. Correspondence truth, however, is not the only way people talk about truth.

A second usage of "truth" is in how we express our appreciation for consistency, such as when we call someone a "true friend." Let's call it "truth as constancy" or constancy truth. Over time, despite changing circumstances, a particularly good friend remains consistent in character, where they continue to express care, loyalty, encouragement, and even constructive criticism. We can count on our true friends. We can be confident with them, even though we cannot know the future in terms of correspondence truth. This is simply because the future, as far we know, has not yet occurred, and thus there are no facts yet to which descriptions can even correspond. People also use this sense of "true" when characterizing their convictions. We have steady and true convictions, meaning that they are reliable even if they do not correspond to any facts. We also use this sense in discussions about good aim, where an archer has a steady hand and a "true" aim. Such an archer can be relied on to make the shot; they are constant in their ability to succeed in sharpshooting. This is quite different from correspondence truth. Yet there is another peculiar way we talk about truth that goes beyond both correspondence and constancy.

The third common use of the word "truth," but also probably the most difficult to explain and grasp, is what we can call "truth as alethic" or alethic truth. *Alethia* is the ancient Greek term for truth. Note the prefix "a-," which negates the root word, by meaning "not," as in atheist, not a theist. The root word, "-lethe," has connotations of hiddenness and even obliviousness. In Greek mythology, the river Lethe is what passengers ride from Hades, the underworld, back to this world. Its role is to make passengers forget their past lives before their reincarnation. Thus, alethic truth has to do with not hiding and not forgetting. It is what we are experiencing when we have "Aha!" moments—where something stands out from an undifferentiated background in such a way that we can no longer be oblivious to it or take it for granted. We talk about stories and other works of art this way when we say that they "ring true" (see Gadamer 2007, 192). It is not that they somehow correspond to facts, but instead that they reveal something to us that we had not noticed with such vividness before. This is also what we emphasized in our development of predicates operative in complete thoughts. Fitting predicates are revelatory about a subject; complete thoughts are true when a subject matter stands out newly in light of fitting predicates. There is a connotation of discovery in this version of truth, literally a discovery or uncovering. When something stands out for discrete attention in light of a story or predicate that "rings true," its cover—the undifferentiated mass of potential meanings forming the horizon of our lifeworld—is removed. Or, perhaps more accurately, it is brought into the foreground from the undifferentiated background.

Note that we can phenomenologically specify a key structure and dynamic shared across all three kinds of truth. In every version, there is a dynamism of unity or identity within or between differences. Our experience of truth is our experience of the unity of identity and difference. Consider correspondence truth: there is the difference between the fact and the sentence, and there is the identity in that they match. Consider constancy truth: there is the difference between one point in time and another point in time, and there is the identity or integrity of something or someone across those different times. Consider alethic truth: there is the identity or unified field of the undifferentiated background and horizon, and there is the differentiation where something stands out from that background. Notice that, despite an inverse dynamic compared to correspondence and constancy truths, alethic truth nevertheless preserves the experience of the unity of identity and difference.

When we are developing the truth of complete thoughts, my preference is to hold to a moderate integration of all three versions of truth. That is, I want genuinely true complete thoughts not only to correspond to facts, but also to be reliable as well as outstanding. Because this may be too high a bar to set for limited and finite thinking like ours, I want us to seek first and foremost alethic truth—complete thoughts where predicates are fittingly revelatory of subjects. Notice that this kind of truth is a function intrinsic to complete thoughts themselves (see Descartes 1998, 35; and Spinoza 1992). There is no need for mapping onto a purportedly "external" world to see if a complete thought is true or false. This helps us preserve our phenomenological bracket or suspension of our natural attitude. That also implies dictionary definitions are neither true nor false. A definition merely tracks and reports contemporary common usage of words. A definition is not a complete thought. There is no such thing as a "true" definition, but there may be a correct one according to current usage reported and recorded in current editions of a lexicon. But even current usage might be incorrect compared to past usage. Just consider the evolutions of words like "queer" or "awful."

This distinction is important to hold down—especially between alethic and correspondence truth. We live in a world where people overemphasize correspondence truth at the expense of other versions of truth. So, our preference for alethic truth serves as an antidote to the hegemony of truth as correspondence. Consider in whose interest it is to get us to believe that "correspondence" is "true truth" or "really true." As scientific theories emphasize correspondence truth, we have witnessed further and further marginalization of poetry and other arts, to the point where art programs are one of the first to be cut in budget revisions in US schools. As long as religious people and scientists share the assumption that truth as correspondence is the only version worthy of the name "truth," I predict we will continue to witness these debates. However, what if we were to see religious language as fitting for alethic truth and scientific language as fitting for correspondence truth? Could that help dissolve the purported debate? Correspondence truth has also historically served the adversarial model of argument that we connected with patriarchy and racism. While descriptive correspondence may be useful at times, we do not need to smear it across all times.

Whether we emphasize correspondence or alethic truth, we can see that—at least for these two—truth is a feature of complete thoughts. This is why premises and conclusions must be complete thoughts. We want to reason from true premises to true conclusions. Sentential truth is what we are after here. Thus, our concern is not with what makes an argument "true," as if that were possible, but *with what preserves sentential truth in reasoning.* Arguments as such are neither true nor false. There are *forms of reasoning that are truth-preserving,* and things that look like forms of reasoning (expositions) that are not truth-preserving.

Truth-preservation is the inverse of what "support" is when it comes to premises supporting conclusions. Conclusions are supported by premises when the conclusions preserve the truth of the premises. Premises support conclusions when the truth in the premises is preserved in the conclusion. We can illustrate the supporting and preserving character of reasoning by looking at Venn diagrams. In many introductions to reasoning and logic, we cover a unit on reasoning with categorical statements. There are four fundamental kinds of categorical statements that form the square of opposition, such as "all" statements, like "All philosophers are mortal." The contrary to that is "No philosophers are mortal." The contradiction of the "all" statement is "Some philosophers are not mortal." And the contrary to that is "Some philosophers are mortal." A categorical syllogism is one that uses a sequence of three categorical statements, such as the following:

Premise 1: All humans are mortal.
Premise 2: All philosophers are human.
Conclusion: Therefore, all philosophers are mortal.

We can plot these statements into a Venn diagram, illustrated in Figure 1.

One fascinating feature of Venn diagrams is that they give picture form to what goes on conceptually in categorical arguments. To plot a diagram of a categorical argument, we create three overlapping circles in a pyramid like stack—two on the bottom and one at the top. When we plot an argument by shading in the relations of categories between those in the premises, we see that a conclusion is relevantly acceptable when its plot is visibly identical to the plot of the premises. In such a case, the conclusion can be said to preserve the content and truth of the premises. Indeed, that is just what a "proof" essentially is—a list of complete thoughts related in a relevant way that preserves truth throughout them.

A question should be on the tip of our tongues: Just what is this relevant relation between complete thoughts in reasoning? How is a list of sentences, an exposition, transformed into an argument? These topics will be addressed in Chapter 5. Before moving there, allow me to point out just a couple more things. We should start to notice some clues about how to criticize arguments appropriately. For example, we need to keep the

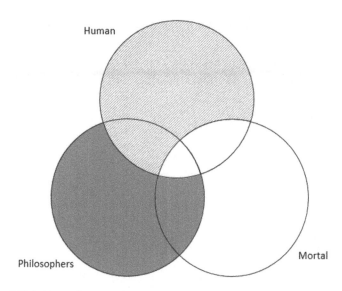

Figure 1 This Venn diagram illustrates the relations between the categories, where what is plotted in the premises is preserved in the conclusion.

following question in mind: Are the premises even relevant to the conclusion? If they are not, then what looks like an argument is not one. Instead of an argument, it is just a list of sentences nearby one another. It is merely an exposition. Just like in cases where something might look like a complete thought but really is not, there are cases where something can look like an argument but really is not one.

Another way we might criticize an argument is to point out that the premises rest on shaky foundations. The arguments that would support the premises themselves as conclusions of precedent arguments, those arguments using such unreliable premises are not sufficiently reliable as truth-preserving. If we cannot trust precedent arguments to be truth-preserving, then we probably should be hesitant to trust the present one. Moreover, and perhaps most importantly, an argument fails if the premises are false. There is nothing to preserve in the conclusion if the premises are already false. Indeed, if the premises are false, then they are not actually premises, and there actually is no argument but just an exposition. Instead, the conclusion is merely a complete thought, a thought in ontological or semantic outer space. *A refutation of an argument, then, is less showing that a conclusion is wrong, but that what looks like an argument is not really an argument.* A refutation is construed usually as a way of showing a conclusion rests on shaky premises or uses an invalid argument form. For us, however, a refutation dissolves an argument; it makes an argument disintegrate into a mere exposition.

Let us turn to examine in detail the relevant relations between complete thoughts in arguments and further roles questions play in reasoning.

5

What Do Questions Do to Arguments?

Chapter Outline

In this chapter, I will focus on two main questions. What is the structure of reasoning? And what relations can we identify between questioning and rationally ordered arguments? In usual approaches to logical validity and inference, we are trained to examine relations of sentences *independent* from their content or meaning—that is, independent from their status as answers to questions we ask. As we will see, logical validity usually is approached as a formal feature of relations between sentences. We do not need to understand the sentences at all. As such, it seems that logical validity has little to do with questioning and understanding as we have developed them so far.

I will examine the structure of reasoning, or the structures definitive for relevance between statements in arguments. Rationality is what explains the difference between a list of sentences and an argument where two complete thoughts have an inferential relation. An additional aspect of rationality is its being structured by a set of laws or rules. These rules provide fitting constraints within which it can be said that we are thinking freely. I will also develop one way to suture together questioning with reasoning. Reasoning strives not only toward conclusions but also toward fundamental premises or grounds. When we have opened ourselves to something's questionability, when we develop responses to our questions, we recognize that they lead to more questions and more responses in an effort to uncover what I called earlier the "unconditioned."

Notice that just as thought aims at unity, a synthesis of subjects and predicates in the copula, so also does reason aim at unity, a synthesis of premises and conclusions. Unity is an aim of understanding as a whole, finding or making unity in differences. Indeed, this pursuit precedes the difference between discovery and invention (see Ricoeur 2003, 291). Is the "soul" immortal? Is there room in the world for free will? Is there a divine being? What do these deep questions suggest about the kind of beings we are as thinkers? While this chapter will develop how questioning opens up reasoning's voraciousness, Chapter 6 will examine four orientations of questioning in the domain of reason as well as how that voraciousness is concretely embodied in metaphors and symbols at the edges of thinking.

Rational Inferences Are Valid or Strong

I want to characterize "rationality" as a theory about what counts as good reasoning in general, and the ability to follow inferences in particular. Reasoning is something we do with complete thoughts, specifically premises and conclusions, just like thinking is something we do with subjects and predicates. An inference is a further complete thought drawn from or developed on the basis of a different complete thought. A conclusion "follows from" a premise, and this "following from" names its inferential power. Inversely, a premise "leads to" a conclusion, and this "leading to" names its inferential power. The kind of support premises give conclusions is inferential support. The kind of derivation conclusions take from premises is inferential derivation.

When we look at the etymology of "inference," the prefix, "in-," indicates a bringing into awareness, and the root word, "-ference," is connected with words like transference and even ferries. When we infer a conclusion from a premise, we are bringing or carrying a different complete thought into consciousness on the basis of the previous complete thought. We also mean to carry over or preserve the truth of the premise into the conclusion. Note, though, that this unfolding is not causal. A premise does not "cause" a conclusion. Recall that premises and conclusions are interdependent. In a way, with some arguments the conclusion is already there in the premise. This is similar to a visual of a triangle with a perforated line, where our mind fills in the blanks of the image. Reasoning uncovers the conclusion from the ground of the premise. To illustrate this point, we can consider some classic forms of what are called immediate inferences. For instance, from the complete thought "No people are mere things" we can infer that "No mere things are people." Or, likewise, from "No cats are dogs" we can immediately infer that "No dogs are cats." Notice what is going on in these cases: we discern that a proposition of the form "No X are Y" serves as the ground for concluding that "No Y are X." In light of the formal structure of this inference, logicians refer to this tactic as *conversion* (meaning, to turn around). As another instance, from a complete thought such as "No people are non-humans" we can infer that "All people are humans." We refer to this tactic as *obversion* (meaning, to reveal a different perspective), because it involves taking a proposition and discerning that there is another proposition of *opposite quality* that can be deduced from it. In this case, the first proposition was a negative proposition; it stated "*No* people are non-humans." From it we deduced a positive proposition, "*All* people are humans." These and similar cases are called immediate inferences because we move from the premise to the conclusion without mediation from any other considerations. If the premise is true, I have sufficient reason to believe the conclusion is true. The argument combining the two complete thoughts is truth-preserving.

Reasons are needed to support your perspective. We use argumentation to tie thoughts to other thoughts through logical relations. Formal logic focuses exclusively on the formal or abstract order of inferences in reasoning and argument. Informal logic focuses on reasoning as it is expressed in ordinary language, looking at word equivocations and definitions, warrants for assumptions, and fallacies as they occur in practical language usage. Inasmuch as complete thoughts are answers to asked questions, arguments are compilations of complete thoughts *and* the questions they answer into coherent wholes. In this way, I think it is helpful to approach argument as a genre of discourse like iambic poetry and autobiography. As such, logic—or rationality more broadly—is a set of principles governing this genre in a peculiar way, distinguishing it from other genres. Of course, there is a logical or structural order to other genres. For instance, fairytales have a beginning, middle, and end. Perhaps more importantly, they involve some sort of magic or enchantment. Without these, it is difficult to say that a story fits in the fairytale genre. Inference is peculiarly definitive for argument in ways it is not for other genres of discourse. If we remove inferences from an argument, we can no longer fit an exposition into the genre of argument and understand what an argument says.

Is there only one rationality or intelligible order, though? Is it universal across all cultures and times, such that we can point at some individuals or communities as being "irrational," that is, as not living up to their intellectual capacities? Is rationality instead always context embedded, differently embodied in different forms of life and traditions (see MacIntyre 1988; and Dickman 2018c)? There seem to be important motives weighing on both sides. Presumably, on the surface, we want to reason with people across cultures. Alternatively, Western models of rationality have proven to be complicit with colonialism, oppression, sexism, and racism (see Herbjørnsrud 2017). A model of rationality is not rationality per se, just as a model of an airplane is not an airplane per se. A (sub)type of a thing is not necessarily exhaustive of the broader category. We might reject some models or types of rationality as complicit with colonialism, and so on, but it would not follow that rationality is per se colonial or oppressive. I think we can preserve this tension between universality and particularity, using the first motive to keep the question open about the possibility of a universal structure to rationality and using the second motive to temper that question with tentative, provisional, self-correcting humility. One of the very topics over which we may seek to reason with others is the structure of reasoning itself, and if we are to do so in a responsible way, we must keep open the possibility that a favored model or type of rationality may be rationally interrogated. Personally, I am attracted to skepticism, where skeptics in the sense of classical Pyrrhonists do not have loyalty to either side. Yet such skepticism through which we supposedly can suspend commitment without taking sides is itself made possible from traditions of thought stemming from Plato and Aristotle. Perhaps it is *the most* Western form of "rationality." All I am saying is that *if* we are going to continue reasoning with one another across cultures, then we *probably* should do it the way I propose in this book—especially in dialogue as I advocate in Part III. However, as many critical race theorists, feminists, queer theorists, and crip theorists have brought to light, what has counted as "rational" is at least partially a social construct complicit with toxic white supremacist ableism, with Eurocentric patriarchal hegemony (see, for examples, McFague 1982 and Kafer 2013). It seems that we are confronted with a difficult choice: either radical revolution that rejects inherited traditions of rationality as unsalvageable in its biases or radical reformation that substantively revises inherited traditions of rationality as sufficiently flexible to be inclusive and accessible. We are gambling on the latter, but through more experience we may need to change and side with the former.

We can identify a few patterns that govern specific kinds of argument. These patterns help provide us with resources and terms within which to question expositions to see whether they are arguments or not. Broadly speaking, there is deductive reasoning, inductive reasoning, and abductive reasoning. Let's start with deduction. We tend to see deductive reasoning as the strictest way to reason because it provides certainty and confidence about our conclusions. Deductions argue for true conclusions from axioms. Deductive arguments preserve truth from premises to conclusion through validity. Axioms are statements assumed to be true from the outset. Inferences are performed via the rules of rationality or logic, such as the Law of Excluded Middle, which is for any complete thought, either it or its opposite must be true. Whatever inferences we make must play within the limits set by this law. Another one is the law of noncontradiction, which is that no contradictions—two contradictory complete thoughts joined by a both/and—can be true. That is, two contradictory statements cannot be true in the same sense at the same time.

A deductive inference is evaluated at two levels: first, in terms of its formal pattern and, second, in terms of the truth-value of its content. If the form or pattern of an inference is such that, *if* (hypothetically) the premises of the argument are true, the conclusion could not possibly be false, we declare that the argument is *formally valid*. If the pattern would not guarantee the conclusion, the argument is *formally invalid*.

The most straightforward examples of deductive inferences are categorical syllogisms, like the one we glanced at in Chapter 4 with the Venn Diagram. A *syllogism* is an argument with exactly two premises, and a *categorical* syllogism is one in which the premises and the conclusion are categorical propositions (e.g., of the form, "All X are Y," "No X are Y," "Some X are Y," or "Some X are not Y"). The following example is used in most textbooks on basic reasoning:

Premise 1: All philosophers are wise.
Premise 2: Socrates is a philosopher.
Conclusion: Therefore, Socrates is wise.

Note that this argument has two complete thoughts functioning as premises, and one complete thought as the conclusion. We can formalize this argument with symbolic abbreviations or substitution instances this way:

> Premise 1: All P are W.
> Premise 2: All S are P.
> Conclusion: Therefore, All S are W.

It seems helpful to formalize this argument with abbreviated placeholders, or substitution instances, rather than words with meanings because, if we can learn the abstract form, we should be able to recognize and transfer this inferential pattern to other contexts. If we can learn it, we can transfer the skill to new arguments. We can recognize valid arguments simply by their pattern.

Validity names the deductive patterns of inference. An argument with deductively rational inferences is a valid argument. Validity concerns solely the pattern, not the content of the argument's complete thoughts. A valid deductive argument is logically or formally valid regardless of its content. We can have a valid argument even if all the premises and the conclusion are, in fact, false. Maybe philosophers are not really wise. Maybe Socrates is not really a philosopher. Even if the premises and conclusion are false, the argument can still be valid. This is because a deductive argument essentially is any argument pattern where *if* the premises are true, *then* the conclusion is necessarily true. If an attempted inference is invalid, then it breaks the rules of deductive rationality, and thus is not really an inference at all. It is a failed inference. *That is, to use an invalid argument is, essentially, not to reason.* It is to do something irrational.

Let us now turn to a second level of evaluation, and to do so let's assume the premises about Socrates are true for illustration's sake ("*if* the premises are true"). When an argument has *both* true premises *and* a valid form, the argument is "sound." Notice what is happening here. Whereas truth and falsity apply only to complete thoughts, validity applies only to arguments. You have probably heard people use "valid" in casual statements like "That's a valid point" or "Your feelings are valid." That's not the type of validity we are after here. We are after inferential validity concerning argument forms only. We can also have true premises and a true conclusion, yet an invalid argument form—mainly because the premises are irrelevant to the conclusion. For example, consider this:

> Premise 1: Bachelors are unmarried men.
> Premise 2: The horizon is where the sky and ground meet in the distance.
> Conclusion: Therefore, competitive games undermine cooperation.

The premises are irrelevant to the conclusion. The premises are irrelevant to one another, too. We have here an exposition, a pile of sentences, but not an argument. If it was intended as an argument, it failed to be one. A sound argument, with true premises and a valid form, is reliable. We can rely on sound arguments. To say an argument is sound is the highest endorsement we can give to an argument! Perhaps fortunately we do not have to start from scratch. Many people before us have worked out a whole list of valid argument patterns, like modus ponens, the disjunctive syllogism, and even the hypothetical syllogism. When we use these deductive forms, we are not just jumping to conclusions or making potentially irrelevant leaps in reasoning. They are vetted and reliable steps of reasoning, the validity of which we can confirm for ourselves (see Bassham et al. 2019, and Tidman and Kahane 1999).

Invalidity, as I said, obtains in any case where the truth of the premises together with the form or pattern of inference is insufficient to guarantee the truth of the conclusion. In short, an invalid argument is one in which the conclusion does not necessarily follow from the premises. Such a form, then, is unreliable. Indeed, *it is not really an argument at all because the very structure of rational relevance (i.e., validity) is missing*. An invalid argument is just a list of sentences or complete thoughts. It is just an exposition. You can often recognize that a categorical argument form is invalid by substituting terms to the point where premises can be true, but the conclusion turns out to be false. Consider this form:

Premise 1: All A are B.
Premise 2: All C are B.
Conclusion: Therefore, all A are C.

Let's substitute the letters with some terms:

Premise 1: All apples are fruit.
Premise 2: All tomatoes are fruit.
Conclusion: Therefore, all apples are tomatoes.

Even if the premises are true (which in this case they are), the conclusion is still false. Invalidity in the realm of arguments is where two or greater complete thoughts lack consistency. Thoughts are consistent when they are neither contrary—where both statements cannot be true though they both can be false—nor contradictory—where only one statement is true and the other is false. Consistency between the premises and the conclusion is necessary for validity, but it is not sufficient. However, inconsistency is not necessary for invalidity because we can have a consistent, yet nevertheless invalid, pattern of premises and conclusion.

We need to be careful here though because apparent or surface inconsistency and invalidity may cover up a deeper consistency. Think of poetry or religious paradox or Socratic irony. Hypocrisy is when we see a practical inconsistency where someone's actions seem to contradict their beliefs. However, poetry, paradox, and irony can involve and often indicate a deeper unity and point. For example, when Jesus is described in Christian gospels as teaching that one ought to act without anyone else knowing, he says that one ought to not even let their left hand know what their right hand is doing. This seems to suggest that with subjectivity comes a right to deceive (see Kierkegaard 1983). Socrates is notorious for having said that all he knows is that he knows nothing. He even underscored that this very belief is what defined his being wiser than all others (see Plato 2002). Ironic statements like this might seem to be irrational, but on a deeper analysis prove to be rational and insightful. To reveal an underlying rationality, we might—for instance—have to attend to and address ambiguities and equivocations where a term is being used in different ways.

With that clarification in mind, let us turn to some key features of inductive arguments in contrast to deductive arguments. A crucial feature to note is that all inductive arguments are technically deductively invalid. Inductive inferences are not about certainty but about probability. Induction is where a conclusion *probably* follows from the premises, where a conclusion *probably* preserves the truth of the premises. Inductive arguments involve premises that are used to support a likely statement of fact. There is no guarantee that the conclusion is true, even if the premises are true. Consider this example:

> Premise: All animals with sharp teeth that I have seen so far eat meat.
> Conclusion Thus, the sharp-toothed beast before me probably eats meat as well.

Or consider this example:

> Premise: The sun has risen every morning so far.
> Conclusion: Thus, it will probably rise tomorrow morning.

Rather than valid or invalid, inductive arguments are strong or weak. Their strength is determined by the weight of evidence, the quality and size of a sample, the plausibility of a generalization, and the coherence of combining various elements into a complete picture like a trial lawyer. Induction often involves reasoning from limited particular instances to wider generalities. Rather than a valid inference, then, induction involves a stronger or weaker inference.

Inductive arguments need not proceed from the specific to general, however, as induction is often described in speech and composition textbooks. They can involve moving from the past to the future, generality to something specific, or even from one generality to another. Such generalizations are fundamental for natural sciences. Notice that since induction is technically invalid, a problem emerges. How can an argument be inductively strong reasoning but deductively invalid? A moment's reflection reveals that we are confident that induction in its various forms provides rational guidance because it has proven effective in the past. What is known as *the problem of induction*, put most precisely, is that the very conviction that (past) observed events are good guides for unobserved (future) events itself rests on (past) observation! It is circular, assuming exactly what it is trying to prove. It seems that we rely on induction without a reliable rational—or deductive—grounding. This is, though, to evaluate inductive argument by standards external to it, standards from deductive argument.

At this point, it is helpful to recognize that *all* reasoning is fallible, but deductively valid and inductively strong reasoning open themselves up to possible error in different ways. In the case of the former, mistakes are found only at the level of the *content* of the reasoning. That is to say, if we have formulated a deductively valid chain of reasoning, a misstep will occur or the possibility of a false conclusion will become possible only if we have one or more false premises. In the case of the latter, deductive errors remain something to watch out for, but there is also another way that the reasoning process can go wrong: even if we have true premises and a strong relation between the premises and the conclusion, the premises will never absolutely guarantee the truth of the conclusion.

A good inductive argument is not valid, then, but strong. And if the premises are true, then the inductive argument is "cogent." Cogency is the highest praise we can give to inductive arguments. They are never a "proof," in the sense of validity or soundness. Cogent inductive arguments yield likely or probable conclusions rather than certain or necessary conclusions. There are, moreover, two types of probability: objective and subjective. Objective probability has a genuine indeterminacy in the world. While it is likely that an observed pattern in the past will happen in the future, too, it is indeterminate until it does happen. Subjective probability, however, is a judgment or complete thought about the level of likelihood of an entertained statement being true, given one's epistemic position. It's a level of our personal confidence in a position being likely. In such cases of decisions, we may need to be subjectively committed and confident in our commitment despite being objectively uncertain. For example, a couple who commits to a long-term relationship may have subjective confidence, but it is always in the face of a technical objective uncertainty that one or the other partner might leave, might die, or might otherwise undermine the relationship. When we lack all the potentially relevant information, we still sometimes have to make a decision or judgment. In such cases, we use probabilistic assessments in causal analyses, analogical reasoning, and generalizations. For example, in Spring 2020, many college administrators had to decide what to do in response to the COVID-19 pandemic from the coronavirus. What will likely happen if we do nothing? What will likely happen if we suspend classes for just two weeks? I will briefly look at each of these inductive patterns, like the deductive patterns of modus ponens, and so on.

One form of inductive argument focuses on causes. When performing causal analyses, we are looking for an explanation of how or why something occurred, or we are looking for someone who ought to take the responsibility for an event. Or we might be looking for a way to control things or predict how things will likely pan out. A cause is an initial condition, or at least one of many sufficient conditions, for the occurrence of something (Conway and Munson 2000, 105). When the house feels chilly, perhaps it was caused by someone setting the temperature too low for comfort. But in many cases there are multiple factors contributing to bringing something about. A chilly house can have several contributing factors. In such an analysis, we use general causal laws to trace causal chains. However, only relevant and significant factors prove explanatory because some essential factors are necessary for something to happen. In the case of a chilly house, there obviously needs to be . . . a house. The house is a constant background condition. But it is the *unusual* or *varying* factors we are after when looking for a probable proximate or triggering cause. Did the furnace stop working? Did someone turn it off? In previous cases where it was chilly, what were the known causes? Are those causes present in this new situation? We can use tests to isolate and identify what is different or the same in varying conditions and experiments, and these tests help indicate the strength of an inductive inference.

Another form of inductive reasoning focuses on analogies. When assessing analogical reasoning, we look at one specific example and apply it to another specific one. It requires seeing that these two things are alike in numerous ways, and so are probably alike in an additional way (see Weston 2009, 20). Are the things compared relevantly similar? They do not have to be completely and exactly the same, or else it would not be an analogy but an identity. The relevance is determined by the point being made through the analogy. The strength of analogical inference is rooted in how the two things compared are similar on the things that they need to be similar about. Some people joke about how we cannot compare apples and oranges, that some analogies we make are as weak as saying that apples and oranges are similar. Yet, if the relevant topic at issue is being a nonpoisonous fruit or being relatively round, the two are similar in those relevant respects.

A third kind of inductive reasoning focuses on generalizations. With generalizations, we move from specific examples to a more universally applicable conclusion. The examples should be reliable and accurate. It is best to use more than one representative example because only one just illustrates, rather than supports, a generalization (see Weston 2009, 11). If the set at issue is large, then examples need to be representative; they must constitute what is called a "representative sample." A representative sample should stand for the entire set at issue. With statistics in particular, we need to be careful about how the sample statistic compares with statistics for a greater set or determine if the isolated set is significant in the first place. We can also look to see if a statistic is too precise—such as whether a certain number is something someone can really know. The precision can give the impression of more authority than there really is. We can also use counterexamples to make our inductive argument more precise. Perhaps we make a generalization such as "All fast food restaurants are unhealthy." Subway purports to be both fast food and healthy (or at least healthier!). So, we could rephrase our generalization to "Most fast food restaurants are unhealthy."

Let us briefly look at abductive argumentation too. Abductive arguments move to what seems to be the best explanation for a phenomenon given what we know about that phenomenon so far. Of course, for any event, there are a number of causes and explanations. The issue is figuring out which explanation is the best explanation for our purposes. Despite inappropriately declaring "Deduction, my dear Watson!" Sherlock Holmes typically uses abduction to solve crimes, not deduction. Some useful criteria for selecting best explanations include the simplicity of the explanation, the coherence of the explanation with other things we already know, the predictive power of the explanation, and/or the comprehensiveness of the explanation (see

Baggini and Fosl 2010, 45). Note that in Part II we are trying to provide a *better* explanation of the relations between questioning and reasoning.

All of these approaches to argument—from validity to generalization to abduction—provide us with a vocabulary for questioning in arguments. And they all provide us with structures within which arguments and reasoning can happen. With this overview of key aspects of inferences, let's move to look more closely at laws governing thought and reasoning.

Rational Laws Set Thinking Free

A quick internet search for "free thinking" will indicate that groups like the Freethinkers Society usually are positioned against religions or other possible forms of apparent indoctrination. This coopting of the phrase should not distract us from the kind of freedom of thought we are concerned with here. For us, freethinking solely has to do with the relations between questioning and complete thoughts, as well as between questioning and reasoning. How can thinking and reasoning be "free" if they are intrinsically governed by logical *laws*, such as combining subjects with predicates, the rules of validity, or abductive inference? What is happening when we "break" logical laws? What does it even mean to tell someone to "think for yourself!"?

This may sound paradoxical, but *laws set us free*. Jesus seems to have been mistaken on this (John 8:32), or at least his follower Paul was mistaken on it (Romans 7:6). Consider this—if we were to take away all the laws for driving, we would not be free to get anywhere! Of course, in some places around the globe, it may already feel like there are no rules of the road to inexperienced outsiders. Or, if we were to remove all the rules for the game of basketball, we would not be free to play it. Or consider the Jewish *mitzot* or Shariah law for Muslims—if we take away these structures, then individuals and communities identifying with these traditions would not be free to be Jewish or Muslim. If one was to be roaming the earth aimlessly, instructions or laws from a divine being would be liberating to them. They might think, "Thank God I know what to do now!" Of course, not all laws and rules are fundamental in this way. Some conventions and laws are more flexible and changeable to new circumstances. Some rules we might decide to change completely by getting rid of them. Think of how US Civil Rights activists have helped show that some laws perpetuate the evils of white supremacy and thus require being dismantled.

The kind of laws for thought and reason at issue here are what I want to call "constitutive rules." Rules and norms that can adapt to changing circumstances or values are what I will call "regulative ideals," and this will be a topic I revisit later in this chapter and even further in Chapter 6. Constitutive rules provide the basic fundamental framework within which something can take place. The rules of driving are constitutive for the possibility of driving. Shariah law is constitutive for the possibility of being Muslim. If we take the rules away, we take away this possibility for being in the world; we take away the freedom to be this or that. This is why governing constitutions are important, because they set forth the possibility for a way of being in the world. Without the US constitution, one could not have the freedom to be a US citizen.

Just as with constitutive rules in other domains, so also with logical laws. *Logical laws, like validity, are constitutive rules for the freedoms to think and to reason at all. Without abiding by these, one is not really even thinking.* I believe this is part of what Aristotle is getting at when he lays out some of what he takes to be the fundamental principles of reasoning. For example, the law of noncontradiction says that both a complete thought and its negation cannot be true in the exact same sense at the same time (Aristotle 1983, 1005b19–30). If someone tries to think such a contradiction, then it is *not* simply that they will have a difficult go at it; it is that they are *not successfully even thinking yet.* The law of noncontradiction is sometimes called the foundation on which all logic is built. Whenever we break the law, we contradict ourselves. And it is not simply that all contradictions are incorrect; it is that contradictions are aborted attempts at reasoning whatsoever. Putting forth a contradiction amounts to saying that something is both true and false in the same sense at the same time, which is impossible for two reasons. First of all, it takes time to think through a complete thought, to predicate of a subject. Second, the purported simultaneity of the opposing complete thoughts cancels each other out.

On the other bookend from contradiction in the domains of thinking and reasoning is tautology. Tautologies are complete thoughts that are intrinsically and necessarily true. That is, they are true in every possible world or circumstance. Instead of a contradiction, where opposing claims are conjoined, tautologies are disjunctive combinations of opposing claims. "Either it is snowing, or it is not snowing" is necessarily true no matter what. This is interesting because it looks a lot like a contradiction, but it is not. All it takes to make a contradiction into a tautology is to change the conjunction into a disjunction. There is a lot of power in coordinating conjunctions, of which conjunction ("and") and disjunction ("or") are two kinds.

My personal favorite instance of a boundary for the freedom to think or the game of reasoning is the self-referential contradiction or what I prefer to call "self-referential incoherence." Consider the sentence "No perspective is correct." Can you tell what might be problematic about this sentence? You got it, I am sure. It itself is expressing a perspective, and since it is saying that all perspectives are incorrect, it is itself incoherent. It contradicts itself. And here is the catch: it looks like a sentence that could answer a question, and so it seems like it could be a complete thought. However, since we cannot understand contradictions, in that they break the laws of thought and reasoning, it is not something we can successfully think. It is an aborted answer to a question that no one can ever ask authentically.

It may seem like what I have just said implies we are not free to think this sentence, "No perspective is correct." That is not the way I am trying to get us to consider freethinking, though. What happens in sentences like these ("no perspective is correct") is that we have run up to the boundary of thinking. In contradicting ourselves, we are not freely thinking because *we are not even thinking.* To demand that we should be able to think contradictions to be "truly free" mistakes crossing constitutive boundaries with spontaneity. Freethinking is not random but patterned. Free-verse poetry, alternatively, need not abide by constitutive rules for thinking as we have stipulated it here. Reasoning is a different genre than free-verse poetry.

Just like learning the rules of music or games and practicing our skills in those domains helps us perfect our freedoms for those activities, so also do we need to learn the laws of logic and practice our skills in it to perfect our freedom to think and reason. Those patterns of argument we glanced through earlier are rules we can get down to perfect our freedom to reason. Being able to recognize the *modus ponens* argument form, for example, makes us more proficient at thinking and reasoning freely. Learning logical laws like the law of noncontradiction helps us be more logically proficient and thus freer in our thinking and reasoning.

In addition, appropriating the rules through practice helps make argumentation and thinking our own rather than merely parroting sentences and expositions. This is an overlooked aspect of freedom. When we consider political liberty, we can see two kinds, what political philosopher Isaiah Berlin called "negative" and "positive" liberties (see Berlin 1969). Negative ones are where we have not been restrained from doing something. For example, we are free from oppression when we gain the right to vote where we had not had it before. Positive ones are where we have the possibility to do something, a freedom to do it. For example, with the rules of basketball in place, we are freed to play it as we please. The laws of reason function similarly. We free ourselves to think by abiding by logical laws. *By so appropriating (making our own) the rules for thinking and reasoning, we become responsible for our thoughts and arguments.* What we are thinking through is no longer simply *an* argument, but my *own* argument. What we are thinking through is not simply *a* complete thought, but my *own* complete thought. What we are asking is not simply *a* question, but my *own* question. Inasmuch as arguments help build lifeworlds or worldviews, learning argumentation helps us make different worldviews our own.

Breaking the laws of reason means *not only that we are not freely thinking, but also that we are not even thinking.* Outlaw attempts at thought are approached usually as "fallacies" of reasoning. Let us briefly note some features of fallacies. There are formal and informal fallacies. Formal ones are errors in the form or pattern of reasoning. For example, consider the valid argument form of *modes ponens.*

> Premise 1: If it is raining outside, then the road is wet.
> Premise 2: It is raining. (Affirming the antecedent.)
> Conclusion: Thus, the road is wet.

In Premise 2, we are affirming the antecedent, the "if" clause of the first premise. However, all it takes is affirming the consequent in Premise 2 to have an invalid argument form.

> Premise 1: If it is raining outside, then the road is wet.
> Premise 2: The road is wet. (Affirming the consequent.)
> Conclusion: Thus, it is raining.

Notice that this conclusion does not follow from the premises. The road could be wet for any number of causes, not merely because it is raining. We cannot rely on affirming the consequent to reason or argue. In fact, when we affirm the consequent, *we are not even reasoning.* Formal fallacies are when we *fail to reason,* solely by virtue of the form of the exposition itself. It might look like an argument; we might perceive the exposition. We might even *intend* it to be an argument, or take ourselves to have reasoned. But we cannot, in the final analysis, understand the exposition as an argument. This goes against how we typically speak, though. We often call contradictions a "bad argument" in casual conversations. That's fine. For us, though, let us say that—technically speaking—those are not even arguments.

Informal fallacies are where we fail to reason not by virtue of the form of the argument, but by virtue of the content of the argument. The faulty inference—which is not really an inference at all, given what we were just saying—rests in the content of the premises and conclusion. There are three general problems of faulty-content inference: those based on ambiguity and the meaning of terms, those based on presumption and assuming too much, and those based on relevance and changing the topic. We are susceptible to fallacies because we have biases, which are rooted in our projections of priorities and regulative ideals. Sometimes we are guilty of wishful thinking or confirmation bias. Other times, we expect—even demand—that there be only one cause or "the" answer. Sometimes we inappropriately appeal to authorities and experts, where we try to persuade others to agree with us because, say, our medical doctor prefers to drive Mercedes cars so we all should. Or we listen to Instagram models for dietary advice.

There is one fallacy almost lost on us now because common use of the phrase gets it wrong, technically speaking. You've probably heard someone say, "Well that begs the question." They usually mean that something *raises* a new question or *leads to* a different question, as if we are begged to ask this new question on the basis of this other question or point. The fallacy called "begging the question," though, is about assumptions, where someone is making a claim and supporting it with a controversial assumption rather than a fitting premise. Perhaps someone developing an argument about the best baseball pinch hitters argues: "Ambidextrous hitters are the best [conclusion] because solely left or right-handed hitters do not hit as well [premise]." While formally valid, the content is not a supportive argument because the premise and conclusion mean pretty much the same thing, so the point has yet to be supported relevantly.

A significant way people change the topic, which we should note, is by committing what is called ad hominem (attack the person) fallacies. This is where we change the topic from the argument's *content* to the *person* making the argument, usually degrading them in the process. Perhaps you have had someone say to you, "Of course you would say that, because you are just trying to win." Just because someone wants to win, that does not make their reasoning incorrect. In fact, the person committing the ad hominem attack has, in a way, just forfeited reasoning in exchange for fighting. In all these ways and more we succumb to fallacies, breaking the laws of reasoning, and *thereby losing our freedom to think.*

Before moving on to coordinate reasoning with inspiration for questioning, I want to conclude this section with some further comments about the unfreedom of what passes for "thinking" and "reasoning." In modern Western societies, there is a fetish character to the phrase "think for yourself." If we are told to think for ourselves, and actually start to do so on the basis of being told to do so, are we thinking for ourselves or doing what we're told? Freethinking is a parody of thinking (see Adorno 2003, 187–97). Consider how free thought is co-opted by militant atheists, where the reification of free thought is put in rigid opposition to the so-called "brainwashing." Their approach to thinking for oneself presumes that there is a mode or space of reasoning without brainwashing, where thinking is free from brainwashing. What we can call such "freethinking ideology" is not local to militant atheists alone or a new cultural phenomenon. Some readers probably objected to the very description of complete thoughts as occurring in subjects and predicates. They see this very approach to thinking as stating that one *has* to think in subjects and predicates, as if an undue obligation is being put on them, and they seek to break such rules to expose that we should be free from such restricted and limited models of thinking. "We can," they might say, "think in pictures rather than concepts."

One way to clarify this rote objection is to point out the difference between imagining and thinking, that imagining happens in pictures but thinking occurs in concepts (see Descartes 1998, 92–3). While we can picture a shape with three sides to count the number of angles it has, we cannot picture a shape with a thousand sides to count the number of angles it has. Yet, we can still figure it out. Let's focus more so on the attitude of the objection, though. Notice how it positions the laws governing thought and reasoning as "obligations" from which we can and should be liberated. This reminds me of the way in which many students experience my courses or going to college in general. They feel that they *have* to do the assignments I force on them. They do not experience their presence in my course or the assignments I give them to learn the material as opportunities to enhance their freedom but as obligations controlling them. This is a repercussion of the general US attitude toward education as something one has to do rather than as something one gets to do. Hence the social degradation of the liberal arts. Learning is not seen as an opportunity to enhance freedom and liberty, but as an oppressive obligation. Similarly, the laws of thought and reasoning are experienced by these sorts of people as oppressive and restrictive rather than enabling and liberating.

The most problematic representation of such freethinking ideology is what we noted earlier which Myer calls "propositionalism" (see Meyer 1995). Propositionalism is the program whereby reasoning and thinking are dislodged from questioning entirely. It is where we are taught that logical relations between complete thoughts solely concern sentential inferences unrelated to questions we are actually asking. It is where we are taught that claims are either true or false independent of the questions they address. Propositionalism creates a space in which we are subjectively convinced we are reasoning and thinking and acting of our own freewill (see Adorno 2003, 188). It is actually *here*, where we succumb to an ideology, that our purported "thinking" is restrained by those very oppressive forces from which we seek to escape.

The parody of thinking is embodied in social media platforms like Twitter where users are constantly demanded to share what they "think" about this or that; they are constantly called on to make a judgment. And we can see the cultic fanaticism emerge in collective shaming for expressions rather than rational engagement. This is not to say that there are not plenty of things that are shameful, such as white supremacy or even naiveté about white privilege. I am focused solely on those instances where thoughts and arguments are silenced by collective disapproval and shaming rather than engagement. Consider how in 2016 some supporters of Bernie Sanders or Jill Stein were shamed for their "betrayal" of Democrats or US values as if they were causing Donald Trump to gain the US presidency. Agreeing and aligning with those doing the shaming does not mean one is thinking freely. Or consider the collective infatuations with film and music reviews. It becomes natural to demand someone share their thoughts about this or that movie or song. Note how all of these are in many ways organized around economic profit (Adorno 2003, 189). Thoughts and arguments become commodities—just picture the surplus of basic reasoning textbooks and the market competition which encourages authors to devise titles that are ever more provocative and catchy, like Christopher Dicarlo's *How to Become a Really Good Pain in the Ass* or Harry Frankfurt's *On Bullshit* (see Hamby 2013). The freethinking industry unfurls in the very direction of being derogatory to freethinking itself by portraying reasoning as merely being "a pain in the ass." We come to expect miracles from crash courses in reasoning, perhaps as preparation for law school or perhaps even more as *the* way to figure out the truth and meaning of life. Despite the surplus of books and courses on reasoning, we can see constant expressions of disappointment—like, "kids these days do not know how to think" or the perennial studies of employers who indicate they want college graduates with better "critical thinking" skills, even though they, themselves, cannot define what critical thinking even is (see Korn 2014). This alarmingly is spread, especially among those who display anti-intellectualism. Consider how often fanatical anti-intellectual US conservatives describe Democrats or liberals as "hypocrites," that is, as committing logical and practical contradictions. Such rhetoric fills up media with pseudo-thinking and pseudo-reasoning, a shadow of them.

Our approach to thinking has been in part an effort to expose vacuity in much that passes for thought today. Let's turn to lay out inspirations for questions in reasoning.

A Phenomenology of Incessant Questions

Reasoning is like a child incessantly asking "But, why?" As Freire writes, "There are insistent questions that we all have to ask and that make it clear to us that it is not possible to study simply for the sake of studying" (Freire 2001, 73). Such questions are precisely what opens avenues of inference toward conclusions or toward premises and grounds. Such incessancy is precisely what many of Socrates's contemporaries found so frustrating, viewing him as an annoying gadfly full of stinging questions creating dizziness and uncertainty (see Plato 2002). With regard to every answer provided, reasoning retorts with an additional, "But, why?" In asking why we are not seeking mere precedent explanatory causes. We are not seeking mere causal explanations. We are, rather, seeking reasons. Indeed, we are seeking ultimate fundamental reasons, secure foundations and principles supporting all subsequent thoughts and arguments—that which earlier we have called the "unconditioned."

In so many ways, we attempt to appeal to higher authorities. In workplace conflicts with fellow employees, we might turn to managers for help or even mobilize support among workers to change business policies that structure the organization. Voters might be one-issue voters, focused solely on the appointment of Supreme Court Justices. We seek advice from others with more experience. Some people even pray to supreme beings for salvation. Reason similarly seeks ultimate authorization. Not only do we reason from premises to conclusions, we also reason from premises and conclusions to grounds for them. Reasoning goes both ways. Reason seems to orient itself in striving for some ultimate first principle, a foundational condition for all other conditions, if there is any such thing. We call it, with Kant, the "unconditioned" (Kant 2007, 311).

The unconditioned unfolds for us in three distinct ways: subjectively, objectively, and totally. I do not want us to get misled here, though. I am not talking about objectivity in the sense of our natural or naïve attitude. I am not talking about subjectivity in the sense of our natural or naïve attitude. Rather, I am talking about reason's quest to uncover first principles of the whole of external life or nature, of the whole of internal life or the mind, and of the whole of both of these in their interrelation or what some call "God." The first route we should call philosophical cosmology, our philosophical theorizing about the world pursing the ultimate objective principle for cosmic being as a whole. The second route we should call philosophical psychology or philosophical anthropology, our philosophical theorizing about the self where we pursue the ultimate subjective principle for conscious being as a whole. The third route we should call philosophical theology or fundamental ontology, our philosophical theorizing about the so-called "higher powers" like gods or the *Dao* where we pursue the ultimate unifying principle of Being itself. Note how these boil down to the three aspects of complete thoughts: the predicate (world), the subject (self), and the copula (being) (see Kant 2007, 297–311). As we will see at the end of this chapter and into Chapter 6, because we reach impasses rather than answers in these three fundamental aspects of life, we end up using metaphors and symbols rather than concepts. Our questioning is driven by, or perhaps even called on by, these symbolic and radiating aspects of the unconditioned of reasoning. Let us consider each of these three in turn.

The world or universe seems to consist of both discrete things and relations or processes between them. In our effort to rehabilitate predication, we have emphasized relations over relata (literally, the entities in the relations), predicaments over things, and will continue to do so here. With regard to the world, reason seems to demand a unity to all these processes and interrelations. Causality, the laws of causal relations, has risen to prevalence as the main way in which we think things are related (see Kant 2007, 383). Everything seems unified in a causal network. If we look closely, we can see reason reach an impasse at the level of the unconditioned, though, where—instead of settling on solid ground—it spins its wheels. Consider, for example, the question of the "beginning" of the world or the "beginning" of time as the origin point of the linear causal chain that seems definitive for the structure of our current universe. On the one hand, given that causality means that every effect has a precedent cause, there seems to have to be a beginning or a so-called "first cause." On the other hand, the notion of an absolute beginning forces reason to think of a "before" time, such as wondering what happened "before" the beginning of time, which—since this is illogical—suggests there can be no beginning. That is, when we reach the unconditioned, our arguments seem reasonable on both sides, such as whether there is or is not an absolute beginning to the universe.

Consider instead the question of freedom or "free will" within the closed causal network. On the one hand, if there are only the laws of nature or causal laws, then there seems to be a contradiction in that there is neither a first causal initiation of a sequence nor an interruption of the causal sequence with specific "free" actions. Hence, we are not free. Just as there seems to be a first cause, however, there also seem to be free initiatives for human beings at least. On the other hand, if there is genuine freedom and free initiatives, the causal network is precarious rather than a reliable grid. How can causality be reliable if it can be interrupted at any moment by a "free" intervention? Thus, since the grid is reliable, there seems to be no room for free initiatives. Reason reaches a level where it can only throw up its hands in a gesture of "who knows?!" The leaps we make in reasoning to things like a "first cause" are never rationally justifiable.

Deadlocks of reason like these indicate a collision with the unconditioned in the domain of the world. Nevertheless, the unconditioned inspires and encourages ever further inquiry where we dig further into precedent conditions, parts and wholes, causality and freedom, and necessity and contingency. Of course, freedom is of particular interest to us, especially as it relates to philosophical anthropology. Freedom helps us make sense of "actions," where we hold people uniquely responsible for actions in ways we do not hold precedent causes responsible for unfolding events. We never ask of a tree losing its leaves, "Why are you choosing to do that?!" Once we reach the level of the unconditioned, though, *we can only work on our fields of intelligibility and not experience.* We do not come to know more about the world we perceive, but we can clarify and refine our intellectual frameworks. We clarify our frameworks through the use of symbols, metaphors, and myths. We only have analogies, symbols, metaphors, and myths at the level of the unconditioned (Kant 2007, 484; see also Anderson 1998).

With regard to the self, we make leaps from processes of thinking and reasoning to theories about the nature of the self as a whole. The "I" or origin point of thinking, what Kant calls "transcendental apperception," makes all categories and concepts possible (Kant 2007, 319). It is a presupposition of all thinking, but not given to thinking as a subject matter. We never have a perception or sensation of the "I." Consider it this way. Pretend we asked you what you had for breakfast. When you tell us the story of what you ate, you split into two: the storyteller and the one about whom the story is told. Pretend then we asked you to tell us the story of you telling the story to us. Again, you split into two: the storyteller and the one about whom the story is told. The storyteller is like the I. It is systematically elusive to consciousness; it cannot be an object of consciousness. As I have emphasized earlier, thinking and perceiving are distinct. For example, a complete thought perceived is a sentence; a sentence understood is a complete thought. Thinking is not the perception of an object—that is, we cannot, as with some followers of Descartes, conclude from the "I think" that, therefore, "I exist as a thing" (see Kant 2007, 355). It confuses or reifies thinking into a specific stable entity. Of course, subjectivity is literally not an object. Rather, thinking is just a process of relating subjects and predicates. It is the determiner, not the determined. It is the determining subject, not the determinable object. Just as with the unconditioned in the domain of the world, when we reach the unconditioned in the domain of the subject, we can see reason spin its wheels.

Consider, for example, arguments about the self or soul as an "immaterial substance" (Kant 2007, 323). Even though the "I" always seems to be the same one, this is a logical characteristic of a unified consciousness and not the permanence of an entity or object (see Dunne 2004). The I, the thinking subject, thinks of substances, as sentential subjects of complete thoughts, but is not itself a substance. At the very least, the I struggles to conceive itself as a substance. Or consider arguments about the soul being the self-consciousness of the body or the soul being an empirically identifiable person (Kant 2007, 326). We can observe a human being, and identify that human as one person, the same "soul." Such an observation and identification is, however, to construct an object unifying the self *as a model* rather than perceiving a subjective unity or the unity of understanding. In no way can the self be merely a function of the causal material network because that would lead us back to the unconditioned in the world rather than the unconditioned in the self. *What this critique of reason illuminates is that arguments about the self can only be a discipline, not a doctrine or dogmatism* (Kant 2007, 353). The self is neither mere material nor mere spirit or mind.

Thinking is happening, and this is the mode of existence of the I. I do not think myself, but only subjects and predicates (Kant 2007, 371). One of the many objects on consciousness's horizon may be an ego with which the thinking I tends to identify, but even my ego is not the "I" (see Sartre 1960). The laws of understanding, thought, and reason—the laws of logic—produce concepts, and this logical production, this unfurling of thinking, is the freedom of autonomous reasoning. This may seem to stand in subtle tension with the sense of responsibility we have to them, as we articulated earlier. Through schemas, we produce varying concepts and options for predication. We *can*, however, be resistant to them. Moreover, we can fail to obey rational laws, and thus fail to think freely. In this light, reasoning is intrinsically ethical.

Despite the world and the I seeming to be radically different to the point where there is no possibility of relation, they nevertheless seem to interact. As such, reason seeks the unconditioned in the domain of the unity or totality of self and world. In Western and some South Asian traditions of reasoning, this has been approached in terms of the nature and existence of divine beings, such as with Islam, Christianity, Judaism, and Advaita Vedanta. However, we can see similar issues in classical Chinese contemplations of the fundamental *Dao* or even in theories about the Dharmakaya or Dharma body of the Buddha in some early Buddhisms. For convenience, we will default to the hegemonic Western philosophical notion of the "perfect" being, a god that is purportedly omniscient, omnibenevolent, and omnipotent—though we will keep in mind that these critiques need to be extendable or transferable to reflections on other figures of supreme beings.

Arguments in fundamental ontology concerning this sort of divine being unfold in three directions paralleling the three features of complete thoughts. On the one hand, tending toward philosophical cosmology, there are arguments urging identification of a divine being with the so-called "first cause" or, rather, a necessary cause for all other apparent events (see Aquinas 1993, 60–2; Kant 2007, 508). The argument at its basis is that since a universe of contingent entities exists, something noncontingent or necessary must have caused it to exist. This first cause, this necessary being, is the god. This argument makes a leap, moving from rational principles to empirical reality, though. Necessity is a logical principle of the understanding, not a feature of the world. Or, put differently, the necessity that we think in terms of causality, that we produce *an objective world structured by causality, is a feature of our mind's* a priori *synthetic judgment* (see Kant 2007, 37–45). We cannot help but apply the fundamental category of cause and effect beyond space and time, not because we know there is a cause but because causality is a structure for the production of any thought whatsoever. Recall the problem with the complete thought: "Everything just increased by ten times its size." The term "everything" tries to point to the whole of time and space, when we know that sentential subjects can only pick out something specific within the content of time and space. For Kant, this approach to a divine being as a necessity or a first cause instead points to the abyss of reason in our confrontation with the unconditioned (see Kant 2007, 513). It leads to the giddy yet smug question: If a god caused everything, what caused the god? This is a natural and predictable incessancy of questioning.

On the other hand, tending toward philosophical psychology, there are arguments that go: because there seems to be intended purposes in us and in the world, there must be an ultimate Artist or Author of it all (see Paley 2002; and Kant 2007, 520). The order of the whole, both subjectively and objectively, seems to be intricately and deliberately designed. Because the universe displays an order like a clock, there must be a divine clockmaker, and that is the god. While this might indicate a principle generator of order, it does not actually get us to a so-called "intelligent designer" as a creator of this all. Instead, we again here witness a desperate leap into the abyss of reason in our confrontation with the unconditioned. Interestingly, Kant claims that both of these angles on divine being—cosmological based on causes and teleological based on purposes—are merely the "ontological proof" in disguise.

This third approach gives privilege neither to the subjective nor to the objective poles of experience and judgment. The ontological proof for the existence of a divine being has been deployed by many thinkers, famously in Western religions by the medieval Christian theologian Anselm in his *Proslogion*. There are a few key aspects crucial for comprehending this argument. The argument uses the very definition of the term to prove the existence of a god (see Anselm 2002). By definition, the word "god" is said to denote that entity the nonexistence of which it is impossible to conceive, whose nonexistence is unthinkable. Anselm defines "god" as "that than which nothing greater can be thought" (Anselm 2002). Second, using this definition, the argument sets out to form a reductio ad absurdum, a valid argument form that reduces an opposing claim to an absurdity or contradiction. Anselm is construed as arguing his point that this god exists by showing that denying it leads to contradictions. To deny this god exists in reality admits that there is something greater than the notion of this god merely existing as in the understanding. This is the third key, something that exists in reality as well as in the understanding is superior to something merely existing in the understanding. Existing in reality is part of the definition of the concept, then, just like having three angles is part of the definition of a triangle. The final key is that if we deny that a triangle has three angles, then we show we do not know what we are talking about.

Similarly, if we deny the existence of this sort of god, then we apparently do not know what we are talking about—because presumably only a "fool" says in their heart that this god does not exist (see Psalm 14:1). We can, perhaps, make this more precise by replacing the word "god" with the word "principle" or even the "unconditioned." To be able to think at all, thinking has to be governed by laws and principles, ordered in a hierarchy—as we noted with the fundamental law of noncontradiction. If we deny that the laws apply to thinking, then we are foregoing thinking as such, which is a foolish thing to do.

The problem with the ontological argument is that existence or "being" is a function of complete thoughts, not things (see Kant 2007, 501). Recall that the copula, expressed in declensions of the verb "to be," combines subjects with predicates. While, once defined, this notion of a god might include existence in its definition, "existence" really is being used as a predicate of a subject. It is as if we are trying to say that "God is is-ing." However, "being" is not a determinate predicate (Kant 2007, 504). We need experiences or sensations to distinguish actualities from possibilities when we come to know that something actually exists. And upon that experience, if a subject matter stands out ready for predication, we might then have something to say about it; we might have something to predicate of this actually existing thing. A more basic belief than such and such a god exists is that "My god is almighty" and similar such predications of one's focal point of veneration or worship. Moreover, as with the truth or falsity of any complete thought, we can reject both the subject and the predicate, even if the subject by definition implies a specified predicate. That is, even if a triangle by definition has three angles, it does not mean that there exists a single triangle or that there exists a triangle in front of us right here and now. Just because there may be a necessity of thought, it does not mean there is a necessity in things.

Probably the most overlooked but also a crucial aspect of this "argument" is that it occurs in a prayer. Some editors and translators say that this rhetorical context is "merely" literary. Yet Anselm speaks not *about* a god, but *to* a god, addressing this being in the second person as "You." He does not really define the word "god" but tells the "You" whom he addresses that "You are that than which nothing greater can be conceived" (Anselm 2002). Anselm is not merely reflecting on this god but talks with his god in a state of ultimate concern (see Tillich 2001). Only in this way, I think, can we say that Anselm's ontological argument integrates the whole of both the highest subjective and the highest objective principles. It is not merely an objective description corresponding to a fact about the world, but an existentially involved proposition. For Anselm, his life's meaning as well as the meaning of the world are at stake in the argument. It is not a mere logical puzzle performed in amusement or performed with scientific neutrality.

As an orientation toward the unconditioned, he can really *only express himself symbolically* and not merely conceptually. Only symbols express ultimate concern. Anything that is taken as an object of ultimate concern becomes one's "god" (see Tillich 2001). If you stake your life on the dollar bill, then money serves as your god. The character of ultimacy or the unconditioned in this existential state transforms ordinary concepts. A dollar is no longer just a dollar in such an existential state. When we extend our notion of "cause" from a specific sequence of time to the beginning of the entire universe as the "first cause," *we have rendered it a religious symbol rather than an empirical concept*. Religious notions for the unconditioned, such as gods, the *Dao*, etc., are better approached as ideals of reason rather than proper names for existing entities. *Ideals have practical power to guide actions even if they do not technically have objective reality* (see Kant, 2007, 486–7; and Anderson 1998). Ideals are not self-contradictory concepts, even if they express our effort to incorporate all possible subjects and predicates. Ideals are archetypes (Kant 2007, 491; and Anderson 1998). Archetypes are nothing but postulates of reason in practical action. Kant calls the ideals of divine being the "crown of thinking," thinking in the service of living well (Kant 2007, 527). If "god" is supposed to refer to or correspond with an entity existing in actual or external reality, no such being exists (see Tillich 2001, 52). To persevere in fanatical commitment to divine beings as entities in time and space, despite our development of thought and reason, we would have to reject this entire approach to thinking. We would have to reject thought itself. Instead of reifying the meaning of "god" into an entity that exists or does not exist, the word "god"—like the words "christ," "buddha," "prophet," "king," "president," "hero," "power forward," etc.—is a predicate, not a subject. We can predicate "god" of someone or something, such as Jewish communities predicating "god" of the person or figure with the personal name signified by the tetragrammaton. To call this figure "god" is like calling the current president "President." This is not merely about contingent experiences that strike us as outstanding and question-worthy. It is about an additional aspect of rationality: *not only does reasoning have constitutive laws; it is structured also by regulative ideals*. Moreover, at the edge of thought and reason, we can no longer rely merely on concepts and categories. Instead, we have to resort to symbols, metaphors, and analogies. In Chapter 6, we will return to further examination of symbols and metaphors in reasoning.

I'm not asking here why we question at all. I'm after what pulls on us to question ever further. In light of this incessant questioning and our striving for the unconditioned, let us turn to elaboration on orientations of questioning in arguments, and then to regulative ideals at the edges of thought and reason.

6

A Rationality of Questioning and Reasoning

In this chapter, I will focus on two main topics. What orientations do questions take in the domain of reasoning? And what repercussions do we face in reaching the edges of thought and reason? In what follows, I will first look at four orientations of inquiry in reasoning, parallel to the four orientations of questioning with regard to complete thoughts. Questioning similarly radiates in four directions. I will then turn to examine the necessity of appeal to metaphors and models to reach intangible aspects of our lifeworlds referred to earlier as the "unconditioned." Some symbols and models provide unifying structure to our worldviews, but—as symbols and models—they must remain open to further inquiry and revision. I will also explicate aspects of worldviews and worldbuilding nurtured through questioning. I will then close Part II with a brief note about how all this opens us up to collaborate with others in communities of inquiry. We cannot and do not reason alone.

How to Question Arguments from at Least Four Directions

Just as there are a number of different avenues for questioning in relation to complete thoughts, there are a number of avenues for questioning in relation to arguments. Before turning to examine those avenues, recall that we repress questioning in part because questioning technically does not *say* anything. We seem able to dislodge reasoning from questioning because questioning disappears into the background in the face of expositions. Just look at the last three sentences all ending with a period—each one technically has an implicit question it addresses, yet none of the questions are written out in detail. This is why propositionalism and free-thought ideology are difficult to confront. I'm not trying to advocate for an opposite or alternative ideology, though, like some reactionary conservative position such as the Tea Party to confront a seeming moderate position represented by, say, the Affordable Care Act. Our confrontation with this ideology consists of having exposed it as pseudo-thinking, as a mere shadow of thinking. The way we are doing this is retrieving questioning from the obliviousness of it in propositionalism.

Despite some crumbs dropped throughout Chapters 4 and 5, I need to explain how questioning works with reasoning overall. In short, just as arguments coordinate premises and conclusions, the broader interrogative context within which arguments even make sense involves a key scaffolding of question orientations. Questioning in thinking coordinates subjects and predicates into complete thoughts; questioning in reasoning coordinates multiple complete thoughts into arguments. That is, while questions open subject matters to predicative possibilities in the domain of thought, questions open premises to conclusive possibilities in the domain of reason. There are four crucial orientations of questioning here: conclusion-centered questioning, premise-centered questioning, inference-centered questioning, and rationality-centered questioning.

In *conclusion-centered questioning*, we ask what we can conclude from a premise. Such questioning opens up premises as radiating possibilities for conclusion. Many questions focus us in on indeterminacy of conclusions. They contain an articulated premise, but open concluding possibilities. Which complete thought can count as a—or even *the*—conclusion to a specified premise or set of premises? What wording of the conclusion best fits for possible strength or valid support from the premises? Take an example: "The car in front of us just put on its breaks! (And?)" A premise is explicit, but the conclusion has yet to be settled. These are conclusion-centered questions because they concern conclusions derivable from a given premise. In addition to all the questions we can ask about complete thoughts, we also wonder about what other complete thoughts relevantly follow from a given complete thought. In essence, *we ask for* conclusions. Given the premise about seeing brake lights, we might conclude, "I should step on my breaks now."

In the opposite direction, we have *premise-centered questioning*. In these sorts of questions, we ask which—if any—complete thoughts might provide support for a conclusion. These questions focus us in on an indeterminacy of premises. Which premise leads to this conclusion? What wording of a premise provides strongest support for this given conclusion? Let us take an example: "We should probably step back. (But why?)" Here the conclusion is settled, but which premise, which reason or motive, leads to this conclusion is yet to be determined. It may be that someone needs to get by and that we want to treat others with the same courtesy we ourselves want. Alternatively, it may be that the bonfire has grown in size and heat. It is as if we have come into an argument midstream, catching the conclusion without having explicit knowledge of the premise(s). Through these premise-centered questions, we try to figure out why the conclusion should be accepted. At bottom, we need to ask why we ought to commit to this conclusion. We are, in essence, *asking for* premises.

On a broader level, there is *inference-centered questioning*. Here the questions concern relations between specific complete thoughts. Are the complete thoughts even relevant to one another? In what way? Is the argument trying to be deductive or inductive? Is it valid or strong? Is it fallacious? In this orientation of questioning, we are asking about the *formal quality* of the argument. Let us examine an illustration:

> Premise 1: If more women are elected to be US government representatives, then the US House will be more genuinely representative of the US populace.
> Premise 2: More women have been elected.
> Conclusion: Therefore, the House is more genuinely representative.

What is the formal structure of this argument? Is it truth preserving? This argument can be symbolized as follows:

> Premise 1: $p \supset q$. (the horseshoe means "if, then").
> Premise 2: p.
> Conclusion: $\therefore q$. (the dots mean "therefore").

It is the valid argument form called *modus ponens*. As such, we know that the argument preserves truth. Consider this alternative illustration of a way racist mainstream media mischaracterized Malcolm X during the US Civil Rights movements of the 1960s. Malcolm X promoted self-defense classes for fellow Black men, but racist media at the time mischaracterized him as "promoting hate" (X 1987). By attacking his intentions and character, they felt they did not have to take the need for self-defense classes seriously. Did the media have a valid or strong argument? No. Their argument was neither deductive nor inductive. They committed the ad hominem fallacy, attacking the person. Such a focus on the person is, in this case, irrelevant to X's position. By changing the topic, they have turned their attention to something irrelevant. Since it is not relevant, it is—as we said in Chapter 5—not even reasoning in an argument. At bottom, we need to ask what kind of argument is being deployed. In essence, *we ask about the form* of argument.

On the broadest level, there is what we have primarily been doing throughout Part II—what we can call *rationality-centered questioning*. These questions are less about this or that specific conclusion, or this or that specific argument form, but about the structure of rationality itself. Is rationality universal, or is it complicit with Eurocentric hegemony? Ought we trust our grasp on reasoning in general? What constitutive laws make specific instances of reasoning possible? How does the unconditioned open us to incessant questions? In such questioning, we are asking for the nature of reasoning itself and at the same time asking about ourselves as autonomous reasoners. By developing a theory of rationality, even if it is merely a folk theory, we can know what we are doing. Such questionings are a matter of both generating and testing arguments. We can test arguments in lots of different ways, such as asking whether an argument is valid or strong, if premises are relevant, or even if an argument is deployed solely in the interests of preserving a dominant class's power. We test arguments to ensure they are truth preserving. Will the conclusion persevere truth or will truth perish in it? Moreover, through testing arguments we can make them and their claims our own. In such appropriation, we grow our confidence in arguments and take responsibility or ownership over them. We are checking them for ourselves rather than merely accepting them passively. In this way, we purge and purify ourselves of falsity and nonsense. In all four orientations of questioning, we experience and express arguments in their mode of being of questionability. This mode of questionability is *the transition point between a mere exposition perceived and an argument understood.*

Our emphasis on these four orientations of questioning available in the domain of reason contrasts with alternative systems used for testing and evaluating arguments. This does not make our approach incompatible with theirs. The worry about potentially being duped by nonsense motivated a number of proposals for testing arguments in the last century. For example, the Vienna School, influenced by Wittgenstein's early philosophical work, proposed the so-called *verification principle* for determining the reference of conclusions. The philosopher A.J. Ayer develops it most explicitly (see Ayer 1952). It puts forth the notion that only claims that can be verified with reference to specific sensations or perceived facts can count as complete thoughts. Other claims are not false; they are meaningless. There are no invisible or intangible things in this approach. The principal question is: Is this claim under examination verifiable by observation and experience? Yet many conclusions are left untestable, such as "All people do things for selfish motives" (see Baggini and Fosl 2010, 137). Any action can be interpreted to fit this claim, such as in discussions of altruistic actions. For example, people have said that Mother Teresa helped others not out of altruism but ultimately for her own access to heaven. Moreover, the verification principle itself cannot be verified according to its own criterion. There is no observation to which it can possibly refer. Even scientific laws fail this test because they purport to apply to the future. The philosopher Karl Popper attempted to correct Ayer's principle with the *falsification principle*. Popper was concerned to delimit the boundaries of natural science, or to distinguish science from pseudoscience. He proposed only those hypotheses that are in principle falsifiable—that is, those which could, hypothetically, be verified or falsified via controlled observation or experimentation—constituted *scientific* hypotheses. His point is that a theory or conclusion is innocent until proven guilty or works until proven unworkable (see Popper 2002). We can already see how this seems compatible with scientific practices. Natural sciences advance by making hypotheses and putting them to tests, perhaps even refuting proposed hypotheses. If they are refuted—falsified that is—then they are replaced by alternative or modified hypotheses. Of course, this works best for general laws, not specific statements. Saying that "I see a purple hippo when I look in the fridge," for example, cannot be modified upon falsification in order to make advances.

We can see that this scientific method is a special instance of the more general process of questioning I described in Part I. What both verification and falsification seem to neglect is that testing arguments involves examining at least two conjoined complete thoughts. They take conclusions out of context as complete thoughts standing on their own. As we saw, questioning, and not falsification, is the heart of testing. Moreover, it is context dependent. It only makes sense within an already-accepted body of concepts, beliefs, and practices, or lifeforms. Testing particular hypotheses with questions only makes sense in light of this broader background. Recall the question, "What year is it?" Or, recall the question, "What direction are we facing?" Toward Mecca? Southwest? Which is true? As I noted, questions involve some presuppositions and assumptions, as does testing with falsification. Kuhn refers to these frameworks of background assumptions a paradigm (see Kuhn 2012).

Questioning in reasoning requires reflection, in the sense of stepping back from pressures and influences of immediate situations. From this broader vantage point, we can take more into consideration. We can clarify, examine, contextualize, critique, interpret, and synthesize notions. How is reflection possible? This is what "universal" probably meant originally. We are not subjected to merely a swarm of random particulars; we experience an accumulation of particulars into groups, categories, and relations. Aristotle uses an analogy with a retreating army (see Aristotle 1983, 100a10–15). First, one slows to a stand. Then another, and another, until the army regroups to form a new front line. Similarly, our unfurling experience of things accumulate into general categories. This perspective on experiences allows us to criticize claims and arguments, and to identify fallacies. It opens up our bullshit detector: not only can we test individual complete thoughts and arguments, we can use this reflection to examine our thinking and others' thinking to see if there is any indifference to the truth of what is being said (see Frankfurt 2005). Someone who is not willing to abide by logical and rational rules for what they assert are bullshitting us. This is not to say that poets and comedians cannot push these boundaries. It is to say that flaunting logical and rational rules shows one is indifferent to truth. This is way worse than lying, because at least a liar has a focus on truth—however hidden they might want it. Arguing from indifference is to argue in bad faith (see Sartre 1984, 47–70).

Rational critique is the analysis, evaluation, purification, and refining of thoughts and arguments. Criticism is not merely stating negative remarks. It tests arguments, with the potential to make them as compelling and accurate as possible. There are many methods for criticizing arguments. We can show a premise is false. We can show that what looks like an argument is invalid and is thus just an exposition. We can show evidence is weak or distorted, like pointing to significant counterexamples. We can show inconsistency between a current argument and another argument in the architecture of someone's worldview. We can show an argument leads to a paradox or even a contradiction. Or we can even show an argument is merely trivial or a simple repetition of the point. All of these may strike us as great ways to demolish our opponents' arguments. However, I am not concerned with "winning" in this sense. All of these methods of testing claims and arguments—indeed, questioning within reasoning—are ways we can improve arguments and take responsibility or share responsibility for them.

Symbols Go beyond the Edge of Reason

A philosophical anthropology is an account of what it is to be a human being. What is the nature of being human? What is the structure of the self? A crucial feature of any philosophical anthropology worth listening to is an account of our "effort-to-be" or some notion of what we can call, with Pamela Sue Anderson, "projection" or "yearning" (Anderson 2001, 197). We are not merely human beings, but human *becomings*. Our efforts-to-become are guided by futural projections, and these projections are structured by what Anderson calls "regulative ideals" (Anderson 1998, 135–7). Since ideas of reason like "the universe" or "god" fall outside the limits of experience and knowledge, they can only operate for reason as ideals. Regulative ideals are what we are left with to guide reason in its practical usage in place of transcendently existing metaphysical entities. Regulative ideals do not, Anderson writes, "constitute knowledge. But they can direct human understanding toward a practical goal *without forgetting the illusion of claiming to know what is beyond* every given experience" (Anderson 2001, 137; my emphasis). When regulative ideals are properly functioning as regulative ideals rather than taken as objectively existing entities, we are humble enough to admit to limits of thought and reason. We cannot get beyond experience, though we can change ourselves by redirecting our energies in such projections.

Thus, besides the constitutive laws governing reason, another feature of reason is this structure of regulative rules. These differ from constitutive laws in that regulative ideals change and adapt, orienting our reasoning and questioning. Given that we have limited opportunities to think and reason, given that we have limited time, we have to make choices and prioritize some things over others. We ask some questions before asking others. What we prioritize reflects and embodies our values—*and* what we say we value can conflict with what we show we value with our actions. The crucial set of regulative ideals is the set of unifying principles—variably called the ultimate grounds, the first principles, and so on, that we examined earlier in terms of the unconditioned. The practical use of reason both preserves and expresses human freedom, the freedom of thinking, but since it is regulative rather than constitutive, we need to determine practical laws in a different way.

Whereas complete thoughts unify experiences into understandable wholes by placing diverse subjects under predicates, reasoning uses regulative ideals to unify complete thoughts and predicates in a broader systematic structure (Kant 2007, 533). Reason unifies thought in fields of intelligibility proper to varying forms of life and language games, as we have gone over with different calendars and different directions depending on a culture. It provides systematic structure to thoughts. Regulative ideals orient thinking for further investigations and inquiries, where we develop further possible responses to our questionings (see Kant 2007, 534). We can change our questions and possible responses through hypotheses that we project beyond rational deadlocks. As regulative ideals, however, we can accept our hypothesizing as undecided possibilities without demanding that this or that undecidability must be the case. We must let go of the demand that others submit to the rightness of our positions on these matters, though. We cannot definitively know things about the soul, the world as a whole, and gods. Our critique of reason exposes its limits, as we have shown with our rationality-centered questioning. Through unification and hypothesizing, however, we cultivate and improve our understanding and knowledge (Kant 2007, 550). Using reason in this way does not increase our knowledge, but improves it. Improvement is merely subjective, not in the sense of personally or egocentrically subjective, but in the sense of logic and reason as functions of the I. Such inspired use of reason helps us avoid the extremes of indolence or apathetic skepticism, on the one hand, and obsession or fundamentalist fanaticism, on the other hand (see Kant 2007, 561–3).

There are two edges to thought. As we saw in Part I, complete thoughts interpret and make sense of experiences. Experience precedes thought, giving to understanding something to refer to in predicating of subjects. What we have not yet addressed in a developed way is the other edge of thought: action. *Whereas experience is before thought, action is after thought.* Of course, we can "do" things without thinking and we can think things without doing them. As we noted earlier, however, only complete thoughts in accord with reason are free. For an action—as opposed to a mere event— one needs to use reason rather than mere psychological motives bound up in the causal chain of nature. We can make sense of this through comparing logical argument with practical argument. In practical arguments, those arguments bound up with action and practices, the conclusion is not merely a complete thought but an embodiment of a complete thought *in action* (see MacIntyre 1981). Actions can sometimes speak louder than words, which is why we can detect contradictions or hypocrisy in people by comparing what they say to what they do. What we commit to do through reason are actions for which we are responsible (see Aristotle 1999, 1110a1–1113a16). We ought to be careful here though. It is useful to keep action and thought relevantly distinct, even if at times we might undertake an "action" analysis of thought, where we analyze thinking as an activity. Here we are approaching action and practice as text, as we do complete thoughts (see Ricoeur 1991).

There are other edges of thinking and reasoning besides experience and action. As I noted, we cannot think the unconditioned in any direct way. There are, however, other impossible thoughts. We cannot, for instance, think of a round-square or a black/white thing. We might picture a square with curved edges, and we might picture stripes like a zebra or just a gray hue. None of those images captures what is at issue here. Such limits are conceptual, referring back to the logical law of noncontradiction. It is not that we are deficient, that we are somehow *unable* to think such contradictions. It is that these are not thoughts to be had. *To worry that such delimitations inhibit or restrict one's freedom to think is to not yet grasp that logical laws actually set us free to think.* Smooshing the words "round" and "square" together looks like a concept—a so-called "round-square." However, these are just perceived words and not a notion that can be understood. Moreover, supposing that picturing or imagining can extend further than understanding and thought is not a helpful way to go either. Thinking extends further than mere picturing. In most imaginations, we can both picture and think what is at issue—say, a unicorn, or a horse with a horn. As I pointed out earlier, while we can think of a triangle as well as picture such a shape, we can only think of a chiliagon but not picture such a shape (see Descartes 1998, 73). Thinking of an object with three sides, we can also picture a three-sided object. Thinking of a thousand-sided object, we cannot also picture it. How many angles does a thousand-sided object have? You can provide the answer not because you pictured the object and slowly counted them, but because you understand the concept. This is not because there is an incoherence in the notion of a thousand-sided object. It is that our capacity to imagine is more limited than we might like to admit. In addition to all this are those thoughts we cannot help but to think or presuppose, such as logical laws and self-evident truths, but even such things as so-called "properly basic beliefs" are concretized in cultural and religious symbols.

As a key aspect of reasoning, regulative ideals are embodied in concrete symbols. Through symbols, we project our ideals for self-realization and values for world-changing action. Through symbols, we project ideals for unified fields of intelligibility for our worldviews. Regulative ideals are concretized in specific symbols and archetypes, and these are configured and reconfigured into narrative wholes or myths (see Anderson, 1998; and Ricoeur 1984–1988). Christian philosopher Paul Tillich develops symbols and myths as concretized or context specific expressions of unconditioned concern (Tillich 2001, 47–62; and Dickman 2017). He provides illustrations of different symbols, such as money for success, the flag for nationalists or patriots, and religious symbols for religious communities like the cross in Christianity. Some key features of symbols are that they cannot be invented intentionally and that they open up aspects of ourselves and reality unavailable without those symbols. This parallels the sociologist Emile Durkheim's explanation of the development of "totems" in many ways (see Durkheim 2008). A group takes some element of their lives, such as an animal, and that comes to represent their community. Symbols and myths open up possibilities for our becoming. They are regulative ideals through which we project our yearning and striving, and reappropriate ourselves for fuller self-realization. This is the fundamental feature of culture, or the cultivation of fully realized human beings. For example, when one sits in meditation or performs *zazen*, one alienates one's self from oneself in striving to emulate the Buddha and in so sitting one returns to oneself having sat in emulation of the Buddha.

We need to be careful, though, because a lot of institutions place restrictions on cultural production symbols, to such an extent that many people are marginalized and oppressed. We lack equitable representation not only in pop culture with TV shows but also in religious imaginaries where many people take it for granted that, say, Jesus is white or that their god is masculine. Irigaray argues that patriarchal societies have a limited, or marked absence of, symbols for projections and reappropriations of feminine subjectivity (Irigaray 2007, 11). The feminist theologian Mary Daly's later work represents a radical effort to create authentic feminine symbols and myths (see, for example, Daly 1990). The quest for equality rather than equity, in Irigaray's eyes, can serve to promote men as the symbolic ideal toward which women strive. Whom are women trying to be equal to? Irigaray points out that "motherhood," if deployed as symbolic of a regulative ideal for cultivating feminine selfhood, can be made complicit with patriarchal social systems. She writes:

> So many young women and so many girls expect their cultural elders to give them a lead on the possibility of their becoming women without an *exclusive* subjection to motherhood, and without, for all that, being reduced to male identity. I think it shows that the goals of our liberation have remained tied to a culture that offers women no subjective opportunities, and that, for want of an identity of their own, many are, in a vague sort of way, trying to find a niche for themselves within a technological era that needs their energy to give itself the illusion of a future. (Irigaray 2007, 128)

Cultures function to cultivate human becomings through symbolic and mythic projections, and these are rooted in specific practices and rituals (see Bell 2009). Yet feminine subjectivity is inhibited by a lack of symbols, myths, and practices that could facilitate its full blossoming, its flourishing. As I have argued elsewhere, I am not inclined to explain this as a result of cultural traditions proper, but as a result of institutionalized restrictions on cultural and traditional productions (Dickman 2018c). Institutional policies and practices control what symbols are promoted and repeated, perhaps in accord with market interests and profit-seeking.

We use analogies in constructing hypotheses, and this helps us to use reason to open new paths for thinking and knowing. For instance, hypothesizing that minds are unified like objects opened up the field of psychology. Without such a model, we would not have frameworks for self-understanding where people describe themselves as "introverted" or "extroverted," for example. Metaphors literally carry reason beyond our current limitations in knowledge. The limits of knowledge are distinct from the limits of thought and reason. Thought and reason are constrained by logical laws and their difference from other dimensions of life, such as experience and action. We experience events; we think thoughts. We know events and laws of nature. But we can hypothesize alternatives based on openings achieved by symbolic quests for the unconditioned.

We should not confuse metaphor as a rhetorical trope with metaphor in complete thoughts. The rhetorical trope approach to metaphor treats it as merely replacing one proper name with a different, unusual, name. As we discussed, a semantic or sentential approach to metaphor helps us see a transition between the literal gravel of life and its redemption in poetry. *The poetic redemption of the real* is that process by which we interpret our experiences, lifting them into the light of discourse and intelligibility. *Such an ontology is against literal reality, resurrecting reality differently to new being and new life.* Indeed, being is metaphoric (see Ricoeur 2003). However, we live in a world of dead metaphors where old predications settle into sediment. As metaphors wane, static metaphysics emerge. We take argument-as-battle as what argument really is. We take time-as-money as what time really is. This demands revivifying thought and reason with new meanings. The poetic redemption of the real with symbols is this transformation of experience into meanings understood.

The practical use of reason preserves and expresses freedom of thought through projection of and unification in regulative ideals. Kant approaches this in his critique of practical reason in order to isolate and develop the laws of morality or autonomy. Let us leave Kant's approach to morality aside. Instead, I want us to look at the development of worldviews.

Regulative Ideals Build Meaningful Worlds beyond Dogmatism

One aim of questioning is thinking, and the ends of thinking are twofold: actions and worldviews within which actions make sense. Consider how people used to explain behavior that did not conform to standards of normality by appeal to spirit or demon possession. Spirits and demons were part of that community's conceptual framework or worldview. In modern societies, most people subscribe to explanations of people's behaviors from psychology and neuroscience, that many behaviors deemed "insane" are causally linked to personality or neurological disorders. Our worldviews or social imaginaries shape the ways in which we act and ways we treat others, and even how we make sense of actions. Thinking and reasoning are not like merely walking through a museum—picture it as an argument museum— where reasoned positions are "over there" hanging on the wall for distanced observation. As existential philosopher Robert Solomon explains:

> Through reflection and by means of articulation and argument, [we are allowed] to analyze and critically examine our ideas, and to synthesize our vision of ourselves and the world, to put the pieces together in a single, unified, defensible vision. Such synthesis is the ultimate aim of [critical]

> reflection, and scattered ideas and arguments are no more [critical thinking] than a handful of unconnected words is a poem. (Solomon 2010, 7)

Our worldviews are personal. They are not merely personal in the sense that we have preferences or biases. They are existentially personal in that they give intelligibility to the "I."

The most basic units of worldviews are concepts and predicates. Predicates give intelligible form to experiences, events, actions, and things. They help us pick out some things from the blur of fluctuating experience. They help us tie together various experiences and events. The etymology of "concept" can help us recognize its tangible meaning as "to grasp" or "to tie" (-cept) "together" (con-). There are a few different kinds of concepts (see Solomon 2010). Empirical concepts apply to experience. We experience orientations under different frameworks of directions, such as facing forward and backward or North and South. *A priori* concepts are prior to experience, making particular experiences possible, such as time, space, number, substance, and more. Existential or teleological concepts are the kind that orient meaning and purpose in our lives, such as ideals of equity or social harmony. Integrating concepts are those by which we make entire worldviews hang together, such as principles, scientific laws, religious destiny, and more. A worldview is an integrated order of varying concepts, a conceptual framework. We usually take this framework for granted as "natural" or "just the way things are." Sometimes we need to examine these frameworks, perhaps due to a surprising experience or a discovery, or due to a person whom we respect seeing things differently.

Sometimes we may participate in or assume more than one worldview, even if they are inconsistent—such as donning secularism during the workweek, hedonism on Friday and Saturday, and Christianity on Sunday. Can all these hang together in a broader complete whole, or must we choose between them? In the academic study of religions, it seems that a default assumption is that people can only belong to one religion. Single religious belonging with exclusive commitment is taken to be the default, and people who participate in more than one suffer from what has been called "ambiguity tolerance" (see Coogan 2003). It does not seem, for instance, that someone can be both atheist and religiously Jewish. However, many people throughout history and across the globe see no problem participating in multiple religions. For example, in many Japanese homes you can find both a Shinto shrine, or *kamidana*, and a Buddhist shrine, or *butsudan*. The framework of these scholars seems to assume single religious belonging as "natural," and that deviating from that is a sort of cognitive impairment in that one has to tolerate ambiguity. If multiple-religious belonging is statistically more usual, however, perhaps the cognitive deficit is really exclusivity to one religion. Maybe we should call it "false dichotomy tolerant"? The point is that what seem like vastly different worldviews are often relevant in a single person's life.

Most *a priori*, existential, and integrating concepts are derived from metaphors and analogies, however much they have become sediment in our worldviews. As we noted earlier, as the greater metaphor and analogy wane, the more ascendant is metaphysics. The problem of substance metaphysics is that it takes conceptual frameworks and worldviews as the way reality *must* be. Thich Nhat Hanh describes this cognitive imposition as a way of constructing things to which we can cling (see Thich 2009). For Buddhists, clinging creates suffering. Wittgenstein describes such metaphysical thinking that things *must* be this way as similar to tracing the frame of a portrait with our finger (Wittgenstein 2009, §599). *Metaphysics takes what is predicative as substantive.* For example, many people do not see argument *as* fighting, but believe that arguing *is* fighting. Many people do not just take language *as* a conduit, but believe that language *is* merely a conduit. Metaphors, analogies, and models help us get at dimensions of reality that seem invisible, those aspects structuring reality besides experience. While these concepts provide cultural coherence, they cannot be taken as transparent conduits to uninterpreted "reality in itself" (if there is such a thing!). That does not mean we are left with mere social constructs. For instance, we know that race and sex are social constructs, but they have been powerful frameworks affecting people with oppression. Social constructs have real effects.

Moreover, while models help us see some aspects of realities, they do so while also hiding other aspects. We need to see our frameworks as fictions, useful in some respects and occlusionary in others. We should be careful here, though. I do not mean "fiction" in the natural attitude of "falsehood." Think of how fictions have changed many of our lives. Did you know that there is an environmentalist organization based on an ethic derived from the *Harry Potter* series? Seeing ourselves or the world in light of different fictions help us live differently, potentially for the better. Useful fictions orient us and provide explanatory power, not explanations like in the natural sciences but in the sense of opening up reasons for why things go the way they do. In light of this, we can see the formation of complete thoughts into things like short stories. Narrative plots function to integrate various features of the world of the story, such as characters, actions, atmosphere, and more. Out of all these emplotted elements, we recognize a complete story. Indeed, a complete thought *is* (and, of course, *is not*) a short story. For those of you familiar with *Star Wars* and the comparative mythicist Joseph Campbell's theories of myth: the subject goes on the hero's journey through the travails set for it by the predicate and comes back to itself greater than it was at the beginning (see Campbell 1991).

We extend or abstract dimensions of experience into broader structures of worldviews. Most—perhaps all—metaphors and analogies have a physical basis (see Lakoff and Johnson 2003). As we emphasized earlier, our bodily dehiscence is the possibility for conscious awareness and understanding of meanings (see Merleau-Ponty 1968). Because our bodies split in two, we are not just aware of the world, but *aware of our awareness of the world*. Our bodies are, however, quite different. This has had two repercussions historically. Because of our differing embodiments, our conceptual frameworks or fields of intelligibility vary. One form of life results in one distinct framework; another form of life issues a different framework. For example, what forms of life gave rise to cardinal directions like East and West? What form of life gave rise to egocentric directions like in front of or behind?

The second repercussion is much more insidious. Different bodies have been differently valued, and thus some people have been subjected to systemic oppression. Conceptual frameworks are, moreover, historically and socially constructed (see Warren 1988). Thinking and reasoning always come from some point of view or standpoint. When metaphors wane and are replaced by specters of metaphysics, frameworks become problematic in that they impose a hierarchical value system where "up" or "above" is associated with more value. It assumes and polices a value dualism, where one point of view is given privilege (Warren 1988). Such worldviews deploy what we can call, with Warren, a "logic of domination." Some worldviews assume an oppressive framework where women's bodies are taken as "naturally" inferior to men's bodies. The bodies of people of color specifically in the United States are affected by hierarchies of values taken as "only natural" (see Lee 2015). Consider how, for Black men, even just being on an elevator in the United States with someone white can create a self-consciousness not experienced by those with white privilege (see Yancy 2015).

Persevering in critical thinking and reasoning involves recognizing assumptions and prejudices, observing observations, and evaluating causal explanations (see Warren 1988). It also requires an open-mindedness. We need to be careful here though. Heroicizing open-mindedness cannot be naïve. *Are you so open-minded that you are open to being closed-minded? If not, then you might not be as open-minded as you imagine.* There is a limit to open-mindedness. It cannot mean to consider all points of view or to give all points of view equal consideration (see Warren 1988). Rather, we need to recognize there are alternative frameworks, alternative points of view, alternative fields of intelligibility, and alternative embodiments.

Such openness requires a healthy humility about our own worldviews, a healthy skepticism. We should be clear about what kind of skepticism is at stake here, though. There are three general kinds of skepticism: methodological, existential, and Pyrrhonistic. Methodological doubt or skepticism makes use of skeptical hypotheses to help clarify or gain information. It is a presupposition of natural scientific methods. In a way, when we are researching a hypothesis, we need to doubt it methodically to see if it survives attempts at falsification. This is the great value of Popper's theory concerning the distinction between science and nonscience, discussed earlier: it tells us to subject hypotheses and theories, even our own or those that we cherish most, to efforts to disconfirm or falsify them (see Popper 2002). Without methodological skepticism, we would have a difficult time imagining things that might falsify our hypotheses. This kind of skepticism applies primarily to empirical dimensions of life.

Existential doubt, alternatively, is a disposition about the meaning and purpose of one's life or life in general (see Tillich 2001). When someone wonders about the meaning of their life or feels like life is meaningless, they are in the throes of existential doubt. Perhaps my favorite form of skepticism is the ancient school known as the skeptics, founded by Pyrrho. Pyrrhonists believed that doubt was like a prayer or meditation, that it helped one realize ultimate fulfillment in a state of tranquility called *"ataraxia."* Pyrrhonists use skepticism not to gain knowledge like scientists and not to face anxiety like existentialists, but to realize ultimate fulfillment in a way reminiscent of religious commitment and practice. *These skeptics challenged all dogmatism with skepticism—etymologically meaning to inquire reflectively—in order to liberate people from clinging to certainty and beliefs.* Of course, all three of these can be said to be genuine. But in some cases, people deploy skepticism halfheartedly, like when people merely play devil's advocate. Often when one plays the devil's advocate, one does not reflectively inquire in the Pyrrhonist sense, committing oneself prayerfully to the interrogation of dogma; rather, it often has the feel of a canned or instrumental performance.

Instrumental Reasoning Lacks Genuine Questions

In light of all this, we need to discipline thinking and reasoning by keeping them within their proper constraints. Recall that constraints do not prevent something from free activity, but instead they free one to activity. The governing laws of music, for example, free musicians to produce all sorts of music, from marches to improvised jazz. Moreover, thinking will always be disciplined by experience, given *what* to think about but not given *how* to think about it. In addition, reasoning will always be disciplined by thought, given *what* to reason about but not necessarily *how* to organize frameworks. Reasoning must also be disciplined by constant reminding that models, analogies, and metaphors are not metaphysical entities. Mathematical models and lexical definitions tempt us to go beyond experience in thinking and beyond thinking in reasoning (see Kant 2007). But we cannot do so without becoming entirely different kinds of things from what we are. That is, only an entirely different kind of being—one not constrained to think in subjects and predicates or not constrained to reason by inferential relations between complete thoughts—can access a supposed "beyond" of what is really "out there." This is precisely the problem with metaphysics: *it expresses the wish to not be what we are* (see Kierkegaard 1982).

Moreover, thinking and reasoning need to be disciplined by recognizing that there is no winning or losing in argumentation. Indeed, all thinking and reasoning, all advances in understanding truth and reality, *are collaborative*. When we disagree with the arguments others make, we are not refuting them. To refute an argument is to show that the argument, not the arguer, fails by virtue of invalidity, weak premises, or irrelevant premises. Even if we cannot or do not want to take the time to refute an argument, we may have other grounds for rejecting it, pointing to inadequately justified premises or conceptual problems like using a concept incorrectly. Regardless, in light of the undecidability of the problems of reason on topics like the soul or divine beings, these deadlocks reached in our addiction to metaphysics, we need the free expression of ideas (Kant 2007, 594–604). If we allow freedom to express reasoned disputes, we can expose the illusions of thinking and reasoning more easily. There should be nothing to fear about disagreement in the realm of ideas. We should even strengthen the arguments of others. Such interactive skepticism and critical thinking does not lead to dogmatic apathy, but liberates us from illusions (Kant 2007, 604). Critique is beneficial for undermining dogmatists on any side.

Thus, *reasoning itself cannot be adversarial*. We must instead advocate for collaboration and mutuality. This is not the norm, though. Argument in institutionalized or academic philosophy is based on an adversarial model (see Burrow 2010, 236). As I have noted, arguing is usually associated with aggressive terms like "fighting," "sparring," "going for the jugular," and so on. This framework for argument and reason itself imposes a value hierarchy and dualism, rooted in win/lose competition. The method often involves undermining "opponents" by "testing" claims against the most extreme opposition or thought experiments (see Burrow 2010, 237). Reason is instrumentalized as merely a means to this end. It is something an individual does alone, calculating what accords best with one's interests. Instrumental reason, this means-to-end logic, is all that counts as "good" argumentation. In women in particular, this "aggression" becomes more apparent because under a sexist and patriarchal system women are conditioned to be passive, subordinate, and accommodating. A cooperative approach to reasoning, alternatively, aims at mutual gains, not winning and losing (Burrow 2010, 236). Cooperative argument aims at mutual respect, consensus, and community. Cooperative argument ought to be seen as moving toward more and more flourishing of rationality, whereas instrumental reason undermines itself in competition. However, women and allies who have tended to promote this have been confronted with hostile audiences, audiences already dogmatically addicted to the adversarial framework for argument.

We need dialogue with others to think and reason. Dialogue is the fundamental dialectic of question and answer. As Plato stated, thinking is a conversation we have with the otherness within ourselves (Plato 1997, 189e–190a). We will now turn to examine questioning in the context of dialogue.

Part III

Make Questions Explicit in Dialogue

Part III: Make Questions Explicit in Dialogue

Let's work through two topics in this part: dialogue and questioning. What even *is* dialogue? How might genuine questioning relate to dialogue? I addressed similar questions in Parts I and II, and so it will prove beneficial to develop how thought, reason, and dialogue might scaffold from one to the other productively. As I laid out, thinking involves combining or separating subjects and predicates into complete thoughts in light of questions. Reasoning involves the combining or separating of premises and conclusions—multiple complete thoughts—into arguments in light of questions. Thus, let us approach dialogue as the combining and separating of arguments into theses and antitheses in light of questions. Moreover, just as complete thoughts are sentences understood but sentences are complete thoughts perceived, so also is reasoning an exposition understood but an exposition is reasoning perceived. For terminological parsimony, I will here speak about dialogue as conversation understood and conversation as dialogue perceived. I want us to distinguish polite conversations from engaged dialogues. Inasmuch as arguments are relevantly combined complete thoughts, dialogues are relevantly interweaved arguments. While reasoning consists of relevantly related complete thoughts, dialogue consists of relevantly related reasonings.

Of course, explicating our main topics are no small task. And, as before, we are fortunate in that we need not start from scratch. Dialogue has been approached from numerous angles, such as scholarship and criticism in creative writing and theater, literary theory and narratology, conversation and discourse analysis, clinical psychology and therapy, and more. Many twentieth-century philosophers and theologians, under the influence of the Jewish philosopher Martin Buber, lifted up dialogue as the answer to cultural divisiveness and global crises (see Peters 1999). Interreligious dialogue in particular became a key platform of liberal-leaning religious leaders. They describe our contemporary age as undergoing an "axial shift" (see Knitter 2013). Premodern societies were defined by dictates of religious authority, which shifted in modern era to the dictates of autonomous reason and the natural sciences. For these thinkers, the shift today is from the modern era to the age of dialogue (see Swidler 1990). This disposition toward dialogue is consistent with our criticism of propositionalism and its accompanying adversarial model of argument. Dialogue is, for us, collaborative argumentation.

The etymology of the word "dialogue" is interesting and is worth looking at for the present moment. At first glance, it may seem that we have a combination of the root -logue (from the Greek *logos*) with the prefix di- (as in "two"). Similar to words like divide, diphthong, or dioxide, dialogue seems like the logical, linguistic, and reasonable exchange between at least two people or two positions. However compelling that picture may be, though, it's spurious. The prefix is actually dia- (from the Greek for "through" or "across"), as with other words like diaphragm, diagram, or even diorama. That is, *dialogue emerged from the attempt to grasp what it is to speak or think something all the way through* or to speak about—as in speak across—a subject matter in such a way as to bring it to its fullest presentation.

Let us take some time to dwell with dialogue and what calls for it. In this third and final part, I will look closely at fundamental elements of dialogue, in a simplified triadic dialectic of thesis, antithesis, and synthesis. I will then turn to examine ways questioning facilitates separations and combinations of these elements in a dialectical way. I will also formulate a schema for at least four orientations of questioning in relation to dialogue. I will close Part III with meditations on responsibility to others in dialogue and on how this responsibility counteracts people's tendency to try to dominate or control others.

7

Dialogue Only Happens in Constructive Reconciliations

Let us stipulate a definition of dialogue so that we can focus our attention on a shared subject matter. The approach to dialogue I want to take can be developed based on what we have previously worked out about complete thoughts and arguments. Inasmuch as reasoning consists of relevantly combined complete thoughts, dialogue consists of relevantly combined arguments. *A dialogue consists of, at the very least, more than one argument.* To put it in a pithy way: a dialogue is just a pile of arguments. Inasmuch as the fundamental particles of a dialogue (noun) are two arguments that stand in some relevant difference from one another, then it seems that dialogue (verb) is the activity of combining or separating complete arguments. In moving from thoughts to arguments to dialogues, we can see that while thinking integrates subjects and predicates, and while reasoning integrates premises and conclusions, dialogue integrates at least two arguments called "thesis" and "antithesis." For our purposes, this defines the essential character of dialogue. Let us break this down in more detail. In this chapter, I will examine key features of conversations and dialogue that underscore their collaborative nature. I will also look at elements of dialogue, often referred to as the dialectic of thesis, antithesis, and synthesis.

Good Conversation Is the Clue to Dialectical Dialogue

Something can look like a complete thought but still not be one. Something can look like an argument and still not be one. Similarly, something can look like a dialogue and still not be one. As I will develop in Chapter 8, just as it takes questioning to understand sentences as complete thoughts, so it takes questioning to understand apparently free-floating conversations as integrated dialogues. Before that, though, we need to lay out some key features of conversations and dialogues. Consider those experiences you have had where you walked away thinking, "Wow. That was a great conversation." Perhaps you have never had such an experience. Perhaps you have only walked away from conversations thinking, "That was a terrible conversation. We got nowhere," or "That was all over the place," or some such expression of frustration. These illustrate we have intuitions about what constitutes a good or bad conversation.

What are some of the things that you know made a conversation good? Perhaps you appreciated how your conversation partner gave you undivided attention and did not react judgmentally. Perhaps you felt like the other person really listened to you. Perhaps you both felt relaxed, and even laughed with each other or felt neither of you needed a filter. What are some of the things you know made a conversation bad? Perhaps the other person reacted in condemnation to what you said. Perhaps the conversation felt one-sided, or you felt you were dismissed before you even got started. Can we generalize these features to broad criteria and constitutive rules for good conversation?

It is a little surprising to have this question and not have a ready answer about which we have all heard already. It may appear we have already settled this topic. Conversation seems to be one of the most common and ordinary of human activities. By ordinary, I don't just mean that we have them anywhere and at any time. One way to clarify the challenge of defining ordinary conversation is by asking what discipline or field should we turn to for its definition and study? We have American Studies programs that study then United States. We have Psychology programs that study the mind. There is no "ordinary conversation" studies department or program, though. Should it be a subject matter proper to Communication Studies? Or is it a subject matter of Linguistics? Should it not be an essential topic in Foreign Language programs? When we consider how often "ordinary conversation" rears its head in polemics about literary (see Fish 1973), philosophical (see

Ryle 1953), and other purportedly more sophisticated forms of discourse, one might get the impression that we have such an adequate grasp on ordinary conversation that there is no merit to making it an independent field of study. How can we make a fitting distinction between "literary" and merely ordinary uses of language without a clear notion of the latter? Is there nothing worse than being ordinary?

Some scholars have asked whether there are essential principles that structure conversation (see Searle 1992). Since a lot of speech aims at eliciting fitting responses, it seems plausible to build a theory of ordinary conversation on how particular speech acts restrain the scope of proper response. Questions—as we saw in the logical and pragmatic approach to questions in Chapter 1—seem to set tight restraints on what constitutes an appropriate answer, so tight that the semantic structure of a question determines the proper form of answers as assertions. Yet, even with questions, we know that is simply not the case. Sure, some questions request assertions, but others elicit promises. A child might ask her parents, "Can we visit the zoo tomorrow?" The proper response is making or refusing to make the promise to do so, not a descriptive assertion. There does seem to be an exchange here between parents and child, however. Maybe this exchange is the basis of conversation? We would not want to call such an instance of making a promise a conversation, though. Further still, changing the topic does not necessarily violate preceding sequences of speech or violate the flow of a conversation itself because, despite such changes, partners might still feel they are having a conversation. In light of these, especially the seeming difficulty with identifying a unique purpose to conversation, we might conclude we cannot construct a complete theory of ordinary conversation. Nevertheless, there are some identifiable features of conversations.

The first thing to note is that ordinary conversation is intrinsically noninstitutional talk (see Levinson 1983). It is a form of talk "in which two or more participants freely alternate in speaking, which generally occurs outside specific institutional settings like religious services, law courts, classrooms and the like" (Levinson 1983, 284). Of course, we have institutional forms of dialogue, like witness interrogation, classroom discussion, or psychological therapy. We also have conversations outside of any easily recognizable institutionalized backdrop. That they are this ordinary—spilling outside nearly every recognizable institutional setting—does not mean they are somehow mundane or uninteresting. Indeed, this form of communication seems quite extraordinary. People hold these conversations without the support of institutionalized roles, without safety nets of higher authorities, and without the aid of scripts. Because it does not have a necessary setting, it also tends to avoid specialized vocabulary and technicalities—except for those that emerge within the conversation itself. Ordinary conversation consists of "ordinary language," the language that, as the linguist Majorie Perloff writes:

> we do actually use when we communicate with one another . . . [It] need not be literal, denotative, propositional, neutral, referential, or any other adjectives equated with it in the ordinary/literary debate. On the contrary, our actual language may well be connotative, metaphoric, fantastic. (Perloff 1994, 901)

In informal conversations, speakers get mixed up and forget what they wanted to say, they make numerous grammatical mistakes, use vague words, interrupt one another, switch styles of speech, manipulate grammatical rules, and even argue illogically and erratically (see Crystal and Davy 1975).

We can isolate further characteristic features of ordinary conversation by way of studying second-language acquisition. Conversation partners bring with them a number of expectations about what conversations are, how they ought to develop, and the kinds of contributions participants ought to make (see Richards 1980). These are crucial for adjusting to conversations in new languages. While conversations consist of multiple "utterances," or minimal units of functional speaking, they are not merely chains of such utterances but instead are a matrix of utterances and actions bound together by a web of reflexive understandings, expectations, and reactions. In other words, conversations occur in the context of a culture and form of life, with its distinctive intelligibility. Moreover, "adjacency pairs" are utterances produced by two consecutive speakers such that the second often is related to the first by being an expected follow-up. Such turn-taking divides into a pattern of either self-selection or other-selection. We can recognize this process in trying to get our bearing in foreign language environments. We can see another person prompting us to respond, even if we do not understand what the other person is saying. In addition, conversational repairs divide into self- or other-initiated repairs. We need to repair the flow of conversation when we recognize there has been a misunderstanding. Such repairs dominate interactions in foreign language immersion, where misunderstandings become apparent and frequent. Nevertheless, some form of turn-taking system seems to be the crux of conversation, where a number of cues are available to the participants for "requesting the floor, giving it up, informing the speaker as to the stability of the attention he is receiving, [etc.]" (Sacks, Schegloff, and Jefferson 1974, 697). These cues indicate whose turn it is to speak or listen in the conversation.

Moreover, participants in conversation don't need to have familiarity with one another. When situations allow for it, such as sitting next to someone on an airplane, complete strangers can find themselves caught up in conversations with one another. Conversation is, then, "any stretch of continuous speech between two or more people within audible range of each other who have the mutual intention to communicate, and is bounded by the separation of all participants for an extended period" (Crystal and Davy 1975, 86). It requires that both participants are at least willing to be in conversation, that they both have a cooperative or collaborative disposition toward each other. If this is not the case, then no conversation is happening. As the linguist Anna-Brita Stenström writes:

> Curiously enough, despite . . . irregularities, conversation may be judged to be successful; the people involved are not prevented from cooperating. *Interrupting, which may result in reformulations and repetitions, may for instance be signs of cooperation and not the opposite.* (Stenström 1984, 21; my emphasis)

Even interruptions can be signs of cooperation rather than the lack of it. Through conversation, in other words, speakers cooperate, working together to develop a common ground and collaborative floor, "where the individual speaker becomes far less significant and what is said is jointly accomplished by all speakers" (Wang 2006, 535). Recall, though, that conversations are not dialogues. Nothing I have developed in this empirical analysis of conversations indicates conversations must include arguments or even questions. Such sequences of turn-taking could consist entirely of exchanges of explanations or anecdotes. You've probably had the experience of conversations with other people who try to "one-up" you, by sharing what they think are better jokes or what they think are even wilder personal stories.

One striking feature of conversation is participants' cooperativeness, which, for instance, "is reflected not only in the way questions are answered, but also in the way they are asked" (Stenström 1984, 262). That is, questioning seems to be an additional key structure of conversation. However, many see questions as inhibiting cooperation. Is it that questions promote cooperativeness or is it that they usurp power and inhibit cooperative conversation? Questions often are put to use by those lobbying for domination and control in conversation (see Wang 2006). When it comes to rank and status in social hierarchies, coercive power can take the form in conversation of how one restrains the contributions of others, when one of the participants usurps others' freedom to achieve self-set goals. Questions can express one's centrality to a group as long as their social status is strengthened and confirmed by responses. Such questioners can take the privilege to control a turn and determine who will be the next speaker, and what sort of answer counts as adequate—such as with yes-or-no questions (see Wang 2006). Restraining discourse in this way is how participants force their own perspective on a subject matter upon others. Moreover, people often perceive closed questions as displaying more dominance than open-ended questions (see Fogler 1980). They are perceived as a display of dominance, an intent to control conversation topics and manage the flow of messages by limiting options for answers. There is a tendency to follow a "chain rule," where one person responds to another's question just to return the floor to the questioner (see Fogler 1980). These chain sequences are a function of the way in which speakers define their relationships along the dimension of social hierarchy. Even the more open-ended wh-question often carries an implicit criticism about the basis or right to perform the action of the prior utterance—as examples: "Why did you say that?" or "What did you do that for?" These questions can convey a strong epistemic stance with an implicit negative assertion and a request for an account of an action, with the accompanying expression of doubt that such an account can be provided (see Heritage 2002). They dare you to answer, and doubt you can do it.

Questions may also be *unwarranted* if the questioner does not have the appropriate relationship to the respondent such that the questioner can reasonably expect an honest answer (see Borge 2007). Whenever an interviewer, for instance, asks a job candidate about political or religious views, sexual preference or what have you, they ask an unwarranted question. A student asking a teacher "Where were you last night?" is quite a personal question, where this student is in no position to expect an honest answer from their teacher. Such a question and the information to be transferred in response are not proper to the context within which the conversation takes place. A question is unwarranted when the person asking is in no formal or informal position to ask rightfully about a subject matter. If the questioner is in no rightful place to ask, they cannot be in a position to expect an honest answer to something that is none of their business. Asking an unwarranted question generates, according to linguist Steffen Borge, "admittures," calculable upon the observation that the participant is *uncooperative*, where an audience realizes that a speaker is withholding something relevant to the matter under question (see Borge 2007). In the latter case, the audience takes advantage of the fact that the speaker is uncooperative by concluding what is most reasonable to assume about the speaker for this uncooperativeness. Consider the teacher saying to the student, "It's none of your business." The student can then infer, "Whatever it was, it must have been bad!" Creating uncooperativeness through kinds of questions—is this still a conversation?

These suspicions about questions in ordinary conversation do not hold for our approach to genuine questioning. Coercive imposition is not unique to questions wholesale because *they do not necessarily* restrain the responses of conversation partners. By setting out some constraints, genuine questions can enable creative response unavailable without those constraints. This is similar to having six strings on a guitar, which can enable the capacity for all sorts of songs. Moreover, while one might put questions to use in institutionalized discourse to gain or display power, this does not necessarily happen in ordinary conversation (cf. Wang 2006). Question sequences within institutions, such as in hospitals, are such that "the professionals largely ask the questions and the lay 'clients' respond with answers" (Kazuko 1999, 251). Prefacing questions with "and," for instance, not only invokes coherence and continuation between sequences of questions, it also displays the "routine and agenda-based nextness of a question within an activity" (Kazuko 1999, 252). Imagine a child's increasing consternation if a parent asks, "And then what did you do? And who did you do that with? And . . . ." And-prefaced questions often do not occur in ordinary good conversations because long single question and single answer sequences are relatively rare, and, in many cases, both participants ask questions. Such switching of roles in ordinary conversation "ensures that fairly short [question-and-answer] sequences 'naturally' form a coherent package of discourse, which does not necessitate the additional use of a conjoining device" (Kazuko 1999, 265). The questioner's purpose and orientation in ordinary good conversations is often to seek new information rather than to acquire control. For instance, the change of state token "Oh!" expressed in moments of discovery is characteristically absent from institutional discourse. Imagine a lawyer saying "Oh!" after every answer a witness gives to them!

A further significant difference between institutional discourse and ordinary conversation is that the primary recipients of answers in institutions are often third parties, such as a judge or jury, whereas in ordinary talk it is the questioners themselves. In addition, while loaded questions lead respondents in a desired direction, genuine questions leave open response options with little indication about the questioner's preferred response.

Moreover, as feminist philosopher of language Robin Lakoff shows, closed questions like "tag questions," regularly described as the most controlling, is a pattern found most often in women's speech and often indicate deference—if not also submissiveness (see Lakoff 2004). In conversational repairs, we often use closed questions as repair initiators. All of this goes to show that questioning is a highly differentiated phenomenon in conversations, and that speakers use questions in a vast number of ways. It is impossible to claim that questions are intrinsically tactics to usurp power or control topics. *Instead, questioning can be an indication of underlying cooperativeness in good conversations.* As I have done throughout the book, here too I will emphasize genuine questioning in contrast to epistemic imperatives and other sorts of questions that involve this sort of control.

Dialogue Has Standards of Excellence

How do we let go and open ourselves to collaboration and cooperation in conversation? Even though there is no empirical or observed essence of conversation, perhaps we can stipulate a deeper meaning through distinguishing dialogue from conversation. Consider for a moment: How many of us would go on an adventure or a vacation completely by ourselves, without taking pictures or notes or ever telling someone else about it? Is it really an adventure if there is no one to share it with? Very few people would choose to do this. It is because sharing experiences enhances them. Think of how we speak with our friends about an experience together: "Do you remember when we did that? It was so funny when we were on the rollercoaster and you totally got scared!" The only way we can know for sure that we are really sharing an experience is by talking about it with another person. Through talking about it with one another, we integrate that experience into the broader storylines of our lives. We enrich that experience by emphasizing certain features of it rather than other features. We remember it from different perspectives. We resolve conflicting interpretations of it. We re-enjoy it, and more.

This is what "studying" something really means. Aristotle identified the heart of human happiness as the life and activity of study. Recall from the Introduction that happiness is not merely a feeling. There are pharmaceuticals and illicit drugs for that, if all that matters is a feeling. For Aristotle, happiness is an activity (Aristotle 1999, 16/1102a5)—something you do, not just something you feel. Yet we often get fatigued doing things. We get fatigued in almost every other kind of enjoyable activity. We have to make use of a lot of equipment for many kinds of enjoyable activities. We have to pay a lot of money for many other kinds of enjoyable experiences. Aristotle believes that the activity of study—not cramming for standardized exams, but the kind of dialogue that enhances experience—is the most complete and self-sufficient kind of happiness human beings can achieve (Aristotle 1999, 163/1177a5–18). It is the most enjoyable yet least fatiguing activity we have. Dialogue about something is just this sort of fulfilling study about it.

How do we make sure we are having a good dialogue? How do we keep things at bay that threaten to undermine good dialogue? I believe we can address these questions by approaching dialogue as a game. Like all games, there are goals to dialogue, excellent actions that facilitate reaching those goals most effectively, and role models who display excellence most profoundly (see MacIntyre 1981, 187–91). These three elements—the goal, the virtues, and the role models—are crucial for any recognizable practice. A practice is, according to the ethicist Alasdair MacIntyre,

> any coherent and complex form of socially established cooperative human activity through which goods internal to that form of activity are realized in the course of trying to achieve those standards of excellence which are appropriate to, and partially definitive of, that form of activity. (MacIntyre 1981, 187)

Virtues facilitate our comportment toward inherited standards of excellence proper to specific practices, and virtues help us realize "internal goods" or goals of the practice. We contribute to the realization of goods through our attempts to excel with regard to those standards. An important aspect of learning practices is that we can transfer those skills we develop in one practice to another practice. Let us specify these three elements of dialogue: the goal, the virtues, and the role models.

What is the goal of dialogue? There are several things we might identify as a goal of dialogue. For instance, the goal of classroom dialogue might seem like it is to prepare us to pass the exam. A problem with that as the definitive goal for classroom dialogue is that preparing for an exam can be done without any dialogue at all. Being prepared for an exam is external to the practice or game of dialogue. Some other external goods to dialogue are camaraderie with others, clarification of concepts discussed, and even painful self-examination. These also seem achievable without dialogue. We can enjoy others' company without dialogue. We can look up definitions of concepts in the dictionary. We can examine ourselves by ourselves. What is something we can get or achieve solely through dialogue, though? Is there anything unique to dialogue? I think there is. There does not seem to be just one word for it. A crucial aspect of it we can call "being at one on a subject matter" for now, though later I will examine it as the "fusion of horizons." When we are at one in a game, we are going with the flow. We have all experienced this flow state when we play—whether it is in music, theater, sports, or what have you. Games draw us in and fill us with their dynamic spirit, a spirit surpassing us as isolated individuals trying to control things (Gadamer 2013, 112). When a game is in full motion, we lose ourselves and get in "the zone." Just like all other games, this happens with dialogue, too. It happens when we are "at one" on a topic. What I want to figure out is how we are "caught up" in a good dialogue about a subject matter. Have you ever noticed that good dialogues just happen to us, independent of our overt control? Have you ever sat someone down and said, "Now we're going to have a good conversation"? Usually it is only afterward that we look back with surprise and appreciation for having had a good dialogue.

Part of the issue here is that dialogues do not seem to have a particular point. As some scholars ask, "What objectives do we have when casual acquaintances bump into each other on the street and start talking?" (Searle 1992, 20). Since dialogues as a whole do not seem to have specifiable purposes like particular statements do, we cannot—according to these thinkers—have a theoretical account of dialogue. We might wonder, however, whether dialogues have a different sort of teleology than those sorts of purposes associated with actions, statements, and intentions. As Gadamer points out in his analysis of "play," play does have a generally shared teleology or end. In games, players comport their behavior into alignment with the appropriate movements such that through the movements the players present the "being" or dynamic structure of the game. The mode of being of play, Gadamer writes, "is self-presentation" (Gadamer 2013, 107). While particular actions within a game have specifiable purposes and points with reference to the whole of the game, the game's purpose is with reference only to itself. Consider, for example, the point of seesaw. How do you know when we are playing seesaw successfully? Just as with play, so also with the kind of dialogue at issue here. While there is a sort of purpose specific to particular discursive actions, there is an entirely distinct sort of purpose to dialogue. Like the purpose of games, the purpose of dialogue seems to be the uninhibited presentation of dialogical movement. Such "being at one" in the domain of dialogue is what we can call "reaching agreement" or "reaching an understanding." This does not mean that we have to believe the "same" thing, because we have all heard sometimes we need to just "agree to disagree." In such a case, there is a productive tension rather than a polarizing division among participants. We are still at one on a topic, despite taking differing stances about it. To be able to disagree means we can at least consider our conversation partners' perspective, respect them as autonomous thinkers, and remain committed to productive community with them over that subject matter. Thus, reaching an understanding does not mean asserting one's own point of view and forcing other people to submit to it. As Gadamer writes:

> [I]t belongs to every true [dialogue] that each person opens himself to the other, truly accepts his point of view as valid and transposes himself into the other to such an extent that he understands not the particular individual but *what he says*. What is to be grasped is the substantive rightness of his opinion, so that we can be at one with each other on the subject [matter]. (Gadamer 2013, 403; my emphasis)

If we are to practice dialogue with one another, then we cannot objectify the other person by speaking about them—to do this, of course, would be to deny their discursive autonomy as a legitimate contributor participating in the transformative event of understanding. We get in the zone when we are "at one" on a topic with each other. How do we get into the dialogical zone, though?

What are some crucial virtues for dialogue? It takes excellent actions, or in other words, "virtues," to facilitate maximal zoning out (see Aristotle 1999, 23/1106a17–23). In Aristotle's view, virtues facilitate flourishing at something, whereas vices inhibit something's flourishing. Virtues help things fulfill their function. Consider eyes: glasses supply virtues to eyes to help people see. Just as in any other sphere of our practical lives, a variety of virtues is necessary for production of a flourishing and healthy dialogue: the patience to take turns, the courage to risk making statements, the hospitableness and respect to share the virtual field of speech, and the wisdom to comprehend the subject matter. These virtues are significant dispositions that contribute to the performance and achievement of a good dialogue, in which the primary aim of understanding is achieved. One further excellent activity necessary for reaching an understanding is listening. According to Fiumara, the ignored and literally "ob-scene" capacity of listening ultimately proves to be a resource for the critique of the hegemonic imperialism and exclusivity of assertiveness

(Fiumara 2003, 142). Listening is necessary, for, without it, assertions would fail to occur. Can someone make a statement if there is no one listening to it? As we have seen, the point of genuine questioning is to listen, to make a dehiscent space so that we can come to understand what someone else has to say about something. Such utterances invert the normal assertiveness of speech, transforming it into receptive speech. To put it concretely, if not also paradoxically, genuine questions are a way in which we listen with our mouths. Thus, the most important dialogical virtue is listening well (Beatty 1999, 287). Without listening, no voices would be heard, and so no dialogue could get off the ground in the first place. Reflect on this for a minute. We hear a lot of people advocating for the freedom of speech, the license to express ourselves. However, why do we not hear people advocating for the freedom to listen? What about whether people have a right to be heard? Now let us turn to identifying role models of dialogue.

Who are some key role models of dialogue? All games have a history. And one important dimension of each game's history is that particular people stand out from the rest of us as role models of excellence in the game. I always think of Michael Jordan in the late 1980s reshaping professional basketball. He changed things so dramatically that the generation after him tried to mimic not only his skill but even his eccentricities, like sticking out his tongue in concentration or pointing his left foot in just slightly as he shot the ball. Who is the—or at least a—hero of dialogue? Is this a difficult or easy question for you? If it is difficult, why is something even more common than basketball harder in which to identify its heroes?

As academics, I think we are beholden to our inheritance from Plato. We get our word "academic" from the name of the garden where Plato taught, the Academy. Imagine that: a garden where we enjoy studying things. For Plato, the greatest hero of dialogue is Socrates. Socrates models numerous dialogical virtues such as creative exploration, perseverance in the pursuit of truth despite discouragement from others and fatigue, and more. Plato's dialogues depict this Socrates picking up dialogue with all sorts of people on all sorts of occasions about all sorts of topics. My favorite is when he speaks with two wrestlers at the gym about true friendship in the *Lysis*. Probably his most famous dialogue, the *Republic*, depicts him speaking with friends about how to be a person of integrity after attending a religious festival. And let us not forget his dialogue about love at a rambunctious party in the *Symposium*.

One thing that many teachers promote is that Socrates is less a dialogue partner and more just an annoying "gadfly." People who read Plato's dialogues often are taken aback by how pushy Socrates seems or how he seems to always find problems with others' arguments. Indeed, we live in an age where we love to see celebrities and heroes fall. Perhaps this interpretation is not too far off, especially considering the teaching method attributed to Socrates, the so-called "Socratic Method." The Socratic Method is a teaching tactic that aims at exposing *aporia* or puzzling paradoxes implicit in people's perspectives. This method uses carefully orchestrated questions to get at underlying assumptions people make to support their positions, and then it sets out to show that some feature or another of the assumption contradicts the original position. This leads a person to experience a state of cognitive dissonance requiring resolution, but in order to reach resolution the person has to rethink both the position and underlying assumptions. The goal would be to establish firmer grounding—not mere assumption or opinion— for establishing a genuine perspective or knowledge on some topic. For this portrait of Socrates, "the unexamined life is not worth living" (Plato 2002, 38a5–6). Apparently, it is only through such rigorous examination that we can realize the good life.

I want to encourage an alternative reading of Socrates's character. I think there is something in addition to this Socratic Method that makes Socrates worthy of memorializing as the hero of dialogue. What allows him to discover *aporias* in people's thoughts is, I believe, his insatiable curiosity. He seems incessantly interested in finding out more and different ways of thinking and the most grounded thoughts. Recall that incessantness is a fundamental structure of rationality, reason's quest for the unconditioned. He expresses this curiosity in questioning, questioning everything that is said—even what he himself says. In the dialogues, Socrates's partners often try to switch roles with him and ask him questions. But these others quickly peter out in their energy and creativity to ask more questions. This is not because they are tired. It is because they have the opinion that they know better! If you assume you know better, then you will not have any questions (Gadamer 1977, 13). This contrast between Socrates and his conversation partners reveals his character to be more like that of an insatiable puppy chasing a ball tossed from who knows where. He simply cannot help but follow where the subject matter goes and where the twists of dialogue go. As Socrates describes it, we need to be ready to follow wherever the winds of dialogue blow (see Plato 1991, 73/394d). Note that this is precisely the point we have made above about getting in the zone or the flow state of dialogue. Socrates seems to rest transparently on the power and dynamism of the dialogue itself. His excellence is not merely in his methodical exposures of *aporias.* That is a by-product of his real virtue: attunement with the topic of dialogue, an attunement that overflows into an unfurling of curious questioning. I believe this is what makes Plato's dialogues worth reading, watching this hero Socrates in action. If this is our hero, then what does someone look like who does not help out topics of dialogue? What does someone look like who goes against the wind of the dialogue? This is the "spoilsport." Let us turn to look more closely at the spoilsport.

Spoilsport attitudes undermine dialogue but listening and questioning enhance dialogue. A spoilsport refuses to play along. The worst kind of spoilsport is someone who looks like they are playing along, but who really is not. A spoilsport is someone who does not take a risk, particularly the risk laid out by the structure of the game. They merely "toy" with playing the game, but protect themselves from the risk because, as we have all heard them say, "It doesn't really matter." They do not really care about the game. But playing games is serious business. Think of how upset children get when you address them by their personal name rather than the character they are trying to play. Think of how devoted some fans are for their teams. One key thing to look out for in the dialogue game is the whether the other person subtly changes the topic. Compare it to this scenario: you and another person agree to play seesaw. You both get on your respective seats, but then, as you're going up, the other person suddenly jumps off to try to get you to slam to the ground. What has happened here is that you thought you both were playing seesaw, but they changed the game to the prank of trying to get you to slam to the ground. The risk in seesaw is to try to achieve harmonious balance, a fluid movement back and forth. A sometimes-difficult task indeed. But the spoilsport, for some motive or other, refuses to take that risk and changes the game in the process. Some of us refuse to play certain games because we do not like the rules of that specific game—or, for some of us who are stuck in adolescent attitudes, we don't like any rules whatsoever. We just do not like feeling as if other people are telling us what to do. Here is a secret: some rules do not control you; some rules set you free. Recall that in Chapter 5 we urged that rational laws set thinking free. Without the rules of seesaw, we would not be free to play it. Without the rules of basketball, we would not be free to play it. Without the rules for driving, no one would get anywhere. These types of rules properly are called, as I described in Part II, "constitutive rules." They are the rules that "constitute" or make a game what it is. So, a spoilsport's refusal of these rules is to refuse the freedom to play that the rules make possible. It may seem as if calling dialogue a game is diminutive, as if it is merely a game. Let us all agree not to say, "It's just a game," but instead say, "It's no less than a game!" Games are serious business for recreation.

One key risk in dialogue games is "openness." Now, be careful with me here. I am not talking about being "open-minded." The naïve promotion of open-mindedness is paradoxical. Consider this: Are you so open-minded that you are open to being closed-minded? If not, then you are at least closed-minded to the degree that you are not open to that. Pointing this out is not just a cute thing to do with words. Pointing this out helps us to see that we need to be more careful about what we mean with open-mindedness. I think it is more constructive to think about it this way: the risk of openness in dialogue is the risk of considering that our dialogue partner may be saying something more fitting than we are. That is, we are open to the possibility of being wrong, and if we accept that, needing to change our mind. This can be a very painful process, as I am sure you all know from your own experience. The risk is intrinsic to considering what another person says. How do we do that? Through asking and sharing questions. In Chapter 8, I will turn to look at these virtues of listening and sharing questions in more discrete detail. For now, we need to turn to the fundamental elements of dialectical dialogue.

Theses Initiate Dialogue

We still need to get at the principal force that fuels the dynamism of dialogue: *dialectics*. We can simplify it in the triadic model of thesis, antithesis, and synthesis. Many deployments of a purported "dialectic" start with two claims that stand in contrast with one another, and from there they formulate some sort of compromise in what is supposed to be seen as a superior position. You have probably heard about the apparent tension between explaining things in terms of "nature" or in terms of "nurture," as in the "nature vs nurture" debate (see Samerhoff 2010). In an attitude approximating the lament "Why can't we all just get along," those who try to deploy dialectics in this way express themselves condescendingly as "It is neither just nature, nor just nurture, but both!" It is as if such a compromise is supposed to be a surprising superior insight about the truth of whatever is at issue. This argumentative tactic often takes the form of whittling down those features that make the two claims opposite to one another until what is left is a superficial common ground between them. For example, many Jews, Christians, and Muslims seeking to preserve a commitment to their religious writings about "creation" while simultaneously preserving commitment to modern physics about the "big bang" claim that science and religion are compatible in a peculiar way. I have heard many say, "Six days might mean billions of years for God." Those who try to work out oppositions this way want to be seen as doing "dialectics." This is incorrect. To put it bluntly, and briefly, dialectical dynamics operate within each side—both nature and nurture, both religion and science— separately from one another and in reciprocity or tension with one another. To see "dialectics" as merely operative in combining two oppositions is naïve (see Jameson 2009). Why is that?

We have inherited this way of simplifying and modeling dialectics from late German Idealism, where Johann Gottlieb Fichte presents Kant's thought on our deepest ideals—recall that these are self, world, and divine being—as a matter of moving from "thesis" to "antithesis" to "synthesis" (Fichte 1982). This description has often been used to summarize fundamental elements of Hegel's philosophy, and in many introductions to philosophy, this triadic structure is attributed to Hegel himself. Once you learn how it works, you start to see it everywhere. For example, this is how the political philosopher Karl Marx's prediction of the rise of communism is sometimes taught: the bourgeoisie class (thesis) is overthrown by the proletariat class (antithesis) to give way to communism (synthesis). As another example, Hegel himself characterized nonmonotheistic religions like Daoism and Indigenous American religions as "natural religions" where people are immersed in the worship of nature immediately (thesis). He claimed that these transform into "moralistic religions"—such as Judaism, Islam, and Confucianism— where people abstract themselves from nature to aim at supernatural ideals (antithesis). Because both of these have limitations or are one-sided, they give way to what he called "the consummate religion"—which (surprise, surprise!) he thought was only embodied by Christianity where people themselves are supernaturally filled via the holy spirit (synthesis) (see Hegel 1988). If you combine hydrogen with oxygen, you get water! Combine a sperm and an egg, you get a fetus! I add these to suggest how this training- wheel version of dialectics is simplistic and prone to distortions. It forces us to conceive of dialectics in light of propositionalism—where it is derived from the purported primary phenomena of propositions or thesis statements. That does not make it entirely incorrect, though. Sometimes simplified models help us gain skill and knowledge in working with phenomena that are more complex.

Let's say that one way to capture dialogue's dynamism is by approaching "theses" as the initiating propulsions of it. While reasoned arguments provide conclusions, argumentation alone does not give a lot of guidance on coordinating multiple conclusions into broader wholes. Sometimes symbols as concrete representations of regulative ideals provide gravitational centers for arranging conclusions into broader worldviews. What about cases where conclusions seem in conflict with one another? Or, perhaps worse, what about cases where conclusions seem completely irrelevant to one another? On a broader level, we can ask similar questions about worldviews or language views. What about cases where partially formulated or even completely formulated worldviews stand in contrast with one another? How does a dialogue even get started? What results from a Buddhist and a Christian in interreligious dialogue? One thing to be cautious about here, though, is that it seems we have to start with some singular claim, a "thesis" statement. This is because as finite and historically conditioned thinkers, we have to start wherever we are. In some ways, where we start may be beliefs or practices we inherited from our guardians or communities. Yet any number of coincidences could start us off in a dialectical dialogue. Perhaps we just learned about atomism, but this initiates in us an exploration of quantum mechanics. Maybe we mishear a holiday song as about "Olive, the other reindeer," and we wonder why Olive was so mean to Rudolph. We are more concerned here with initiative than this or that conclusion or broader worldview. The point is that we are less concerned with a specific thesis statement, and more concerned about triggering initiatives. Theses name those moments of triggering initiative.

Antitheses Move Dialogue

An additional aspect definitive for dialectics is that instance of negativity, indicated by the prefix "anti-" in "antithesis," a negativity that propels the motions of thought, reasoning, and dialogue further. It is not a vacuous negativity, but a productive negativity. Consider how we have to add qualification to our notion of "criticism" to indicate when we intend to be productive, such as in the so-called "constructive criticism." All criticism—criticism worthy of the name anyway—is *intrinsically* constructive. It is redundant to call it constructive criticism. It would be interesting to develop a social or psychological explanation for our perceptions of criticism as so negative that we now have to reassure everyone that we are not out to be cruel. Criticism is not cruelty; it is not simply negation for negation's sake.

It brings to mind for me how my students perceive Socrates as a bully in Plato's dialogues, as if questioning is intrinsically negative. It surely is, if we believe—incorrectly—that "everyone is entitled to their own opinion." However, as we pointed out earlier where we selected Socrates as a hero of dialogue, Socrates's insatiable curiosity is embodied in questioning not for the sake of destroying opponents but for the sake of all to realize truths. Critique is productive. This is the heart of Hegel's notion of *aufhebung*, or determinate negation, where what is at stake is "thrown upward" (*aufgehoben*) or further elucidated in the light of rigorous thought (see Hegel 1977). I consider it like polishing tarnish off a lamp to bring out its radiance. Dialectics are tied to this productive negativity, and this negativity provides an explanation for why the *logos* or dialogue moves like wind. Dialectics make the *logos* more than mere piles of discrete sentences and questions, more than mere piles of arguments and questions. Dialectics make the *logos* move, integrating parts with a projected whole.

Movement is a crucial feature of dialectics. This has been true since the apparent historical invention of dialectics as an explicit form of reasoning. Most accounts of philosophy's early history in Ancient Greece explain that the Eleatic philosophers, namely Parmenides and Zeno, posed difficult metaphysical questions about the nature of being and nonbeing. Note how we can immediately "see" the triadic model of dialectics: being (thesis) stands in opposition with nonbeing (antithesis), and the opposition can be overcome through becoming (synthesis). These accounts position later philosophers like Plato and Aristotle as providing solutions to the Eleatic problems. Consider, for example, Zeno's critique of motion in the so-called "Achilles and the Tortoise" paradox. Imagine these two are in a race, and the tortoise gets a head start. For Achilles to catch up, he must cross that place where the tortoise has been. And then to catch up from there, the same thing must happen. And so on, into infinity. Therefore, it seems that for our ordinary conception of movement, it is an illusion because it is impossible to cross an infinity of halves (Curd 2011, 68–9). Aristotle, for instance, responds by saying that infinite in divisibility is distinct from infinite in extension of space, and so this puzzle equivocates on the notion of "infinity." Another of Zeno's paradoxes is the one called the "Arrow" paradox. Here, for an arrow shot at a target, it must be in one place at a specific time in its trajectory, what we can call a discrete moment. In each moment, there is no movement (Curd 2011, 69). Thus again, it seems that our ordinary conception of movement is an illusion. Aristotle, again, responds by saying that time is not composed of individual "nows" like frames in a filmstrip. Notice that in both cases, we are positioned to think primarily about what is at issue, time and movement. We are purportedly talking about what is really real. However, the brilliance of Zeno comes from his masterful unfolding of speculative dialectics—dialectics that provoke and unfurl thinking. What is moving is neither arrows nor individuals in a race, but thinking, our thinking in confronting such paradoxes. An irony here is that in training us about ways to think about movement, our thinking moves. How can there be oneness despite diversity? Why are identity and difference interrelated? What differentiates integration from mere mixture?

For Plato, education and initiation into the art of dialectics requires some maturity. Only those mature enough can handle it. Only those with proven character and intellectual virtues are responsible enough to use it well rather than just to contradict people. Plato imagines an education system designed precisely for nurturing and testing individuals' maturity and excellence in dialectics. This is because the negativity of dialectics "destroys hypotheses," or mere opinions and mindless conventions, to expose our fundamental intellectual foundations (see Plato 1991). People not sufficiently prepared for such critique of their precious opinions may fall into existential crises. Indeed, some may turn to take up a pseudo-dialectic and become contrarians, or devil's advocates, merely deploying dialectics as a method of undermining others for the sheer sake of undermining. Like children who first learn about contradictions, they become trigger-happy with accusations of and impositions of contradictions. Immature appropriation of dialectics allows a more sophisticated expression for the basic whine, "But that's not fair!"

Note the productive negativity for Plato, though. The path, or what he calls the "song," of dialectics opens up horizons of fundamental grounds, what is sometimes called his theory of Forms. It exposes the "hypo-," as in "under" or "subordinate," character of hypotheses. We should also note here that, for Plato, it is all about the interrelations of these grounding ideas, not each taken by itself in abstraction like "Treeness" or "the Beautiful itself." Isolating forms from their integrated network misses Plato's true insight (see Gadamer 1976). Plato's approach to dialectics is crucial for us because he always situates dialects within the life of dialogue. This should address any objections readers might have about why I use dialectics in the plural rather than in the singular, dialectic. In the singular, especially if accompanied by a definite article, as in "the dialectic" (or even "the new dialectic"), reifies the embodied nature of dialectics. Dialectics manifest only on occasions of specific dialogues. Thus, I promote using dialectics similarly to physics, aesthetics, hermeneutics, and economics, where these name comprehensive fields of inquiry including many varying instances of this or that particular hermeneutic or aesthetic or physic, rather than like the singular rhetoric, which suggests there is really only one ("true" or "consummate") rhetoric.

We can bring out a further feature of the "antithesis" moment of dialectics through briefly engaging Hegel, for it is really Hegel who isolates the productive negativity of dialectics. Rather than the reified model naming moments from thesis to synthesis, Hegel isolates *aufhebung*—a determinate and productive negation that raises what came before into a higher plane of understanding. He exposes and illustrates how dialectics operate in various domains of life. For example, in the unfolding of different art forms, he points out that paintings determinately negate the limited aspects of architecture and sculptures (see Hegel 1997). Space is transcended in paintings in ways it cannot be transcended in architecture and sculptures. For another example: sensation gets frustrated rather than fulfilled in its devouring of sense-data, literally in that abstract "data" is not discrete enough to be fulfilling (see Hegel 1977). This negative frustration prompts reflection and the use of understanding to grasp obscure data into clarified concepts. That is, we elevate, through negation, the opaqueness of sensory information into the elucidation of conceptualization. As I examined already, the subject is negated and sublimated by the predicate in a complete thought. As Gadamer writes:

> Even Hegel's doctrine of the speculative proposition seems to me to have its place here, and always takes up into itself its own sharpening into the dialectic of contradiction. For in speaking, there always remains the possibility of canceling out the objectifying tendency of language, just as Hegel cancels the logic of understanding, Heidegger cancels the language of metaphysics, [Asian philosophers cancel] the diversity of realms of being, and the poet everything given. But to cancel [*aufheben*] means to take up and use. (Gadamer 2007, 368)

The key here, like with Plato and the Eleatics, is movement. Indeed, under this model, we can see that *the entire system of concepts is moving rather than our individual thinking moves through stable and essentialized concepts.* Instead of focusing on "antithesis" as an alternative thesis statement to a preceding proposition, we emphasize it as creating more movement, a furthering of dialogue.

Syntheses Reconcile Oppositions

If dialogue is both initiated and furthered, where is it going? One element we want to edit out of our incorporation of Hegel is his insistence on an actual moment of totalization, where all determinate negations are sublimated into a complete and complex whole system. This would finish dialectics into a final synthesis. The notion of "totality" does not seem to have functioned as a mere regulative ideal for Hegel, but instead as a—pretentious and inflated—assumption about his own historical position in the unfolding of the grand human dialogue of history. Obviously, life and thought have moved on since Hegel's time. In this, we return to Kant (see Ricoeur 1995b, 208–9). Kant exposed a suspicious feature of transcendental dialectics as always leading to metaphysical illusions. While reason seeks ultimate foundations or the unconditioned, it cannot resolve problems such as the existence of a god or the soul in confidence and certainty, because—as we showed—it involves the application of concepts beyond their proper domain of experience. Does a god exist? Is there freedom in this world of natural laws? What is the soul or self? Any answer to these questions that is not taken as symbolic is a metaphysical illusion not because there is no reality there, but because all knowledge claims here are misapplications of concepts. Thus, with Kant, we can affirm an openness or ever-renewing character to dialectics that—although oriented by an ideal totality—is never fully completed. Perhaps even Hegel—on a certain charitable reading—would agree to this. As Gadamer writes:

> Hegel simultaneously meant that being itself may never be apprehended in the unrestricted presence of some *unus intuitus* (unitary intuition) or of an infinite monad in the sense of Leibniz; but, as with all human clarity and lucidity, it is clouded over by opaqueness, passing away, and forgetfulness. Diotima knew this when she compared the knowing proper to humans with the life of a species that has its ongoing being only in the relentless process of the reproduction of its individual instances. (Gadamer 2007, 342)

Despite a human desire for immortality, our finitude forces us to compromise with time, where we can find a version of immortality, that of reproduction with children and handing down ideas in traditions and cultures.

Every productive dialogue includes growth, where we learn from one another. This growth, seen from a broader perspective of human history, seems to proceed into infinity. Hegel calls this incomplete or unrealized infinity a bad or spurious infinity, like a line extending beyond the visible horizon, in contrast to "good" infinity like a circle (see Warnke 1987). This distinction, however, imposes a false opposition between either a line ("thesis") or a circle ("antithesis"). I'm confident that there are some who are tempted to respond to this with, "It's both—a spiral!" This would be to think of synthesis in the same problematic ways of thesis and antithesis, where we conceive of all of them as standalone propositions. We are tempted to trace out a triadic dialectical unfolding in the following way: Life is an infinitely extending line (thesis). No, life is an infinite cycle (antithesis). Actually, life is a radiant spiral (synthesis). For us, we are not so concerned with particular synthesis statements, but the furthering reach of dialectical dialogue. Just as theses initiate and antitheses further dialogue, syntheses paradoxically give a sense of closure as well as a sense of ever further openness for more. Like moving up a staircase, when we complete a step, it starts another step. A synthesis is not a completion in the sense of an end, but in the sense of an overcoming.

Let us turn to examine questioning's role in dialectical dialogue.

8

What Do Questions Do to Dialogues?

Our investigations about thought, reason, and now dialogue have brought out that questioning is not something that happens in isolation, but instead is intrinsically something we do with others. Of course, insofar as we ask ourselves questions, this otherness includes an otherness within oneself (see Ricoeur 1995). Dialogue is the sustained movement of question and answer complexes moving through dialectical initiatives, furthering, and completions. Whether written, signed, or spoken, utterances do not yield meaning outside a social or intersubjective context made up of (at least) questioners and answerers. I need to stress questioning *with* others because, just as questioning facilitates the transformation of sentences perceived into complete thoughts understood as well as facilitates the transformation of expositions perceived into reasonings understood, so also does questioning facilitate the transformation of conversations perceived into dialogues understood. A conversation is a continuous stretch of perceived speech; dialogue, though, is an understanding of the dialectical dynamism among the complete thoughts, reasonings, and questionings. As dialogue is something we do with others, though, this sort of questioning needs to be properly rooted in listening with others. In this chapter, I will first distinguish dialogue from debate. I will also develop how genuine questioning is, paradoxically, a form of listening. It is a way we listen with our mouths. I will then examine what genuine questioning achieves for reaching an understanding with others about a subject matter. We can share questions, and through this sharing we can understand what others have to say. I will close by determining what "reaching an understanding" is with more precision in terms of fusing horizons. Let us turn to develop genuine questioning as a mode of listening.

Dialectical Dialogue Is Not Debate

Maybe your school did not have a debate club; maybe it did. If it did not, you have probably at least heard about debate teams and competitions. Did your school have a dialogue team? Were there dialogue competitions? Of course not. Why do you think that is? In whose interest is it to train and habituate us into debate forms of argument rather than dialogical forms of thinking? Because debate teams face off in competitions, there have been numerous occasions where teams have tried to win by whatever means necessary or have shown how the very debate structure is complicit with white male privilege (see Kraft 2014). This happens not only on the academic competition level, but even—and perhaps especially as a consequence of what is tolerated and promoted in schools—at the US national political level such as with former US president Ronald Reagan's "debategate" scandal (see Kondracke 1983). The etymology of the word "debate" hearkens back to our identification of ambiguity in the word "argument." The root word, "-bat," means fight or battle. Here the suffix "de-" works as an intensifier to mean "completely," as in "A battle to the bitter end." A debate ends with the decision of a judge or panel of judges assessing the quality of argument, the defense of a thesis, or the critique of an opposing team's thesis. Notice how the propositionalist ideology fits well with this surplus of debate. It is all about defending a conclusion, conclusively.

Debate imposes and maintains certain conditions of intelligibility not necessarily shared across other communities or lifeforms. It is intrinsically adversarial. But it goes further. I have often heard debaters announce things like "You cannot say that." They use things like fallacy accusation to police what others say. They unconsciously make logic serve their political and economic interests. Think of how exclusivist Western monotheisms say you cannot belong to multiple religions at the same time. For them, it is only "logical" that only one religion can be true. For them, one must choose—and of course they always assume that their own religion is the true one. Wouldn't it be amusing to meet this sort of person, but they were to claim that a religion other than their own is the true one? Imagine it: "Only one religion can be true, and it is Daoism. I happen to be a Reformed Christian, though." This is a clear example of the subordination of reason to self-interests.

Despite their apparent differences, dialogue and debate do share the presupposition that in order to have differing views there must be underlying common ground. How can disagreements be specific without this? Debate and apologetics, however, start from preestablished positions where we deploy reason instrumentally to defend, clarify, and persuade others of our views, views that we already hold as correct and true. Thus, debate does not lead to a new understanding on our own part. In some extremely defensive debates, where people merely argue to defend their own conclusions, they do not even set out to support their conclusions. Instead, they try to persuade others that they are *at least not irrational* (see, for example, Plantinga and Wolterstorff 1991). They change the topic from supporting their position and to conditions of intelligibility. They set out parameters on what counts as rational and what is irrational, and simply defend themselves by saying that "at least we are not irrational to maintain our beliefs." This also functions as a threat to others, that they must avoid being "irrational." Of course, it is their own version of rationality. They demand that others play by their rules, rules to a game that they seem to be making up as they go. "In our understanding, which we imagine is so innocent because its results seem so self-evident, the other presents itself so much in terms of our own selves that there is no longer a question of self and other," writes Gadamer (Gadamer 2013, 311). Yet what is the point of demonstrating that we are at least not irrational if the order of intelligibility itself is in question? This strategy simply lets us rest complacently in an exclusivism, an unchallenged commitment to our own views on things. Saying something *to* others— defending one's beliefs or position—is not to be in dialogue *with* them. Think of how people sometimes leave telephone conversations with "Talk to you later." The word "to" is ambiguous. Does it mean "at" or "with"? People trying to demonstrate that they are at least not irrational are often merely speaking at others, not with them.

Dialogues, however, do not stop at a concluding thesis statement like debates do. Dialogues reach toward understandings that touch off further dialogues. Conclusions are not the end. In dialogue, they are dynamically serving multiple roles, often simultaneously. As we have seen, a conclusion can serve as a premise to a further argument. Debates stop at a conclusion. For dialogue, though, these stops are mere interruptions not conclusions. Dialogue preserves our historical dynamism. The world and thinking do not end with the stopping of a debate. Consider this: Why do good dialogues come to an end? Do they really end? Genuine questioning facilitates further dialogue. If we have differing perspectives, we enter into dialogue to work out our differences, and perhaps even resolve them in fusions of horizons. However, as Gadamer writes, "every dialogue also has an inner infinity and no end. One breaks it off, either because it seems that enough has been said or because there is no more to say. But every such break has an intrinsic relation to the resumption of the dialogue" (Gadamer 1977, 67). Besides running out of things to say for the time being, any other practical matter and pressure also interrupt dialogue, such as fatigue or hunger. But the fact that these are *interruptions* rather than conclusions show dialogue's orientation toward infinity.

It may seem that in my advocacy for genuine questions, then, that I am advocating the inverse of debate. It is as if instead of persuading others to accept our conclusions through debate, genuine questioning might merely lead to being persuaded and absorbed by others, where we open ourselves to being imposed on by them. Absorption into and subordination to their worldview or conditions of intelligibility is no better than contented exclusivism. Enabling someone else to impose on us is not the alternative, contra Levinasian ethics of the hostage. Indeed, it is not something we can seek anyway because every time we try to walk a mile in another's shoes, we bring our own shoes with us. Instead, such questions indicate a readiness to follow unfolding subject matters whichever ways the winds of dialogue blow, as we noted Socrates describes dialogue as being like wind (Plato 1991, 73/394d). Dialogues and whatever understandings we reach are unpredictable. Subject matters radiate predicative possibilities, and topics radiate reasoning possibilities. The *logos* is like the wind blowing every which way it may please. Questioning in dialogue presupposes that we are aware of our limitations and do not know ahead of time what will come of developing responses to diversity.

Because we cannot think everything all at once, we have to draw it out bit by bit (Gadamer 2013, 422). Dialogue *does* presuppose that we start from some standpoint or perspective. But responsible dialogue—the kind that engages rather than evades—need not require imposing conditions of intelligibility. One need not, indeed cannot, cling to one point of view or even a kind of point of view. Instead, while we always literally start from the position we are already in, this position opens us to changing horizons of potential understandings. Insofar as we are always moving in dialogue, however, our particular positions and the horizons these positions open up are also always changing—even if we misrecognize this dynamism under the illusory security of a stable essence. What if one questions, not as a representative of a particular political position, but as a student of political science? What if, instead of as a parent, we take the perspective of a child? What if one shifts away from psychological questions to sociological ones? Yes, it is, as Ricoeur writes, "always from somewhere, from a particular point, that we perceive, that we observe, that in imagination and sympathy we approach foreign convictions, in a movement of gradual transfer . . . " but our standpoints are far from fixed (Ricoeur 2010, 38). Levinas's emphasis that "proximity is a difference" applies here: our dialogical proximity "is not simply a passage to a subjective point of view" (Levinas 1998c, 82). It "empties me of all consistency," he writes. Participants do not have a rigid essence embedded in some purportedly stable and sedimented tradition as the sole source of their contributions. Someone claiming to be a Republican at the start of a dialogue does not actually inform us about where the dialogue might go, if they use genuine questioning.

Dialogue is instead a fragile achievement. There are so many ways in which dialogue is discouraged, though. Political leaders, for example, sometimes say that, "There is a time for talk, and there is a time for action. Now is the time for action." Have you ever noticed that it is always time for action? There are lots of dialogue or conversation stoppers. Bias is probably the most significant. Bias is sometimes mischaracterized as simply *having a viewpoint*. While that is a necessary element of bias, it is not sufficient. A bias is an unthinking habit in someone's disposition toward a particular position, involving an unconscious or conscious refusal to consider reasonable or dialogically available alternatives and often resulting in unfair actions. Biases are cognitive shortcuts, so we do not have to think every single thing all the way through. Sometimes, of course, these shortcuts are useful, perhaps even beneficial. We do not have time to do it all. We have to prioritize our time and investments. More importantly, biases shape how we see the world, others, and ourselves (DiCarlo 2011, 44). They are the prejudices definitive for our perspectives. They cause problems when we apply them inappropriately, such as with stereotypes and oppressive discrimination. They even shade our very thinking about thinking itself.

There are a few sources of bias. As I noted, prejudices are a function of our historical situation and our biological finiteness. The desire to eradicate all our prejudices is itself a prejudice against prejudice. It is not about escaping them, but understanding them and using them well by putting them at risk. Our biologic predispositions, brain chemistry, health or illness, and even emotions, can cause biases in our thinking. Cultural biases come from our family background, ethnicity, constructions of in/out-group identities, peer pressure, the media, and more. The worst kind of conversation stopper, or perhaps the root cause of all discouragement of dialogue, is what we can approach as "bad faith" (see Sartre 1984). To accuse someone of bad faith is to show that *they cannot really mean what they are saying.* For Sartre, it is bad faith to use your freedom to argue that you do not have freedom or to live like you do not have freedom. I always think about students who voluntarily take a course but then say the professor is "making" them do a particular assignment. We live in a society and world where bad faith abounds, and we can see it in the surplus of colloquial statements that earlier we called self-referentially incoherent. Perhaps you have heard someone say, "No one knows what they are talking about" (or no one knows what they are doing). Perhaps you have heard, "That's just your opinion." Or, "I couldn't help it." These are examples of bad faith because someone cannot possibly own them, yet they say the statements anyway. This is not the same as lying. When you lie to someone, you still have the truth in mind—in fact, you care very much about the truth. Speaking in bad faith instead is "bullshit," where one does not even care whether what they say is true or false (Frankfurt 2005). Why do we tend toward bad faith? Are we lazy? Disinterested?

My proposal is that the propositionalist ideology is *the* fundamental conversation stopper. We already examined the propositionalist ideology in general but let us examine its *insidiousness* in more detail. An ideology is an unconscious comprehensive distribution of material and symbolic power accompanied by a view of the world bolstering that distribution, which is governed by a system of binary notions hierarchically ordered. All this serves the material and symbolic interests of dominant economic and cultural classes (see Baggini 2010, 223). Note that "ideology" is not synonymous with "worldview." We need to emphasize this. Ideology often—perhaps usually—gets used that way in colloquial language in popular media and even in scholarly works. This helps isolate the insidiousness of ideologies: *it is in the interests of ideologies for us to believe they are synonymous with mere worldviews.* Worldviews are, on the whole, conscious conceptual or intelligible frameworks within which knowledge is built up. We have explicit representatives or spokespersons for worldviews, such as self-identified Buddhists or Republicans. An ideologue, alternatively, is one whose thinking, speaking, and acting serves the interests of a particular institution, without explicitly knowing or recognizing it. For example, in the United States, citizens cannot send mail on Sundays—an inheritance from Christianity. So even if a specific citizen holds to an atheistic worldview, they nevertheless serve Christian interests unintentionally. Crucial to note here is that it is not merely that an ideologue does not recognize their own ideology; they *misrecognize* it (see Bell 2009). This misrecognition is what makes it so insidious. Do you really believe that propositionalist ideologues will be persuaded by my argument? No. Is it possible even to persuade them through direct rational argument, since they rest contentedly and exclusively on what counts as rational persuasion? No. The critique of ideology cannot be to address it directly, to argue with it directly—especially since it has already co-opted the very conditions of "argumentation." *The critique of ideology instead must involve exposing the strategies and tactics of preserving material and symbolic domination for the sake of emancipation of those who are marginalized* (see Freire 2001). The father of existentialism Soren Kierkegaard proposes using "indirect communication" (see Poole 1993). The political philosopher Jurgen Habermas proposes approaching society itself as if it were a patient in psychoanalytic therapy, where we must approach societal expressions with a hermeneutic of suspicion (see Habermas 2002).

The strategy we have advanced throughout this book is genuine questioning. As I pointed out, we cannot simply eradicate our prejudices and ideologies wholesale. We are structured by finitude and historicity. With each overcoming of a bias, new ones are established. With each conclusion reached, we have a premise for further reasoning. This is the sediment aspect of tradition. Questioning, though, allows us to put our biases, prejudices, and ideologies at risk—at risk of critique, response, transformation, and fusion of horizons. Indeed, questioning represents a crucial opening for the innovative aspect of tradition. Such an opening corresponds with our ability to listen.

Questions Are a Way of Listening with Others

In our theory of genuine questioning in Chapter 2, one thing I did not stress sufficiently is that genuine questioning is essentially a mode of listening. Our fundamental objection to other approaches to questioning—such as theories in erotetic logic or earlier phenomenologies of questions—is that they start from complete thoughts or judgments and derive their theory of questioning from there. They give privilege to answers, and so questioning comes off as parasitical rather than an irreducible phenomenon in its own right. They mention dialogue only cursorily rather than analyze it as the context in which questioning flourishes in its fullest form. Husserl, for example, brackets out considerations of dialogue in his analysis, and focuses solely on the solitary ego's experience of frustration expressed in questioning. For Husserl, as in the erotetic model examined in Chapter 2, questions express an experience of frustration over an uncertainty that strives for satisfaction in a decisive judgment (Husserl 1975, 309). Unlike an objective judgment, questioning merely expresses a subjective feeling according to Husserl. Genuine questioning, on the contrary, does not merely express my experience like the interjection "ouch" expresses my subjective experience of a pain. Instead, questioning is "tied intrinsically to its being addressed to some other person" (Schumann and Smith 1987, 372). Just as reading is always reading to another, so is questioning done with another.

In the twentieth century, thinkers saw nihilistic crises and threats of meaninglessness as their definitive problems to address, but today those problems have given way "to a more fundamental problem than the notion of [existential] crisis—the situation of confronting otherness" (Klemm 1987, 445). In facing up to otherness, we experience uncertainty about giving others their "due," because the alterity of others exceeds our instrumental reasoning and logic of equivalence bound up with technocracy. Many people are disenfranchised in the narratives dictated by the privileged few, and they are left with few options but to protest. Consider how while the US government decided to provide citizens and documented immigrants with financial support during the COVID-19 pandemic in mid-2020, they did not provide support to undocumented immigrants who make up a large proportion of the essential food production workforce such as agricultural workers and even proposed to lower their wages. Even with protests, we are left wondering whether people have been heard. Consider how—despite their informed and peaceful protests against racist police brutality— professional athletes were harassed by the Trump administration and Trump supporters. The task set to us in our increasingly diverse world is to "uncover what is questionable and what is genuine in the self and the other, while opening the self to the other and allowing the other to remain other" (Klemm 1987, 445). I want to contribute to this task by developing an account of genuine questioning that explains how we listen to and with the other.

It is important to note that, contrary to appearances, we are not granting a privileged status to the sense of "hearing" over other bodily senses. Listening here is a dialectical operator juxtaposed not to sound, but to speech. A person with impaired hearing can ask genuine questions and is capable of reaching an understanding with others through sign language. Ears are only the focal organ of sensing sound; we actually hear with our whole body (see Idhe 2007). The key is that genuine questioning is receptive, expressing receptivity, rather than being merely expressive or assertive. As I emphasized, questions do not say anything. It is, writes the phenomenologist Don Idhe, "to the invisible that listening may attend" (Idhe 2007, 14). The auditory field is an opening people have to networks of significances that constitute our worlds. As an existential structure, all things present themselves to us within it. We can change our focus from one sound to another without much bodily comportment, without even—say—moving our head. The auditory field is omnidirectional, not unidirectional like vision. We are surrounded by sound. Even in an anechoic chamber, we hear the sounds of our own bodies covered over in ordinary contexts. As Idhe writes, "My breathing, the 'whine' of my nervous system, and the inhibited flow of my bloodstream suddenly appear in the quiet as noise" (Idhe 2007, 81). Meaningful sound, by contrast to mere noise, appears as voiced. That is, meaningful sound can be seen as speaking a language. Meaningful sound is speech. For example, the teakettle whistle calls to us.

Spoken discourse, or voiced word, is only the center—not the entirety—of significant sound. Spoken discourse is only present in and with a wider horizon of unspoken significance. Everything people explicitly state said carries with it everything that is unsaid. Thus, to listen with understanding is more than the mere recognition of words, but an entry into a wider situation of significance. Listening, then, is an important avenue for comprehending the whole or unity of our experience. As Gadamer writes:

> There is nothing that is not available to hearing through the medium of language. Whereas all other senses have no immediate share in the universality of the verbal experience of the world, but only offer the key to their own specific fields, hearing is an avenue to the whole because it is able to listen to the *logos*. (Gadamer 2013, 458)

Listening is not the opposite of the inability to hear, but the opposite of speech. Thus, it is not that listening is somehow more primordial for the human relation with existence than other senses. But as the dialectical accompaniment of speech, it is the avenue to reaching an understanding.

Discourse can be embodied in alternative ways besides sound, however, such as in sign language and writing. Written discourse in particular is another embodiment of meaning. A basic difference between spoken and written discourse is the way in which they relate to a broader significant context. When we say or sign a single word, the unspoken context is simultaneously present with the word. We make other noises and gestures; even our facial expressions can enhance what we say. When we write a word or sentence by itself on a blank page, however, the reader must supply the context. More words must be added to approximate the context that accompanies spoken discourse. Moreover, speaking adheres to writing, which is most apparent in learning to read through phonetics where words must be "sounded out." As we gain more and more proficiency in reading, the less and less we require the liaison of sounded voice. In other words, as I elaborated earlier, we gradually reach the stage where we can read silently to ourselves.

My point here is that whether spoken, signed, or written, discourse requires understanding's receptivity. We do not merely make statements in ontological outer space. Listening is foundational for other acts in the practice and play of dialogue. It is a condition of the possibility for decision about what the other says. It is, in essence, the fundamental openness definitive of human being. Human beings need, as Irigaray notes, "to preserve an opening starting from which it would be possible to listen to the other as other, as the one whom we cannot appropriate and whose speech we cannot appropriate, while remaining receptive and listening to them" (see Irigaray 2002, 36). Human being is opened within the world with others. Without such openness, writes Gadamer, "there is no genuine human bond. Belonging together always also means being able to listen to one another" (Gadamer 2013, 355).

Listening is not passive, though. Skill in the art of listening involves concentration and interpretation of what others say. We need to "evacuate" areas of the dialogical field such that others might assume those areas. Listening is "a process of contraction, of stepping back and creating a void into which the other may enter" (Lipari 2004, 137). Listening well involves suspending prejudices; openness includes a relative detachment from our own needs and interests (see Beatty 1999). The listener's perspective must yield in importance to what others say by suspending one's own claim to accuracy of categorization and by regarding one's interpretations as revisable. As Gadamer writes, "Openness to the other involves recognizing that I myself must accept some things that are against me, even though no one else forces me to do so" (Gadamer 2013). This suspension applies both to prejudgments and to responsive reactions to what others say. We might find, for instance, what another says incites our anger, but in attempting to listen to what is said we must suspend the application of this reaction. As Fiumara writes, "Listening involves the renunciation of a predominantly moulding and ordering activity; a giving up sustained by the expectation of a new and different quality of relationship" (Fiumara 1990, 123). Giving up our pretension to order and control, we listen with good faith, where others can recognize in our interpretations their own view of what they mean. Listening stays focused on others' meaning rather than letting our "inner voice" intrude. Effort is put into guarding against distractions by our own hang-ups and interests. As Fiumara states, "A discerning act of listening . . . demands a strength and rigor that are difficult to subjugate and that deserve constant exercise. A listening environment is not improvised. It is, on the contrary, the product of a strenuous process of conception, growth, and devoted attention" (Fiumara 1990, 60). In all these crucial ways, listening is constitutive for discourse. Discourse requires both an utterer and a receiver. Receptive listening is the condition for the possibility of following and opposing what another person says. In this receptivity, we can see there is revealed "a mode of being which is not yet a mode of doing and which avoids the alternative of subjection and revolt" (Ricoeur 1974, 451). It is how we follow along with what is said, inasmuch as what is said commands the attention of our listening. There is a connotation of "obedience" in such following along. The Latin root *obaudire* for the English literally means "a listening 'from below'" (Idhe 2007, 81).

Our openness to following along is fundamental to any particular instances of listening. We can bring this out by considering all the ways that listening is embodied in speech. Listeners are rarely silent but express their listening in words. We can observe numerous response tokens in dialogues. Response tokens are typically monosyllabic utterances listeners make, say, to encourage a speaker to continue (as in saying "mmm . . ."), or to acknowledge and taking note of what a speaker says (as in "oh!"), or to mark a readiness for a topic change (as in "okay") (see Gardner 2001). We literally speak out our listening, displaying to others we are listening to them. Response tokens differ from contributions to content such as agreement or criticism. Contributions indicate an attitude or position with regard to what is said; response tokens merely indicate a listener is taking note of what is said (see Bublitz 1988). Taking note of what is said is necessary for taking up an attitude toward what is said, whereas the opposite is not the case. Moreover, just because someone is not speaking, that does not entail that this person is listening. Consider a phone call where the other person has gone silent. Are they even still there? This is why we need to display to others that we are listening, not merely with body language and eye contact, but with our very words. Listening is not merely a faculty for sensation like hearing, but a mode of speaking.

Listening is embodied in speech, and genuine questioning is one crucial way in which we embody listening. *It is a way we listen with our mouths.* We preserve our openness in genuine questioning. We ask questions to ensure we are hearing what someone is saying, to take note of what is said and understand its meaning. In this way, we are open to what others say. We also construct tentative interpretations of what is said and we test these constructions against what they say, sometimes through asking, "Is this what you mean?" Moreover, we need to get down that "taking note" of what is said is not merely the recognition of vocalized noise, a recognition that speech is happening. Taking note requires that we understand what is said—we need actually to ask the question to which the sentence answers. Of course, some questions are so deficit driven, so structured by anxious need, that we cannot hold ourselves open in them. Such questions are not an embodiment of listening, but a demand placed upon others. These assert control on dialogue, demanding "the" answer. The surplus character of genuine questioning, alternatively, issue forth from a passion for more. It is difficult to describe such questions as acts of deliberate or intentional control. Genuine questions are ones that occur to us. They happen to us when we are caught up in the play of dialogue. As I described in Part I, they are the unfurling radiance of a subject matter—and I add here—inspiring us to further dialogue. We ask them with invitational enthusiasm out of a surplus of love for more life. Insofar as genuine questions render listening audible, *in receiving a genuine question from another we are hearing ourselves being heard.*

By rooting our account of genuine questions in listening, we can now see that such questioning is not only hospitable to answers but also hospitable to *answerers.* That is, in genuine questioning we embody and display respect for others. This is the new and different quality of relationship established through listening, through giving up our need for control over others. Such questioning practices of good listening display respect for the others' authority over their own speech. Asking such questions shows we are listening to what others are saying rather than telling them what they are saying or having an ulterior aim other than the dialogue and reaching an understanding with them. Through posing these questions we demonstrate that we are trying to listen to what others say. Rather than imposing our own constructions upon the discourse of the other person, we hesitate in insecurity about whether we have heard it correctly and so pose the question.

Note that our questions concern what the other *says*, not the other as such. We sometimes say things like "Oh, I get you" to try to indicate we understand another person. The other person, however, is not a complete thought, and so cannot be understood. Understanding is not about getting inside other people and reliving their experiences—though this is the aim of interpretation in Romanticist and other modernist hermeneutics. We *might* approximate that through empathy or even sympathy. *We cannot, however, confuse empathy with understanding*. We can understand without empathy and we can empathize without understanding. As Gadamer writes:

> It belongs to every true [dialogue] that each person opens himself to the other... to such an extent that he understands *not the particular individual but what he says* . . . Where a person is concerned with the other as individuality—e.g., in a therapeutic conversation or the interrogation of a man accused of a crime—this is not really a situation in which [different] people are trying to come to an understanding. (Gadamer 2013, my emphasis)

Responsive questions in dialogue neither assimilate otherness nor impose hegemonic conditions of intelligibility onto the other. What we come to understand in genuine questioning is not the otherness of the other but what she says. (I use "she" because many authors refer to people exclusively as "he" even when we do not know the person's identity.) The other with whom we engage in dialogue is not and cannot be the subject matter or the complete thought we have about the subject matter.

Dialogical responsivity to the other does not make the other understood, as if the other were a complete thought. As Levinas writes, "The other to whom the petition of the question is addressed does not belong to the intelligible sphere to be explored. He stands in proximity" (Levinas 1998c, 25). Why do we speak with others at all, and not just feel satisfied with thinking our thoughts to ourselves? *That we say what we think is an excess*. Speaking with others, especially in the form of questioning, is excessive, an unnecessary emission of surplus (see Levinas 1998a). By asking others questions, we address and invoke them rather than reduce them to mere cognitive representations. The relationship established in questioning cannot be reduced to a representation because we cannot control what others do with what we say. This is why genuine questioning cannot be reduced to the imperative mood. In dialogue with others, our questions remain open without the power to coerce or command another to reciprocate, though we can so manipulate our cognitive representations. We respect the other person's autonomy; we do not reduce the other to a mere thing. If we are trying to understand them, rather than what they say, we treat others as a topic or a mere object. In respecting them, we treat them as equally legitimate contributors to our dialogue.

Genuine questions, questions through which we invite and listen to the contribution of others, are a mode of listening that contributes to the unfolding of a dialogue. In such questions, we listen by speaking. We do this in dialogue with others. Genuine questions are the concrete act in which we suspend judgment on what another says and contract ourselves in order to receive it. We expose ourselves and situate ourselves in proximity with the other person in a responsive rather than merely reactive way. It is only with such vulnerability that what the other person says might "enter" us—enter our dehiscent body, enter our world, enter our field of significance. While this appears counterintuitive with regard to those dialogues that take place when we are bodily nearby another person, we must presuppose it if we are to make sense of the possibility of dialogue with another person who is not physically proximate. For example, on the telephone we respond to the "call" (the ringing phone) with a question: "Hello?" However, answering services do not begin with a question, but a statement: "Hello." This is the convention by which callers are informed about whether they will be speaking with the intended individual or be leaving a message. *The question, not bodily contact, establishes the proximity.* In dialogue, the otherness of the other is otherwise than understandable. We should not feel disappointed about this, this limit to understanding. As I discussed before, understanding is limited to complete thoughts—no more, no less. Let us turn to a surprising aspect of genuine questioning with others in dialogue: the transformation of "you" and "me" into "us."

Share Questions to Understand What Others Say

As I have indicated, genuine questioning is intrinsically intersubjective. It is not really something the solitary individual can accomplish. It is not merely a form of thinking that someone can do by themselves. It is a mode of speaking, and all speaking is speaking *with* others—or "at" others, as the case may be. Some influential philosophers of the last century, though, urged that we should not confuse questioning and thinking. As Heidegger writes, "the authentic attitude of thinking cannot be the putting of questions . . . The true stance of thinking cannot be to put questions, but to listen to that which our questioning vouchsafes" (see Heidegger 1982, 72). If genuine questioning is a form of listening, then we must make some distinctions here. Do we "put" genuine questions? And can that to which we listen only be received via genuine questioning? Surely, as I have emphasized throughout this book, we only understand complete thoughts through actually asking questions to which the complete thoughts answer. Thus, what we "listen to" in thought, what we think, is only opened and available to us through questioning. However, questioning seems to be a paradoxical phenomenon. Is it something we *do*, or is it something that *happens* to us over and earlier our willing and acting?

Questions occur to us. They arise. They present themselves. Questions even strike us. We say such things about questions. They are as much a passion as they are an action. They are not something we simply "put." It may be true that we "put" calculative questions and other typical interrogatives—those we can translate into commands. This point develops another aspect of questioning's hermeneutic priority in addition to questioning's priority for the reception of meanings, and we can use it to draw out genuine questioning's *intrinsic intersubjectivity*. Recall that understanding questions does not belong to the same order as understanding meanings. Questions are not answers, so they do not "mean" anything. Answers do, and do so predominantly in the form of judgments, complete thoughts with a subject and predicate. Questioning is necessary to catch judgments as meanings. However, we do not have to "mean" a judgment even if it answers our question. A judgment is a meaning because we can consider it as among numerous possible answers, but it takes appropriation to "mean" it. By contrast, the only way to understand a question—to "mean" it—is to ask it. As Gadamer writes, "There can be no tentative or potential attitude of questioning . . . A person who thinks must ask herself questions. Even when a person says such and such question might arise, this is already a real questioning that simply masks itself, out of either caution or politeness" (Gadamer 2013, 383). We might decide to not utter a question publicly, but we cannot decide whether a question occurs to us. For a question to be what it is requires adoption of it. Getting caught up in genuine questioning, though, is less an intentional activity and more a passivity. Genuine questions occur to us. While we might decide to command others with interrogative sentences, genuine questioning's *occurrent* character—not its intentional character—distinguishes it as questioning.

Such questions not only occur to us, they also expose our vulnerability. Invitational questions are speech correlates to the vulnerability of our ears. This is a form of love. For Kierkegaard, those who love others do something to themselves—namely, they make room for others (Kierkegaard 1995, 210). This kind of questioning does that. The kind of questions we are after here are those that make room for both the contributions of others and the subject matter itself. It is an act of love to open spaces of genuine dialogue. In listening to others, then, we risk our very selfhood by taking the other's questions and answers seriously as possible disclosures of truths. As Levinas writes, "It is in the risky uncovering of oneself, in sincerity, the breaking up of inwardness and the abandon of all shelter, exposure to traumas, vulnerability" (Levinas 1998c, 48). Speaking is certainly a risk, particularly the risk that we might be misunderstood. Questioning as active listening seems to be an even greater risk.

Genuine questions are a way in which we establish and perceive proximity with regard to others in a responsive rather than merely reactive way. One cannot merely react to such a question. It must first be asked before it can be answered. Imagine being asked, "Are 'good books' also 'good reads'?" Do you respond by immediately and reactively answering? Or do you repeat the question with a "huh," to clear space for responsiveness? This is not to say that the world places no demands on us. A child needs to be taken to the hospital at a moment's notice. Members of one's community are struck by catastrophic weather. Political and social forces make us move. We react. These forces are often such that they cannot be negotiated with. This is in no way unique to human being, though. In the domain of language, that medium within which all our forms of life take place, reaction can be sublimated into responsivity. Genuine questions communicate that one is receiving the world in a responsive rather than merely a reactive way. It is a hesitation, the sort of hesitation that helps us resist naïvely projecting our prejudices and biases on our experiences (see Al-Saji 2014). Paralleling bodily proximity in many ways, in asking a genuine question we put ourselves "out there" in order to attain responsive proximity with the other person. Not all of our questions are mere attempts to get others to answer. Many of our questions, like listening well, are ecstatic events in which we are caught up in something greater than our intentions.

Due to genuine questioning's being more a passion than a deliberate action, when we hear another ask a question, we must ask that question too if we are to understand it. That is, *their* question becomes *our* question. We share in genuine questioning. Not only does the hermeneutic priority of questioning explain how it is possible to understand meanings, it also explains how it is possible to *transfer* meanings. To understand what others have to say not only requires that they answer my questions. I must ask their questions, too. What they have to say might not be an answer to a question I am currently asking. Instead, they may be responding to questions *they* are already asking. Can I position myself to ask their question? Can we orient ourselves so that we can share others' questions, and consider their answers to those questions? If not, then it seems we forego dialogue. Genuine questioning uniquely indicates our being in relationship with another and makes it possible to consider their responses to that questioning. In our very considering of their questions, we are already asking them. Whereas our answers often divide us, this peculiar quality of questioning allows us to relate in ways beyond mere assimilative empathy. Contact in questioning is not absorption. It neither annuls others' alterity nor suppresses my own. When I hear another's question and I ask it with her, it becomes our question, and *this difference-preserving relationship* makes it possible for me to consider her answers as meanings. Levinas urges that questioning embodies a different intentionality than assimilative absorption in egoistic consciousness. If information is all we need in this DRIP (data rich, information poor) culture of ours, we need not question one another at all. If I want to know someone's name, I can just as easily look at their nametag. Does questioning have to consist of consciousness seeking fulfillment in knowledge? Levinas writes, "Must we not admit, on the contrary, that the request and the prayer that cannot be dissimulated in the question attest to a relation to the other person . . . ? A relation delineated in the question, not just as any modality, but as in its originary one" (Levinas 1998a, 72). Questioning is not about getting the answers, but embodying relationship with others.

The difference-preserving relationship established in shared questioning makes reaching an understanding possible. Yet even more, it preserves respect for others. When I hear or read another asking a genuine question, I necessarily ask the question too if I understand it. When we both ask the question, though, whose question is it? The other's or mine? When I hear you ask a question and I understand it (and thus ask it), it transforms into our question. You might initiate it, but here it is shared. In whose interest is it to "possess" a question in claiming "*my* question is . . . " rather than be possessed by sharing questioning? Think about it this way. Have you ever read a page of text from an author, and at the end wondered what it was that you just read? I have. This is, in part, because we do not ask the questions to which the sentences on the page answer. I have seen this play out in classrooms. For example, students sometimes have a difficult time grasping Aristotle's theory of friendship when they do not share Aristotle's questions to which his theory answers. His question is: What is the most fulfilling or complete kind of friendship? Yet, notice, that the question is not really Aristotle's. It is not as if Aristotle invented friendship as something through which to think. Traditional college students are often uniquely positioned to ask questions about—to study!—friendship because they are in transition from high school to adult life. They wonder who their true friends are. When students suture their questions with Aristotle's, when they all share in the questioning, they are enabled to consider Aristotle's theory as a possible answer, and so his conclusions can be understood as meanings. Moreover, they can then evaluate the quality of Aristotle's theory for its adequacy to addressing the question.

This shared quality of genuine questioning, moreover, keeps it ethical rather than exploitive. Some critics claim questioning subordinates other people to one's domination. If questioning demands an answer, it seems oppressive. Again, as Žižek illustrates, the authoritarian says, "It is I who will ask the questions here!" (Zizek 1989, 182). While perhaps fitting for epistemic imperatives, genuine questioning circumvents this because the questioners' positionalities are indeterminate. Genuine questioning is without deliberate domination. Since only answers count as meanings to be understood, the other is respected as a co-explorer and is not assimilated. What we understand is not the other, but what the other states as potential answers to our shared questioning. It allows us to listen to what another says, opening a space for the other's unfolding. Genuine questioning proves not to be a privative need to subordinate others, but a desire for a surplus of possible meanings through shared exploration.

When such shared questioning is achieved, whose question is it? The indeterminacy of "us" asking the question helps maintain orientation toward the real subject of conversation: it is neither you, nor me, nor even us, but the subject matter. Can we feel assured that we ask the "same" question? Our purportedly private subjective perspectives seem to inhibit this. The suspension of our natural attitude toward questioning applies here, too. People influenced by Western individualism and Cartesian subjectivity tend to assume that all people are isolated subjects of experience. This leads us to ask questions about whether we can really know other people. It leads us to ask questions like, "How do I know your 'red' is not my 'green'?" We can approach how we share questions through looking more closely at language. To share the same question is to share a language, the conventions for identifying subjects and enframing them with predicates. Grammatical conventions help us speak about the "same thing." To share a question is to know the same language or to translate proficiently between languages. Subject matters stand out as topics in part because cultural traditions hand them down as important. By inheriting a language, moreover, we appropriate fields of predicative intelligibility or language games that reflect our cultural *Lebensform* or lifeform.

To illustrate, let us ask the question, "What year is it?" Our responses depend on our forms of life. To answer "2021 CE" is to bring secularized Christian coordinates to bear, or at least a secular lifeform bestowed to Western civilization by Christendom. Yet for Muslims, it is "1442 AH." To ask what year it is in genuine questioning rather than to get information, we can reflect on what time itself is (the subject), and the politics of era-dating systems (the possible predicates). We can also reflect on relations between languages and truths, because both dates are true, yet both seem unable to be true in the same way at the same time—though it seems equally absurd to ask which is "truly true." The point of a genuine question is not so much for another person to answer it as much as it is for another person to ask it with us, and thereby share our question. So, when I ask a question, and you consider it, the question becomes our shared question because we both are simultaneously asking it. It is only in light of sharing questions that we can come to consider each other's responses. Sharing the questions is what makes a statement a response within a dialogue rather than just some random expression coming out of nowhere and receding back into nowhere. *Questions facilitate the transferal of meaning from one person to another.* Understanding another person's question entails that I also ask it, that the question becomes "our" question rather than merely hers or his. Achieving this shared asking of the question transforms the other person's meaning into a possibility that one may consider, and thus makes possible our coming to a new understanding.

This is why it is crucial for dialogue that we come to share questions. What is the subject matter about which others have something to say? In what ways do others apply predicates to their subject matters? Do we even have a shared language in which to think together? Moreover, how do I come to consider subject matters about which the other asks questions and has something to say? Is what they are saying inferentially related to other statements? If we do not share the other's questions, then the other's answer—indeed, the other's very voice—is lost on us. Given our limited standpoints, how might one come to share the other's questions? How will this be possible given not only the difficulty of learning entirely different languages but also the difficulty of learning idiosyncratic uses of purportedly shared language? As the myth of Babel suggests, our condition here is one of dispersion in different language games. We live in radically different cultures, to the point where our values seem incommensurate (see MacIntyre 1988).

What if our language games are incommensurable? Perhaps we can reenvision cultural diversity and individual differences as both analogous to and intertwined with linguistic diversity. If this is possible, sharing questions only occurs through the arduous labor of learning new languages and language games—in other words, *translation*. As Ricoeur writes, "There is no universal language; nevertheless anyone seems capable of learning an additional language . . . We have always translated . . . Indeed, is it not with something similar to this linguistic hospitality that we achieve a gradual understanding of . . . beliefs we call foreign?" (Ricoeur 2010, 38). To assert that we cannot translate or assert the untranslatability of our language games reflects, for Ricoeur, a false sense of self-sufficiency which grounds exclusive hegemonic ethnocentrisms. We believe that our own cultures are self-contained and complete, and we implicitly assume our culture is superior to other cultures. These assumptions are reflected in someone despairing that translation is impossible. However, like our mother tongue, our inherited cultures constrain our starting points, but make possible opportunities for building bridges instead of barriers. Under the aegis of our analogy between cultures and language, we can see that this lateral movement of understanding in dialogue proceeds aoristically, perhaps even to the extent that one's previous commitments no longer hold influence. In sharing questions, we yield our horizons to the importance of what the other asks. As Levinas writes, "If one is deaf to the petition that sounds in questioning . . . everything in a question will be oriented to [an exclusive] truth, and will come from the essence of being. Then one will have to stay within the design of this ontology" (Levinas 1998c, 26). This is why translation, learning another's language, is fitting. Through learning more language games, we become increasingly fluent and keep possibilities fluid. The indeterminacy of "us" asking the question helps maintain orientation toward the real subject: it is neither you nor me, nor even us, but the subject matter. Like absorption in games, genuine questioning draws us in and fills us with the animating spirit of the subject.

I want to emphasize one more time that genuine questioning just makes it possible to *consider* meanings. It does not force us to "mean" any of them. While understanding a question is to ask and appropriate it, we can understand a meaning without assuming responsibility for it. Considering which year it is, or even considering *whose* year it is, does not entail adoption of one or the other era-dating systems. But to take up one option as our answer—especially as "the" answer—is to take responsibility for determination within the indeterminate predicative possibilities opened by the multitude of cultural options. In shared questioning we are already co-responsible on the way to fusing horizons.

A Phenomenology of Integrating Questions

Recall that the primary aim of dialogue is being-at-one on a subject matter. We also described this as reaching agreement or reaching an understanding. A more precise determination is available to us now. Because shared questioning makes it possible to transfer complete thoughts to one another, shared questioning makes it possible to share meanings. In asking a genuine question, I do not necessarily intend to know something, but instead I intend to hear what someone else has to say, to enter into dialogue with her in such a way that something new and unpredictable emerges for the both of us. Not only does such questioning establish a relationship of mutuality, it also makes shared meanings or "fusion of horizons" possible. Consider Tillich's explanation for ineffective Christian evangelism:

> The difficulty with the highly developed religions of Asia . . . is not so much that they reject the Christian answer as answer, as that their [conception of] human nature is formed in such a way that they do not ask the question to which the Gospel gives the answer. To them the Christian answer is no answer because they have not asked the question to which Christianity is supposed to answer. (Tillich 1964, 204–5)

I do not quote this to give people ideas about how to be better Christian evangelists. My point is not about forcing others to ask our questions. Refusing to ask another's question—or refusing to learn their language—may be in one's own best interest, especially if such others are complicit with imperialism and colonialism. My point is simply that an answer makes no sense abstracted from asking the question it addresses, and reaching an understanding requires a shared language.

A fusion of horizons is concretely realized, according to Gadamer, when dialogue partners reach some form of agreement concerning a subject. But if we cannot even get to the point of agreeing that we are talking about the same subject, then we will not be able to fuse horizons. People talking past one another is not a dialogue, as we have seen. I take "subject" here in a particular way: the subject of a sentence. A fusion of horizons is realized when we find shared predicates fitting for that subject. A genuine question is not a judgment, not a synthesis of subject and predicate. And yet, a genuine question is not the negation of that one or any other synthesis. The peculiar nature of genuine questioning is, as Gadamer writes, "that it stands closer to a statement than any of the other linguistic phenomena, and yet it allows no logic in the sense of a logic of [assertions]" (Gadamer 2007, 102). Such a question is not deficit driven in need of one particular settled answer, but is surplus driven, more in awe at the possibilities before any specific possibility is tried out. It is by virtue of the shared question that I can start to try out these predicative possibilities for a specific subject, and when I find a predication that works, it expands my horizon and enriches my world. As we have developed earlier, genuine questions are an articulate listening signal. Through them we indicate to others that we hear and understand what they are saying, and that we are willing to continue speaking with them. Moreover, through the partnership of questioning, they determine a horizon within which the transferal of meaning is made possible. In this way, hearing what another person has to say, accommodating them in discursive space, and suspending resolution with regard to that which they speak about precedes all "striving to reach a resolution" definitive of typical interrogatives. Thusly does a genuine dialogue between (at least) the two of us ensue. If we reach agreement concerning those pertinent predicates, then we also can be said to "fuse horizons."

Horizons are fields of intelligibility giving shape to our forms of life, and are articulated in language games. It is because we come to share a language that we come to share a world. Understanding subject matters must take the form of language, because being that can be understood is language. As Gadamer writes, "It is not that understanding is subsequently put into words; rather, the way understanding occurs—whether in the case of a text or a dialogue with another person who raises an issue with us—is the coming-into-language of the thing itself" (Gadamer 2013, 386). In language, we illuminate and elevate aspects of life held in relief. Things are revealed for the truth of what they are. However, as feminist phenomenologist Gail Weiss writes:

> One must always be cognizant of the fact that sedimentation of everyday experience into recognizable patterns can serve to codify oppression as readily as it can promote a reassuring sense of existential stability . . . To avoid complacency, one must be attentive to continual possibilities for transformation offered by those aspects of the world that cannot be rendered intelligible within established horizons, and that therefore demand new ways of thinking, feeling, and being. (Weiss 2008, 5)

Some aspects of experience, as well as some predicates, can settle into stagnation. Through dialogue with others, though, we can resist such sedimentation and be attentive to new possibilities for transformation available in others' languages as well as our own. With ever new predicates available for shared subject matters, we can unfurl ever-broadening horizons. It is important to have breadth of horizons because horizons are what help put what is right in front of us into proper perspective. Consider how intense some people feel in anger about a particular experience. With time and a broader perspective, people can see that experience in a better light. Moreover, there is indeterminacy within every questioning. These immediate experiences, where people feel righteously justified in their anger, can be dislodged by questioning. Through this indeterminacy, we hesitate and can be deliberate about making a determination. We can share a determination through having first shared an indeterminacy.

Languages have a history. As we have seen, thinking is affected by prejudice, and prejudices are effects of history. We are affected by our culture. Our horizons and fields of intelligibility are shaped by history and traditions. People brought up in Buddhist homes tend to become Buddhists. People brought up in Muslim homes tend to become Muslim. Tradition names this dynamic of historical transmission. Tradition is a dynamic and dialectical process including both sedimentation and innovation (see Gadamer 2013, 293; Ricoeur 1986, 125; and Bell 2009, 123–4). Yet the word "tradition" is usually associated with only one side of that dynamic, making it seem as if it denoted some ahistorical sedimented and unchanging entity. Consider how people against marriage equality defend their position as holding to "traditional marriage." Or consider how people associate Confucius with outdated values in labeling him a "traditional thinker." One of my biggest concerns is the way some philosophers argue for the existence of "the traditional god" (see Dickman 2018c). Traditions are historically effected practices structured by symbolic and mythic conventions, in response to contextual contingencies. Indeed, such contingencies are often the stimuli by which innovations occur. This dialectic definitive for traditions can be observed in evolutions of musical performance. Each occasion a musical score is performed changes the history of the piece. Each occasion is affected by contingent circumstances, from the acoustics of the space to the quality of the instruments to the skill or talent of the performer. This can also be observed in traditions of Quranic recitation (see Sells 2007, 163–5). Yet for some instances, these factors coincide in a performance that sets a new standard for the tradition of recitation. In coming to learn another's language and hold a dialogue where we reach and understanding then, is less an intentional act of a subjective ego and more *an event of tradition* (see Gadamer 2013, 302). Recall that in Chapter 1 we asked about the nature of the thinking I, where Aristotle and Spinoza approach the thinker as merely a reflection of a god thinking thoughts. We give privilege to the prejudice and pretense of subjectivity in believing that we choose to "enter" into dialogue and in believing that we "decide" to agree with this or that. When we look deeply, we see collisions of linguistic sediment and unfurlings of linguistic innovation in dialogue. Students studying to become musical performing artists sometimes research improvisation, believing that they need to improve their skills at improvisation. What they overlook, though, is that their very question asking about improvisation *is itself improvised.* They improvised their very question about improvisation. This is how subtle the dynamism of sediment and innovation is in tradition and the event of fusion of horizons.

Historically effected and effective horizons are operative in events of understanding. Indeed, what seems worth asking about is already an effect of history (see Gadamer 2013, 311). Politicians, scientists, professors—indeed all people—try to use objectivity where "facts" speak for themselves to urge this or that action. We tend to believe that we can stand apart from the vicissitudes of history and reach an objective perspective. Propositionalism positions us to take mere expositions as valid reasonings. We conceal from ourselves that our views and beliefs are "situated in the web of historical effects" (Gadamer 2013, 311–12). The reality is that our views depend on "the legitimacy of the questions asked" (Gadamer 2013, 312).

We are situated. Our genuine questionings reflect and express our historical situatedness. Our situatedness opens us to a horizon of possible meanings. Because we are always in a situation, our understanding of it is always unfinished. Hence, the need for the application of the concept "horizon" here. We need a superior breadth of vision in trying to reach an understanding and fuse horizons. As Gadamer writes, "To acquire a horizon means that one learns to look beyond what is close at hand—not in order to look away from it but to see it better, within a larger whole and in truer proportion" (Gadamer 2013, 316). Propositional expositions lack such proportion of historical vision. Reflective arguments, for example, have the feeling of someone trying to bowl us over, but this show of strength inadvertently signals their weakness. For example, we have the abstract method of reductio ad absurdum against skepticism and relativism. The claim that "there is no truth" is often attributed to skeptics. But this claim is logically self-referentially incoherent because the statement purports to be true! A relativist view is supposedly similarly self-contradictory. The claim that "what is true for me is true for me, and what is true for you is true for you" is often attributed to relativists. Yet, this claim is logically self-referentially incoherent because it assumes that it is universally true. These accusations of incoherence miss the point, though. They may be formally correct, but they do not show superior insight. They do not tell us anything (see Gadamer 2013, 353). No matter how often people expose the contradiction, both skepticism and relativism return in different forms (see Levinas 1998c, 167–9). They both seem to disclose some truth missed by the accusation of contradiction, the truth about multiple fields of intelligibility. Moreover, the strategy of logical refutation suggests that reaching a conclusion is merely a subjective act. Rather, understanding is an effect and an event of traditions. Horizons include all that can be seen from this or that specific point of view situated within evolving traditions.

Yet the notion of "fusion" of horizons seems to imply that there are two separate horizons—mine and yours—which fuse when we reach agreement (see Gadamer 2013, 314). It seems as if there are distinct individual subjects with points of view opened to distinct horizons. This would entail that there are "closed" horizons. The notion that a horizon is closed, however, is incompatible with the relativity and situated character of horizons (see Warnke 2016). Horizons move as we move, preserving an opening with us. There is no such thing as a closed horizon. When we reach an understanding, we are not empathizing with another person where we try to enter into their situation and horizon. As we have noted numerous times, we can empathize without understanding and we can understand without empathizing. We do not try to understand others, but try to understand what they have to say in response to our living questions generated by historical situations. In this way, *we are all part of one great horizon.* By reaching an understanding and fusing horizons, we "rise to a higher universality," a greater breadth of perspective in which it is possible to share meanings with one another or to consider things from multiple points of view (Gadamer 2013, 314). The term "universality" is not some metaphysical truth that stands eternally. Instead, hermeneutic universality indicates those complete thoughts and their questionings that can be shared by ever greater swaths of humanity.

Fusing horizons transforms us because we open ourselves to new possibilities of meaning not only for consideration but also for appropriation and ownership. How can we tell whether we are listening well? One clue is when the other recognizes in our questions her own view of them. Can we pose the questions without slanting them? Can we reiterate their answers without subtly undercutting them? As Gadamer writes, "A person who is trying to understand . . . has to keep something at a distance—namely everything that suggests itself, on the basis of one's own prejudices, as the meaning expected" (Gadamer 2013). All understanding involves an alienation, what Ricoeur refers to as "productive distantiation." Even if all understanding is self-understanding, we always and continually understand differently, if we understand at all. Responsible understanding involves coming to speak otherwise than I have ever spoken before. Insofar as speaking differently reflects being differently, to what extent might one also become otherwise in responsible service to the other within dialogue? Completely otherwise if one is loyal to responsible understanding. But are we not then faced with a hard choice: Either loyalty to understanding or commitment to my current identity?

Reaching an understanding also involves a transformation of ourselves (Beatty 1999, 295). When we understand what one another says about something, we cannot help but be transformed into a communion in which we are no longer the exact same person (Gadamer 2013, 371). Understanding, in other words, expands our horizons. Notice here, too, that we do not technically understand another person in themselves. We understand what the other person says (Gadamer 2013, 387). It also implies that we are putting our very selves at risk. Regarding our perspective as revisable entails we regard our very selves as revisable. As Beatty writes, "To listen to another with openness is, then, to open the self to the possibility of taking seriously meanings of the sort that can transform it. Such openness requires, therefore, not merely the willingness to rework and rethink experience and its ingredient opinions but the willingness to rework character" (Beatty 1999, 295). Every time we listen, in other words, our very selfhood is at stake.

This event is transformative, because in it "you" and "I" become "us." We can explicate the way in which we are at one in reaching an understanding through dialogue by returning once more to Gadamer's development of the structure of games. A game moves and has its essence beyond the particular intentionalities of the players. Hence Gadamer's saying, "all playing is a being played." Games draw us in and simultaneously fill us with their dynamic spirit, like "team spirit," a spirit surpassing all of us as isolated individual intentionalities. In other words, games mediate and moderate intentionality by transforming each of us into parts of a greater whole. And just as with games, so also with being-at-one and reaching an understanding. As Gadamer writes:

> A [dialogue] does not simply carry one person's opinion through against another's in argument, or even simply add one opinion to another. Genuine [dialogue] transforms the viewpoint of both. A [dialogue] that is truly successful is such that one cannot fall back into the disagreement that touched it off. The commonality between the partners is so very strong that the point is no longer the fact that I think this and you think that, but rather it involves the shared interpretation of the world which makes moral and social solidarity possible. (Gadamer 2007, 96)

In games, players comport their behavior into alignment with the appropriate movements such that through their movements they present the being of the game. As the game of seesaw perfectly illustrates, a "good match" consists of the uninhibited performance of the to-and-fro movement. This movement is irreducible to some further end or purpose; there is nothing more excessive than play. Participants in games are overcome by the playfulness of the movement and animated by it. A game only fulfills its purpose when the participants, so to speak, "lose" themselves to the movement or get in the zone. As Gadamer writes, "It is at this point that the concept of the game becomes important, for absorption into the game is an ecstatic self-forgetting that is experienced not as a loss of self-possession, but as the free buoyancy of an elevation above oneself" (Gadamer 1977, 55). Something is at stake in games, and we play for the sake of that something, namely *recreation*. We literally recreate ourselves in games. The form that the recreation takes is determined by the task set by the game to the participants. This task, though constraining the field of possible action, is experienced not as restraining, but rather as liberating. Without the game situating players thusly, they would not be freed to play. The constraints governing the field of the game are the condition of the possibility of the playful variety of activity. *Furthermore, the goal of recreation is fulfilled not in winning or solving the puzzle of the game, but with simply exhibiting the dynamic form of the game.* This is quite distinct from the goal of a debate, with winners and losers. The mode of being of such an alternative game, as we already discussed, "is self-presentation." What the game means for the participants does not depend on completing the task of the game. Rather, players "spend" themselves on the task of the game and "play" themselves out in it. In this way, the game takes a stand in and through the participants. This excursion into the concept of play shows us the way in which "who we are" is at stake in play, and even more in listening to what another person has to say. Dialogue presents dialogue.

Let us go back to thinking about seesaw. Subject matters are like the fulcrum on which the plank sits. Our questions and responses are the to-and-fro movement in playing seesaw. The subject matter, like the fulcrum, regulates and guides dialogue. Questions and responses are the shifts we make with our bodies whereby we reach to the fluid back and forth movement. Just like good actors disappear behind the characters they play on the stage or screen, the dialogue partners disappear and the subject matter speaks volumes through them. We want to find out what "it" has to say to and through us. It is only through sharing a subject matter in this specific way that we can come to consider what others have to say about it. We share subject matters and the questions that occur to us as we play. To understand what someone else has to say is to understand what they say as a response to a question. Other scholars echo this point insofar as dialogues involve what can be called "shared intentionality," or collective behavior (see Searle 1992).

Such a form of intentionality is not just a conjunction of individual intentions. We can illustrate this through the example of pushing a car with another person. It is not that "I" am pushing the car and "you" are pushing the car. My so doing and your so doing are a part of "our" pushing the car. If "I" discover that "you" were merely faking it, then not only was I wrong about what you were doing, but I was also wrong about what I was doing. As Searle writes, "In collective behaviors, such as [dialogues], individual intentionality is derived from the collective intentionality" (Searle 1992). Dialogues are collective activities, and the intentional contents of a participant's I-intention, even though it may differ from the content of other participants' I-intentions, conjoin in some way to a common we-intention. As we have emphasized earlier, it is through sharing questionings that we can come to consider others' responses as meanings to understand and own. A dialogue is not the sum of the individual actions having the same intentions, such as when individual and solitary hikers all take shelter from a storm in the same bunker. The understanding achieved in dialogue is more than the sum of its parts. Understanding and dialogue are something we accomplish with others, not by ourselves. Coming together in this way is the aim of dialogue as a discursive practice.

Let us turn to elaborate on four further foci of questioning definitive for dialogue.

9

A Dialectic of Questionability and Responsibility

Not all of our questions are primarily attempts to get others to answer. In genuine questioning, we attempt first to *share* questions with others. Moreover, many of our questions, like listening, are ecstatic events in which we are caught up in something greater than our intentions. In asking a genuine question, I do not necessarily intend to know something, but instead I intend to hear what someone else has to say. My desire is to enter into dialogue with her in such a way that something new and unpredictable emerges for the both of us. We have examined several factors that contribute to questioning and dialogue leading to ever new understandings. In this chapter, I will return to the elements of dialogue represented by the triadic model of dialectics: thesis, antithesis, and synthesis. We will see that questioning similarly radiates in at least four directions just as with questioning in relation to thought and as with questioning in relation to reasoning. I will also turn to uncover how dialogical dialectics undergirds erotetic logic concerning epistemic imperatives. All questions, even those instrumentalized to gain answers, have their depth in genuine questioning. I will close this chapter and Part III overall by ending with a meditation on personal responsivity as our fundamental responsibility constitutive of subjectivity. We will see that while dictatorial monologue lacks genuine questioning, dialogue facilitates the emergence of originary responsibility.

By emphasizing dialectics as intrinsic to the kind of dialogue enabled by genuine questioning, we can resist a naïve celebration of infinite dialogical cacophonies (see Bakhtin 1981). Of course, reaching agreement in dialogue includes respect for differences, but dialogues are not merely a practice for recognizing differences. Dialectical dialogues uncover truths within or across such differences. They are not activities of assimilative hegemony where we reduce others to just reflections of ourselves, but openings for reaching more vibrant and more thorough understanding among one another. We can see this through a glance at the etymology of dialectics. The suffix, "-tics," comes from the ancient Greek *techne*, which means the art or craft of something. We get our word technology from it. The prefix, "dia-" we have seen before. Recall that it means "across" or "through." But it can also mean "thoroughly" and "entirely." (The word "diaper," for instance, means "thoroughly white.") The root word, *-lektos*, derives from another word we have come across already, *-legein*, to speak or to gather. Dialectics, or dialectical dialogue, is a technical practice, a technical kind of dialogue. It is, in part, a systematic method of reasoning working with contradictions and conflicts of interpretations, attempting to arrive at truths through this exchange.

How to Question Dialogues from at Least Four Directions

Just as both thinking and reasoning are bound by questionings radiating in at least four directions, so also is dialogue bound by questionings radiating in at least four directions. Recall once again that because questions do not technically say something and only complete thoughts do, questioning is susceptible to misrecognition. We tend to forget it is even there, despite knowing that without it we would not understand anything said. Not only do we dislodge thoughts and arguments from their proper situatedness within questions, we also dislodge dialogues from questions that operate to initiate, sustain, and complete them. I'm not advocating to have different dialogues other than we already have, as if I'm here to invent a new way of speaking and thinking. I am instead urging that without valorizing—and even venerating—questioning as the fundamental context within which dialogues take place, without making questioning more explicit, then we are not experiencing the dialogues we have *as dialogues*. I am attempting to expose question-less dialogue as pseudo-dialogue. Despite some suggestions throughout Part III about ways questioning interplays with our approach to dialogue, we need to lay out dialogical orientations of questioning. Just as dialogues coordinate what I have called "theses" and "antitheses," the broader interrogative context within which dialogues even make sense involves a key scaffolding of question orientations. Questioning in thinking coordinates subjects and predicates into complete thoughts. Questioning in reasoning coordinates premises and conclusions into arguments. Now, as we will see, questioning in dialogue coordinates theses and antitheses into fusions of horizons. While questions open subjects to predicative possibilities in thinking, and while questions open premises to conclusive possibilities, questions in dialogue open theses and antitheses to synthetic possibilities. There are four crucial orientations of questioning here: antithesis-centered questioning, thesis-centered questioning, synthesis-centered questioning, and dialectics-centered questioning.

In *antithesis-centered questioning*, we ask what reactive possibilities or possibilities for negation are available from a thesis. It may feel counterintuitive to begin with the antithetical dimension of dialogue. Consider it this way—negativity often seems much more vibrant and pervasive in our experience of life, sometimes to such an extent that we forget that negation necessarily presupposes a precedent positivity. War, deaths of loved ones, breakups, and more all stand out to us as outstanding experiences. Loss even seems to accumulate throughout our lives, to such an extent that some people choose modern cynicism or even nihilism. We worry about potential pitfalls. We focus on what we want but do not yet have. In a way, it is in this negation or negativity that we wake up to dialogue, *dialogue that is already underway*. We come too late if we merely want to settle wherever we already are, as if movement is not actually happening. Perhaps an illustration may help. Imagine a dialogue about tax rates: "We have been saying that a progressive marginal income tax rate of 70% is not unreasonable. Why do we live in a world based on money anyway?" I select this sort of question because we can take it in two ways. On the one hand, it can sound like a deflationary cynicism, probably expressed from someone with at least moderate financial privilege. In this way of taking it, it is a conversation stopper, undermining the very topic itself. It is what we can call a nihilating negativity. On the other hand, if conversation participants ask the question with one another, then it brings out larger possibilities for imagination and action that may be even *more* progressive than a tax rate, possibilities hidden by the dialogue so far. This we can call a productive negativity, the kind of moving negativity we said is essential for genuine antitheses.

In *thesis-centered questioning*, we try to get back to the thesis that seems to have set off our dialogue. This effort is inherently reconstructive, not an actual return to some purported origin. We might ask, "How did we get here again?" And the partners try to retrace their steps. The act of "retracing" however is not a pure and transparent access to a past but is instead something that happens in the present. Just as we know that memory is constructed— which is why eyewitness testimony is unreliable—our "memory" of the thesis is produced rather than recovered. This is why we are left to formulate a hypothesis, something a little less than (hypo-) a pure thesis. We ask what we are or have been talking about, as if we are trying to return to the main dialectic after having traversed a seeming dialogical tangent. Yet even such a return from the tangent should expose us to an otherness of the thesis, not only because the thesis has changed but also because we have changed. We are now people who have tried to return to the topic after having traversed a tangent, a specific tangent. We can only really know a thesis from within the negativity of the antithesis.

In *synthesis-centered questioning*, we are less oriented toward the idyllic past of the thesis and more oriented toward an idyllic future. We sometimes, perhaps often, experience impatience in listening to others: "Where are they going with this?" Such a question can have at least two connotations, similar to antithetic questions. It may, on the one hand, express an attempt at being a conversation stopper. In such a case, it expresses a desire that the other stop talking. On the other hand, it may express an anticipatory excitement (see Anderson 2001). Such anticipation is inescapable for active listeners. We cannot help but project possibilities for fulfillment and completion in listening to what another says, and we correct our anticipations upon receiving what they actually are saying. This is why we experience surprise at what others say if we are listening to them. If we were not projecting anticipations of meaning, we would not feel surprised, but merely collect and accumulate more information. What makes synthetic questioning distinct from thetic and antithetic questioning is that such anticipatory projection concerns completion and fulfillment. Is the dialogue as a whole complete? Have we covered everything needed?

What have we been really doing throughout this book? We have been focused primarily on *dialectic-centered questioning* or dialogue-centered questioning. Dialectic-centered questioning is not about this or that thesis, antithesis, or synthesis. It is instead about dynamics of dialectics itself (see Jameson 2009). Is the triadic model the best way to even construe the dynamism of dialectics? Is it possible to even have a complete dialogue? Note how different this question is from the anticipatory question of "Are we there yet?" Again, the question of "What if we never get there?" can be taken in two ways. On the one hand, it could express a deflation, a giving up of courage to keep talking. It dismisses everything that has come before as failure if we do not reach a complete resolution. It is, really, a function of Romanticism, the romantic delusion of utopic completion (see West 2008). If we cannot have the whole thing, what is the point at all? On the other hand, it can express a genuine engagement with the dynamism of dialectics. Maybe the grand conversation will continue without us? So what? Can we not feel grateful for where we have been so far, and see what we might do better next? Dialectic-centered questioning fundamentally resists the temptation toward the "final answer." Such an answer would be the end of questioning. The final answer makes questioning absurd (Cage 1973, 118). The final question makes no answers absurd, but opens to ever further answering.

Erotetic Logic Has Its Depth in Dialogical Dialectics

We can see more clearly now what we can mean by a dialectics of question and answer, beyond the mere logic of question and answer. It is not that erotetic logic and dialectics stand in opposition and need to be resolved into a synthetic compromise. The same goes for "question" and "answer" themselves. Each on its own unfold in its own dialectics, which mutually inform each other. That is, questioning—as we have seen—has its own intrinsic dialectics; answering—or forming complete thoughts—has its own intrinsic dialectics. When genuine questioning collides with genuine answering, these dynamics unfold in the direction of a dialectical dialogue. And, like all Plato's great works, the dialogues do not really end in a complete comprehensive answer as if there were some eternal principle integrating all the parts and tangents and questions of the dialogue. Plato's *Lysis*, for instance, poses the question of true friendship, and leaves the reader wondering and dwelling with the question of friendship—inviting readers themselves to take up their own responsibility for questioning and answering concerning friendship.

We defined thinking as the process of combining and separating subjects and predicates in light of questionings to which these combinations or separations are relevant. There is a unique interplay of questioning and responding forming the crux of thinking. With as much trouble we have in pinpointing the identity or nature of the thinker, we know from this interplay that there is a fundamental split in the thinker between the thinker as questioner and the thinker as respondent. The I is twofold: the I as questioner and the I as answerer (cf. Buber 1970). These two roles are taken up in turn, an internalized turn-taking system. Thinking is an internalized dialogue. Because thinking does not comprehend all it knows and all it has to express in one single glance, it has to present itself to itself "as if in an inner dialogue with itself" (see Gadamer 2013, 422). We have inherited this model for thinking from Plato, in his dialogues the *Theaetetus* and the *Sophist*. Socrates teaches Theaetetus that "thinking" is "a talk which the soul has with itself about the objects under consideration . . . It seems to me that the soul when it thinks is simply carrying on a discussion in which it asks itself questions and answers them itself, affirms and denies" (Plato 1997, 189e–190a). When Theaetetus in a different context gets caught up in dialogue with an unnamed visitor, the visitor asks, "Are not thought and speech the same, except that what we call thought is speech that occurs without the voice, inside the soul in conversation with itself?" Theaetetus answers, "Of course" (Plato 1997, 263e).

There might be many objections here. For example, some people will claim to "think" in nonverbal ways, outside of or without language (see Wittgenstein 1922; cf. Wittgenstein 2009). They might lift up images and assert that they think in pictures instead of concepts. Or they might lift up the body as having its own intelligibility more fundamental than or even otherwise than cognition (see Vilhauer 2016). As we saw earlier, there is a relevant distinction to make between imagination and thought. We can picture a triangle and understand it; we cannot picture a thousand-sided object, but we can still understand it by determining how many angles it necessarily has. Imagination and thinking are different. It is not to say that we should only think and never use our imagination. It is simply that we do not need to smear them together. With regard to the body, it may have organizing principles of its own. Indeed, we may discover that thought is a function of embodiment. It would be committing the genetic fallacy however to reduce thinking merely to a function of embodiment, as if we have explained it away or subordinated it. Dance and athleticism can be rigorous, and require concentration. To think, however, is to do something distinct from those. I believe one way of relating embodiment and thinking is through the notion of internalization and reflection. Thought is a new phenomenon emergent from the adapting awareness infusing the human habitus.

I want to explain this through a parallel internalization, reading literacy. For people who can read, our earliest experiences of reading are always situations in which we read aloud. Perhaps our guardians read to us. At the very least, learning to read involves always reading for someone else, namely the reading teacher who can assess one's quality of reading (see Raphael 1986). Indeed, reading is always reading for someone. The verb "to read" is not merely transitive in requiring a direct object. Of course, to read is to read something—a book, a poem, a blog, a sign, or what have you. In this sense, it is transitive. It is also transitive in requiring another someone, the one to whom the direct object is read. Reading aloud is like a musical performance (see Gadamer 2013, 400). In reading, we bring the resounding words and sentences into harmony with meaning (see Gadamer 1989, 47; see also Sells 2007). A paradigmatic example is the guardian who sounds out the voices for the wolf and the three little pigs in different registers for their child's bedtime story. Readers graft their reading voice to the code given to them by the lines of text. We encourage readers learning to read to "sound it out." We can tell by the sound of their reading voice whether they are comprehending what they read. Is it monotonous? Then we likely have sentences perceived but not complete thoughts understood. The same principles apply to silent reading (see Gadamer 1989, 47). Just as in reading aloud we read to someone, so also do we read to someone in silent reading. Namely, we read to ourselves. This reflects that split in the I that we noted earlier between questioner and answerer. Here, though, it is the I who reads—the one saying something— and the I who is read to—the one to whom this something is read (see Dickman 2014). We are recognized as literate when we can demonstrate to our reading communities that we are able to read to ourselves (see Raphael 1986). That is, we internalized a social activity and practice of reading as something we can do on our own, silently to ourselves.

Just as with reading, so also with thinking. Inasmuch as thinking is a dialogue we have with ourselves, thinking is the internalization of the practice and play of dialogue. Our habitus is structured such that we are enabled to internalize this social practice. How we speak with others, and in turn how we speak with ourselves, becomes of crucial significance in our current notions of mental well-being. Clinical therapy is premised on the internalization of the voice of the therapist. We do not merely need to change our beliefs, as with cognitive behavioral therapy, but we need to change the very way we think with ourselves—we need to change our inner dialogues. Is our voice of conscience condemning with its demands and accusations? Or, perhaps, might we benefit from a voice that asks us genuine questions (see Dickman 2018b)?

I approach Plato's dialogues as just this sort of therapeutic script for internalization. Perhaps you have heard of Plato's argument(s) for the immortality of the soul or his arguments for the doctrine of the Forms. Indeed, on the basis of many of these positions attributed to Plato, Plato has been the object of criticism of many other philosophers trying to make a niche for themselves, beginning with his student, Aristotle. The term "Platonist" has in some circles been a reproach. Yet, I believe we should ask why Plato writes in dialogues rather than merely laying out his arguments for these transcendent entities. Surely Plato could have just written that way. So we must assume that the genre of dialogue is somehow essential to his teachings (see Moors 1978). His writings belong, in many ways, to the ancient genre of aretology, similar to biography, where someone's life story is given. In this genre, though, authors take artistic license to present the hero of the biography in the best light possible, even if that means constructing what they would or even should have said rather than merely record what they in fact said. The authors try to capture the *arete* or virtue of the narrative hero. This can be seen similarly in the Christian gospels as well as Diogenes Laertius's lives of the philosophers. Plato gives us a portrait of a hero whom he believes we readers ought to emulate, to imitate, and through habituation, internalize this excellence of character. In reading Plato's dialogues, we are initiated into dialogical excellence, that is, excellence in thinking. In this way, Socrates is our regulative ideal for what it is to be a thinker.

Responsibility Emerges through Dialogue

Let us dwell briefly on what all this can add to contemporary philosophical discussions of responsibility. The end of questioning in our age of answers is not to get more or better answers. I want us to object to describing us as "answerable animals" or claiming that we need to "give an account of oneself" (see Butler 2005). Questioning is the fecund ground enabling the flourishing of responsibility. Our effort to be, our effort to become, is supported and facilitated by dialectical dialogue rooted in genuine questioning. It is only by way of questioning that we are enabled to respond, whereby we are response-able. This runs counter to our inherited traditions of reflection on the transcendental enabler of responsibility. Rather than elicited into action through a "call," as in "the call of conscience," we are "in question." This criticizes both the critical queer studies philosopher Judith Butler (1997) and Marxist philosopher Louis Pierre Althusser (1994) on the call, who claim that only through the call does one become a "you," who claim that through such subjection is one constituted as a subject or person.

Both Levinas and Heidegger construe the transcendental enabler of responsibility as a "call," too. For Levinas, the face of the other calls one to responsibility, demanding that one live up to the adventure of subjectivity. The face expresses suffering to which one must respond. The other inaugurates responsive discourse because, in facing me, the other makes my activities public. As Levinas writes, "The relationship with the [other]— responsibility extending beyond intention's 'range of action'—characterizes the subjective existence capable of discourse essentially" (Levinas 1998a, 22). Through this confrontation, this "face-to-face," humanity dawns on one, urgently demanding responsible action and generating reassessment of our egocentric perspectives (Blum 1983, 161). I—as a reflective and contemplative solitary individual—cannot situate myself like this through some solitary self-examination. Rather, only in the dawning upon me of the face of the other is a call to me made that does not request mere information but appeals to me as response-ability (Levinas 1998b, 165). There is an asymmetry here in that the other calls from a height such that it constitutes me or the I. Such a structure of accusation posits one as "guilty." The one and the other do not have a relationship of mutuality and reciprocity, but only a disjunction. The other calls to us in a form approximating divine proclamation, and I respond in guilty responsibility.

Heidegger locates the call within the discursive structure of self, an otherness within oneself (see Ricoeur 1995, 319–55). Authentic responsibility is realized when the one called—specifically *Dasein* in the mode of "the they"—heeds the call issued by oneself in the mode of uncanniness. As Heidegger writes, "'It' calls, against our expectations . . . [Yet] the call without a doubt does not come from someone else who is with me in the world. *The call comes from me, and yet over me*" (Heidegger 1996, 254; my emphasis). This call not only attests to the possibility of being authentic, for Heidegger, it also "demands it" (Heidegger 1996, 246). We call ourselves out of our complacency and irresponsibility. Without the call, human beings are lost in the they and their "idle chatter." As Heidegger writes, "robbed of [our] refuge and this subterfuge by the [call], the self is brought to itself by the call" (Heidegger 1996, 252). The caller, however, is systematically elusive to everyday language because it does not answer to a name or any other form of address. The uncanniness and mysteriousness of the caller grounds its authority over one, for Heidegger, an authority that cannot be questioned. "It goes against this kind of being," writes Heidegger, "to be drawn into any consideration and talk" (Heidegger 1996, 253). All counter-discourse is rendered impossible (Heidegger 1996, 272). Rather, the call situates us—just as with Levinas—as "guilty," but not in the moralistic sense. The guilt we bear is that we are thrown into being without recourse to "the" answer. The call releases us to take up our own possibilities for ourselves rather than merely conforming to inherited traditions. In other words, we become our own ground (the ground of a nullity) in authentic responsibility (Heidegger 1996, 261).

Anxiety can clue us into an affection distinct from guilty subjection. Anxiety clarifies that the human task is "to maintain a unity of self, integrity, within ever threatening disintegration into boundless chaos" (Gadamer 1986, 122). Despite arrested horror, the human effort-to-be stubbornly projects possibilities for self-preservation. Rather than paralyzed suspense, anxiety can engender care and reflection. Anxiety as a negativity contributes to the opening for reflection and discussion. So a peculiar gift of anxiety is that it distances us from things and opens us to language, particularly dialogue. "It is through the *logos*, through [being possessed by] language," Gadamer writes, "that a person is able to think something and at the same time hold certain possibilities open" (Gadamer 1996, 157). As the hermeneutic philosopher Charles Taylor defines us, "The human agent exists in a space of questions" (Taylor 1989, 29). As Milan Kundera has his philosophical femme fatale Tereza put it: "Questions set the limits of distinctively human possibilities" (Kundera 2005, IV.6). This space is a fertile field for the human spirit's flourishing in taking up answers. "Humans give themselves divine representations [or answers] as supports for becoming," writes Irigaray (2002, 140). "But," she asks, "what are these worth if they do not favor natural growth?"

Our perspectives are exposed as incomplete by anxiety and its opening of us to language. Perspectival incompleteness provides potentially infinite opportunities to reorient toward the good rather than restrict ourselves to egocentric grabs for dominance. As Taylor writes:

> To know who I am is a species of knowing where I stand. My identity is defined by the commitments and identifications which provide the frame or horizon within which I can try to determine from case to case what is good, or valuable, or what ought to be done . . . [Orientation toward the Good] is the horizon within which I am capable of taking a stand. (Taylor 1989, 27)

In anxiety, we recognize our time is limited. Because our time is limited, we have to prioritize things and make the best decisions we can in light of the information we have so far. In so needing to come to a decision with an aim at the Good, one cannot but engage in dialogue with oneself and others. Dialogue requires self-forgetting, a sort of release from particular defensive constructions of self in order to be free to pursue the good wherever the *logos* goes. As Gadamer writes, "One must lose oneself in order to find oneself" (Gadamer 1989, 57). The risk is crucial in all questioning generated by desire. Desperate preservation of oneself—the anxious need to "take care" of oneself—inhibits what Levinas calls an "ethics of sacrifice." He writes, "Sacrifice cannot find a place for itself in an order divided between the authentic and the inauthentic" (Levinas 1998b, 217). Rather than taking a resolute stand within anxiety, responsibility for others—even to the extreme of dying for others—signifies a genuine transcendence within life. What sacrifice reveals, claims Levinas, is a beyond being, that there is something more to life than mere self-preservation—but which is not an "afterlife." The excessiveness of sacrifice, beyond the limits of self-preservation, prioritizes others over the self. Only through responsibility for others does a truly human "I" emerge that is neither substantialist identity nor resolute authenticity (Levinas 1998b, 217).

With regard to the Good as a principle for decision-making, there is no complete body of information at our disposal and no other to whom we can defer with complete confidence. Rather, as Gadamer writes, "one has to ask oneself, and in so doing, one necessarily finds oneself in discussion with oneself or with another" (Gadamer 1986, 41). In dialogue with an orientation to the Good, one can navigate between extremes that tug at our willpower if one holds fast to dialogue unswervingly. As Taylor asks and answers:

> Do I know what I'm saying? Do I really grasp what I am talking about? I can only meet [this challenge] by confronting my thought and language with the thought and reactions of others . . . The transcendental condition of our having a grasp on our own language, that we in some fashion confront it or

relate it to the language of others. This is not just a recommended policy of the kind that suggests if you check your beliefs against others' you'll avoid some falsehoods. *In speaking of the transcendental condition here, I am pointing to the way in which the very confidence that we know what we mean, and hence our having our own original language, depends on this relating.* The relating and (ontogenetically) inescapable context of such relating is the face-to-face one in which we actually agree. We are inducted into language by being brought to see things as our tutors do. Later, and only for part of our language, we can deviate, and this thanks to our relating to absent partners as well and confronting our thought with any partner in this new, indirect way, through a reading of the disagreement. (Taylor 1989, 37–8; my emphasis)

We can come to share questions only through the arduous labor of learning new languages and language games. But it is in relating with others that we come to understand things. The relating constitutes me as both responsive and responsible. We need this framework of responsibility to humble our hubris. We are tempted to smear understanding across all things. We are tempted to expect all things are understandable. However, we can only understand discourse in dialogue with others through the opening of genuine questions. The best we can do is dig down to our fundamental questions, whereby we start to transmute experience into discourse. There are many things I do not understand. This is not because of my personal limited capacities—which of course are many. It is because there are things that simply are not understandable. May we have the serenity to accept what we cannot understand, the courage to understand what we can, and the wisdom to know the difference between these two.

Dictatorial Monologue Lacks Genuine Questions

It is difficult to imagine a conversation where no one asks each other questions. Two parallel monologues do not make a dialogue. Living alongside another person does not mean that you live *with* them. As Aristotle says, "In this case of human beings what seems to count as living together is this sharing in dialogue and thought, not sharing the same pasture, as in the case of grazing animals" (Aristotle 1999, 1170b10–15). Our age of answers is really an age of monologues. We do not yet seem to have recovered from either the monological age of religious dictates or the monological age of Eurocentric

"Reason." This is reflected in current neoliberal and advanced capitalist interests that lead to us being bombarded by answers. Advertisements tell us what we need. Political leaders tell us what we need. Academic researchers produce surpluses of publications that no one reads to earn tenure. In these ways and more, we are given answers to questions no one is really asking.

Dictatorial monologue is oppressive to dialogical responsibility and the freedom it engenders. Oppression cuts of our freedom to enhance and amplify our existence (Beauvoir 2015, 87). While we might feel nature oppresses us, it is really just the friction or resistance of experience that gives us things about which to think. Only other people can be oppressive because they force us to take sides. Surely you have heard some leaders say, "Either you are with us, or you are against us"? Are you a hostile or are you an ally? Through such division, oppressive people change others into a thing (see Yancy 2015). This is often camouflaged in the language of what is only natural, such as women being perceived as the weaker sex or racial stereotypes. The key attitude underlying dictatorial monologue can be put this way: "You are oppressing me by not allowing me to oppress you!" (Beauvoir 2015, 96). Consider how many US Southerners refer to the civil war as the "War of Northern Aggression," as if it was an act of aggression to seek the liberation of slaves. The disposition of dictatorial monologue seems to assume that we are only really free if we deny another's freedom.

Why are we so susceptible to dictatorial monologue? We can become complicit in our own oppression (Beauvoir 2015, 90). This is the existentialist writer Fyodor Dostoyevsky's key insight expressed in the parable of the Grand Inquisitor (Dostoyevsky 1950, 292–314). The point the Grand Interrogator seems to make is that human beings cannot be trusted with freedom, and that they do not really want freedom anyway when they can have food and amusement instead. People do not want freedom and responsibility, but prefer feeling happy. Why do the necessary work it takes to be responsible for ourselves when we can turn to—in this case—the church for the answers? From the Grand Interrogator's perspective, human beings do not eat to live, but live to eat. We seek gratification rather than the struggle to flourish.

There is a deeper reason we are susceptible to this. Beauvoir calls it our "tragic ambiguity" (Beauvoir 2015, 6). We are radical subjects experience or individual I's, systematically elusive to categorization. Yet at the same time, we are objects for others. This is why it is so easy to gossip about people, to make them the topic of conversation rather than engage them in dialogue. We do this even to ourselves when we treat ourselves as objects, as having an essence. There is a certain comfort that comes with this, an alleviation of the struggle of responsibility. The final answer, the final solution, is intrinsically a resistance to and an evasion of the responsibility (see Beauvoir 2015, 109–18). Dictatorial monologue, contentment with provisional answers taken as absolute, is an evasion of genuine questions and dialogue. More should be said here and has been said by others to whom we can turn in further research. Let us conclude with a meditation on the joy of genuine questions.

Conclusion
The End(s) of Questions

I do not have a conclusion, as if I could end a book on questioning with a final solution. In fact, I want to resist the very making of conclusions—as these are construed in propositionalist ideology. Perhaps I could point to possible applications of my theory of genuine questions, such as in therapy or classroom discussions. My worry is that specific applications open genuine questioning to mere instrumental value, as if it is only worthwhile if we can get this or that specific social or natural profit from it. Let us instead end here with a reflective meditation on the joy of endless questioning.

The Joy of Questioning

The symbolic value of the question mark is its openness toward broadening horizons of understanding. Through questioning we enhance and amplify our existence. As a symbol, the question mark provides representation for a religious-like community of inquirers, however wide we questioners might be spread across the earth. Questioning itself is an enabler of confidence and faith, not an enemy of them (see Tillich 2001, 18–20). Indeed, it is a vital expression of faith. What we see in communities that suppress questions is a fanaticism, literalism, exclusivism, and complicity with norms of oppression and exploitation. In 2019, for example, the United Methodist Church (UMC) voted to maintain and more strongly enforce their ban on people in open non-heteronormative relationships in church leadership positions, claiming "homosexuality is incompatible with Christian teaching" (UMC 2012, 220). Some people had decided to bypass the UMC order and to ordain people regardless of their orientations and identities. Note that the direct statement does not say "some," or even specify that they are speaking about peculiarly Methodist interpretations of Christian teaching. This purports to be a final answer, one that does not to respond to questions but gets rid of questions. Consider this: for other organizations that also claim to be Christian but who do not see any incompatibility about who people love and marry with Christian teaching, such as the United Church of Christ (UCC), does the UMC mean to say that it does not recognize the UCC as Christian? The UMC's wording purports to represent "Christian teaching," not merely Methodist teaching. The decision to enforce a ban directly inhibits questioning. Indeed, UMC ministers were explicitly told not to speak on the issue from the pulpit after the vote to maintain the ban.

Such ultimate conclusions and final solutions, such discouragement of questioning, creates feelings of anxiety and guilt in those who find themselves unable to quiet their questioning. Such people see something wrong, a hypocrisy or a contradiction in their community of practice or in their leaders. They might wonder, "Our community teaches love, but all we seem to do is express hate toward those who are different from us." Instead of this anxious guilt in questioning, my text has promoted ways to take joy in it. Instead of compulsively tying ourselves to answers, to a desperate need for "the" answer, we instead are empowered to open to further resources disclosed in our ever-renewed questioning.

Rather than an apocalyptically impatient attitude toward our bewilderment, praying daily for its ultimate end, let us be eschatologically patient, relaxing into our daily questioning. Indeed, relaxation into questioning is similar to the state of *ataraxia* or tranquility promoted by the ancient Greek school of skeptics, the Pyrrhonists (see Thorsrud 2009). By calling into question our very pretense toward answers, the belief that we must have all the answers and that all questions must be answered, Pyrrhonists instead encourage suspending both our belief and our disbelief. By suspending our compulsion to believe, we can realize a state of liberation. We often express a demand, an impatient anticipation in need of immediate resolution. Instead, let us dwell with questioning, where we seek ever-broadening horizons, a seeking where it is possible to accept the continuing tension of living with unfolding questions.

Questions are a reality we can affirm with a resounding "Yes!" Taking joy in our questions is life-affirming; compulsively seeking to end questions is life-denying. In our joyous affirmation of endless questioning, we can pass from death to life. Our dialogues might proceed without end, in a surplus of understanding. A possible role model for this experience of joyous questioning in Western philosophical and religious traditions is the Platonist Christian theologian Augustine. Religious Studies scholar Charles Mathewes, in his close study of Augustine's *Confessions*, argues that Augustine's choice to include the last half of Book 10—as well as Books 11-13—reveals that for Augustine "questioning . . . is not simply a prolegomenon to faith or praise but, in fact, a vital expression of it" (Mathewes 2002, 542). Some readers of the *Confessions* expect the narrative to end with the seemingly climactic moment of Augustine's conversion experience in Book 9, expect it to such a degree that some editors simply leave the subsequent parts out. Mathewes develops an interpretation that Augustine's story is about learning to ask questions in the right way, and that Augustine achieves this in the latter books of the text. He writes:

> Augustine's new perspective was one of learning to be "eschatologically patient" rather than "apocalyptically impatient." This allowed him a more relaxed attitude than permitted by the habituated demand for a complete comprehension of previous foretastes, a demand that expresses an impatient anticipation of (and implicit demand for) a nearly immediate resolution and end to his questioning. . . . It was when Augustine realized the character of his life as [seeking after the depth of divine mystery], that it became possible and necessary for him to 'endure' the 'continuing tension' . . . of living with ever unfolding questions. But it should be clear by now that "enduring" the "continuing tension" of such questioning is in fact not merely something one suffers regretfully; it is, rather, a mark of being alive. To come to see the joyous endlessness of such questioning, and to begin to inhabit it, is to pass from death into life. (Mathewes 2002, 551–2)

Like Augustine, we too can come to affirm life through questioning without end. While we undergo questions as they occur to us, while we literally "suffer" them, they are not something to regret to rid ourselves of. They are a way we express and enhance our experience of being alive.

Recall that neutrality is not merely about not biasing answers, but is also about neutrality with regard to finality. What my study of dialectics opens up for us is a movement without a totalizing completion. While a completion can function as a regulative ideal toward which we strive, it is not something we need to demand happen here and now. We need to give up on our compulsive need for immediate gratification or satisfaction in completion. Open questions contribute to cultivation of openness to further experience, more dialogue, and greater understanding. It is like realizing the perfect game of seesaw. Subject matters are like the fulcrum on which the plank sits.

Our questions and responses are the to-and-fro movement in playing seesaw. The subject matter, like the fulcrum, regulates and guides conversation. Questions and responses are the shifts we make with our bodies whereby we reach to the fluid back and forth movement. Just like good actors disappear behind the characters they play on the stage or screen, the conversation players disappear and the subject matter speaks volumes through them. We want to find out what "it" has to say to and through us.

This is quite different from the demand for the "right" or final answer, particularly as we develop technologies for solving perceived problems efficiently. The philosopher Jacques Ellul critically interrogates this aspect of the natural scientific attitude, observing that it gives privilege to mathematical precision to such a degree that "only that is knowable which is expressed (or, at least, can be expressed) in numbers" (Ellul 1964, 17–18). To get away from the so-called "arbitrary and subjective," to escape ethical or literary judgments (which, as everyone knows, are trivial and unfounded!), the true scientist must get back to numbers and statistics. What, after all, can one hope to deduce from the purely qualitative statement that the worker is fatigued? But when biochemistry makes it possible to measure fatigue numerically, it is at last possible to take account of the worker's fatigue. Then there seems to be hope of finding a solution. However, an entire realm of effects of technique— indeed, the largest—is not reducible to numbers; and it is precisely that realm which we have investigated in my book. Yet, since what can be said about it is apparently not to be taken seriously in science, it is better for the "true scientist" to shut "his" eyes and regard it as a realm of pseudo-problems or simply as nonexistent. People often dismiss philosophical dwelling with phrases like "I do not do 'qualitative' research" or "That's too deep for me." The "scientific" position frequently consists of denying the existence of whatever does not belong to current scientific method, narrowly construed. The problem of the industrial machine, however, is a numerical one in nearly all its aspects. Hence, all of technique is unintentionally reduced to a numerical question (see Ellul 1964, 18).

With Ellul, I seek to expand on Sartre's claim that "statistics can never be dialectics" (Ellul 1964, 206). There is an opposition, even a mutual exclusion, between statistics and dialectics. They differ not merely in their mode of explaining but also in their very mode of apprehending the world and action. Statistics is necessarily a univocal method that expresses an aspect of reality which is not combinable with any other (except other statistics) and which cannot tolerate contradiction or evolutionary development. Both contradiction and evolution are intrinsic to dialogue and the fusion of horizons. Statistics conceives evolution only in its formal aspect, fastening on its strictly numerical element and proceeding discretely along the numerical continuum which it connects by extrapolation. It sets up this linear formulation as the very essence of evolution. But it is incapable of grasping in any degree the internal and continuous mechanism of evolution and the interplay of negations involved in the affirmations. Statistics (and every technique) can proceed only by affirmation, by exclusion of negations, refusal, and destruction. It implies and prescribes a logical evolution of accumulation, but not a dialectical evolution of changes and growth (see Ellul 1964, 206).

As we have seen, dialogue integrates multiple perspectives not in the accumulation of further refined statistics but in the broadening of horizons for understanding. Diversity of meanings often implies—although it need not—divisiveness among and between, for example, those who are committed to particular religious traditions as well as those who are committed to forms of anti-religiousness. Divisiveness is, in part, a function of the ways in which individuals are committed to their particular religious (or nonreligious) traditions. Their answers are, they believe, *the* answer. The terrifying and murderous consequences of divisiveness need not be rehearsed here. What must be stressed, however, is that the divisiveness takes not only such extreme forms, but also more subtle forms such as the simple dismissal of another person's voice in dialogue or the exclusion of individuals from communities. Divisiveness in whatever form threatens the integrity of humane social life: while many answers threaten to divide human beings and generate various states of alienation, genuine questions promise to bring human beings together in solidarity while simultaneously disclosing our primordial belongingness within the world and with one another. Questions can only be genuine, really, when shared.

Dialogue, as living language, is not a means to some precalculated end. It is not something to be submitted to a purpose as if it were a tool employed for acquiring some end, such as the transmission of one's will. It is a life process in which we cultivate and develop our being in a world, a common ground that supports our individual and collective endeavors. It does not have a point like that of other actions, but rather the process appears to be the point itself. As Friere writes:

> It is also false to consider seriousness and joy to be contradictory, as if joy were the enemy of methodological rigor. On the contrary, the more methodologically rigorous I become in my questionings and in my teaching practice, the more joyful and hopeful I become as well. Joy does not come to

us only at the moment of finding what we sought. It comes also in the search itself. (Freire 2001, 125)

How might such seemingly pointless practices like dialogue help liberate us from the hegemony of instrumental calculation? What is the point of doing something pointless? Is freedom when we find joy in pointlessness?

Appendix for Instructors

Chapter Outline

I want to provide a number of suggestions for professors to help students engage with my book. I do this instead of providing chapter exercises, where students could quiz themselves on the material and could potentially get away with using this book on their own without engaging with others in dialogue. My goal is not to have students memorize and regurgitate facts, and not to have them methodologically practice a specific set of skill steps. I want students to be engaging in the practice of dialogue, and so these suggestions reflect how I approach creating classroom discussions among students. I will move from my general teaching strategy for promoting classroom discussion, and then move to chapter specific suggestions. Of course, professors should feel welcome to adapt my book to their courses as they see fit. One preliminary remark I want to make here is that my book design is structured to move through it in terms of the table of contents or to move through it in this way: Chapters 1, 4, and 7 focusing on the scaffold of thought, reason, and dialogue; then Chapters 2, 5, and 8 focusing on the roles of questioning in these domains; then Chapters 3, 6, and 9 focusing on the underlying coordinates and principles definitive for each domain.

The Word-Phrase-Sentence Strategy for In-Class Dialogue

Each day that I assign reading for a class period, I use an adaptation of the National School Reform Faculty's protocol called the "text rendering experience" (see NSRF 2014). Before explaining this strategy, I want to point out that if the reading is especially difficult, I also provide students with four to five reading guide questions from which they select one or two. I create between three and six groups of students, with at least three students per group (rotating them roughly four times over the course of the semester). The rotating of students forces students to create dialogues with others in the classroom as opposed to grouping merely with their friends. The students use their materials to create group dialogues. This is somewhat more advanced than "think, pair, share," because the text rendering experience as well as the reading guide responses require that students come to class prepared for dialogue. Sometimes I will even say to them that, "I require these from you so you prove to me you did some of the reading assignment—because if I was a student and could get away with not reading, I probably wouldn't!"

The word-phrase-sentence assignment requires students to select a single word, a single phrase, and a single sentence that they feel was especially meaningful to them from the reading selection, particularly with regard to the main topic for the day's lesson—as it is titled for the day in the syllabus schedule. These "three things" (as we affectionately refer to them after a couple of periods) also have to have specific author and page number citations, as well as a brief one- to two-sentence explanation as to why those three things stand out to the student as significant. In class, the student groups each go around their small circle, first with each student sharing their word selections and why these words stood out to them, second sharing phrases and explanations, and then their sentences and explanations (see Ritchhart, Church, and Morrison 2011, 207). This routine not only helps students capture the essence of a text or what "speaks" to them, but also prompts dialogue about why this or that stands out. I ask that each group be prepared to share between one to two things for the entire class, and I use these as prompts for more thorough lecture or generating more discussion with all of them as an entire class.

The National School Reform Faculty characterizes all their protocols as aids to group dialogue. They protect time for active listening rather than running into anticipatory interruptions where students speak over each other. They promote equity of voices rather than default to the few dominant speakers. They help students feel safe to ask questions and receive feedback rather than make students feel attacked or defensive. They focus students on specific texts and words to address understanding rather than allow for endless complaining or going over the same problems. They also help students gain enhanced perspectives and empowerment with optimism about the next steps, rather than leaving the room with no clear sense of progress. I have personally tried other protocols, such as the "Four A's" strategy where readers bring in something they agree with, want to argue with, aspire to, and an assumption in a text. I found this protocol left too much room for misunderstanding reading assignments because—as many of us are wont to do—we are on the ready to argue before understanding. The "three things" strategy helps students stay focused on understanding, and realizing just how difficult it is to understand complicated texts. I also want to point out that students regularly express satisfaction with and appreciation for the "three things" practice in end-of-semester evaluations. And, I see remarkable improvement in student performance on formative and summative writing assignments. I share these two anecdotes to motivate interest in the "three things" strategy but also to suggest that further quantitative research could be done to measure significant improvements in student performance.

I recommend using this strategy for engagement with my text throughout each reading assignment, regardless of whether my other chapter-by-chapter recommendations are used.

Introduction: An Age of Answers

I believe the best way to get into the book is just to ask some solid open-ended genuine questions. I suggest using a simple "think, pair, share" strategy with the following:

1. (To say to students) Take a moment to write a short response to the following question: Would you rather be free or be happy? Why? Do you have to be free to be happy? Introduce yourself and talk about your responses with students nearby.
2. (To say to students) Is happiness a feeling or an action—something you do? If it is just a feeling, do we have a pill for it?

For the instructor: Ask for a few volunteers to share their answers and reasoning, and riff on them, particularly in connection with Aristotle on flourishing. You might even show the BBC History of Ideas clip on this.

3. (For students) What are some of your favorite questions to think about? What do you wonder about when you are doing laundry or taking a shower? Do you have any favorite questions?

For the instructor: Ask for a few volunteers to share their answers and reasoning, and riff on them as you can.

Chapter 1: Thinking Only Happens in Complete Thoughts

For this chapter, I suggest just a few activities in addition to the "three things" strategy.

1. The first thing is to focus on grammatical components of sentences. One fun way to do that is what we can call "Yoda grammar." It is easy to find examples of Yoda speaking with some clips. Ask students to figure out what the order of parts of the sentence are for typical English ones, and how Yoda switches those parts around—using the terms "subject," "copula," and "predicate" as best as they can. They should be able to tell that Yoda uses the order: predicate, subject, copula. In more technical linguistic terms, it is: object, subject, verb (see Lafrance 2015). Try also to revisit the question of whether "everything" can work as a subject—recalling by definition that subjects pick out specific things from everything else. What other words might not work as subjects? There are words that do not work as predicates either—such as "being," "space," and "time." Ask them to form sentences using those as predicates.

2. I think it is useful to delve into some of the "deeper" topics the chapter leaves in suspense. Use think, pair, share to reflect on and discussion the question: Do thoughts originate in us (the thinkers), in the gods (as Spinoza and Aristotle suggest), or with subject matters themselves? Why or why not?

3. Reiterate that what makes thinking "critical" is being reflexive about the specific context within which a thought is taking place, using any of the disciplines or methods available.

Chapter 2: What Do Questions Do to Complete Thoughts?

In addition to the "three things" protocol, I suggest a few activities related to chapter content.

1. For some general activities about questions, have students think of song titles with questions, such as "Are you gonna go my way?" or "Who can it be now?" Have the students look at the questions made famous in the "36 Questions That Lead to Love" phenomenon (see Aron et al. 1997), such as "What constitutes a 'perfect day' for you?" or "What do you value most in a friendship?"

2. Practice translating informational questions into commands, such as "What is your name?" into "Tell me your name." It could be convenient to use an exam, where the prompts are questions to which the teacher already knows the answer. Also use these examples to pull out assumptions being made by the questions, such as the assumption that "This person has a name."

3. To become more comfortable with the phenomenological suspension, have students discuss what it is like to get in the mood to watch a fantastical movie or fantasy novel. How can they enjoy it when they know the actions and plot are not real?

4. Try a think, pair, share activity with the following question: Can you have empathy without understanding (in the technical sense of "understanding" defined in the book) and understanding without empathy?

Chapter 3: A Logic of Question and Answer

For this chapter, I have just a couple suggestions for engaging the content in addition to the "three things" protocol.

1. Practice using the four orientations of questions: predicate-centered ones, subject-centered ones, copula-centered ones, and questioning-centered ones. Consider bringing up the *Schoolhouse Rock* song "The

Tale of Mr. Morton" to prime students to think about grammatical parts of sentences. Select a number of sentences, perhaps at random, to illustrate each of the questioning orientations.

2. Use think, pair, share to have students address the questions: Can we pose a question without meaning it? Can we understand a meaning (in the technical sense of a complete thought) without meaning it?

Chapter 4: Reasoning Only Happens in Explicit Arguments

In addition to the "three things" protocol, I suggest a few activities related to chapter content.

1. Try using think, pair, share to reflect on differences and similarities between arguments and fights. How is "argument" defined technically in this book?

2. Have students discuss the differences between deduction, induction, and abduction. Can an inductive argument be valid? Is a valid argument true? How so or how not?

3. Challenge students to come up with a number of potential "self-referentially incoherent" statements and positions, such as "No perspective is correct."

Chapter 5: What Do Questions Do to Arguments?

For this chapter, I have just a few suggestions for engaging the content in addition to the "three things" protocol. The two most important concepts here are the "unconditioned" and recalling the three main elements of complete thoughts—the subject, the copula, and the predicate.

1. (To help get at the "unconditioned") Try a think, pair, share exercise where students address the question: Do you recall when you were a

child and your guardians (or grandparents, or teachers, etc.) would respond to you asking, "But why?" with "Because I said so."? What makes that answer unsatisfying? What did you seem to be looking for with your "why" question?

2. (To help get at the "unconditioned" in the domain of the subject of complete thoughts) Try a think, pair, share on the topic of the soul: What is it? Do people have one? Is it immortal? What limits our ability to know about it?

3. (To help get at the "unconditioned" in the domain of the predicate of complete thoughts) Try a think, pair, share on the topic of the universe: Where is the universe? Does it have a beginning? What makes it difficult to know about this?

4. (To help get at the "unconditioned" in the domain of the copula of complete thoughts) Try a think, pair, share on the topic of divinity: Is there a *Dao* (a fundamental generative principle unifying all things)? Does an all-good, all-powerful god exist? If God caused the universe to exist, what caused God to exist? What limits our ability to know about these things?

Chapter 6: A Rationality of Questioning and Reasoning

1. In addition to the "three things" protocol, I suggest a few activities related to chapter content: (a) Practice using the four orientations of questions: conclusion-centered ones, premise-centered ones, inference-centered ones, and argument-centered ones. (b) Consider bringing up a few arguments to prime students to think about parts of arguments. (c) Select a number of arguments, perhaps at random, to illustrate each of the questioning orientations.

2. Use think, pair, share to have students address the questions: How are poetic images (symbols) similar to yet different from concepts? Can we understand a thousand-sided object without picturing it? How do we access areas of our lives that show us ideals for living?

Chapter 7: Dialogue Only Happens in Constructive Reconciliations

For this chapter, I have an activity to assign along with the chapter, and just a couple of suggestions for engaging the content in addition to the "three things" protocol:

1. Assign the students to try out "Socratic Dialogue" after reading the chapter. For this exercise, have students attempt to ask a peer or parent or teammate a question, and sustain asking them questions (if they can) for up to fifteen minutes. For example, maybe they are at lunch with their roommate, and their roommate says, "This is a good burger." Then the student could ask, "What is 'good' really?" And then when the roommate provides their answer, the student should select a word from that answer, and perform the same action, "What is 'survival' for really?" And so on. They should try to be Socrates—insatiable about asking more and more questions. The students should bring with them a 200-word report summarizing the conversation content as well as a brief reflection on the activity itself. What is it like to try to sustain questioning rather than trying to debate or provide your own answers?

2. Use think, pair, share to have student address the question: Recall a recent good conversation or a recent bad conversation. What are three things that made it good or bad? What seems to be the point of conversations?

3. Use think, pair, share to have students reflect on rules: Do they restrict us or set us free?

4. Provide some examination of dialectics—the dynamic movement from thesis, to antithesis, to synthesis. Perhaps use the 8-Bit Philosophy clip on Hegel titled "Will History End?" and/or the 8-Bit Philosophy clip on Marx titled "What is Marxism?"

Chapter 8: What Do Questions Do to Dialogues?

In addition to the "three things" protocol, I suggest a few activities related to chapter content.

1. Try using think, pair, share to have students discuss their answers to the following question: Why do good conversations come to an end?

2. Provide a transcript of a telephone call, and pinpoint with students all the ways the people on the call indicate they are listening, perhaps with listening tokens (mmhm . . .) or with questions.

3. Make sure to clearly distinguish between empathy (or sympathy) and understanding, as these are approached technically within the book. Empathy is being able to feel like another person, but might not require understanding. Understanding is being able to grasp the complete thought in what another person says, but does not require empathizing with them. Perhaps use think, pair, share to have students discuss how this applies in the following case: As a woman, men will never understand my experience, what it is like to be me.

4. Try using think, pair, share for the following question: What happens to another person's question when we ask it too?

Chapter 9: A Dialectic of Questionability and Responsibility

For this chapter, I have just a few suggestions for engaging the content in addition to the "three things" protocol.

1. Practice using the four orientations of questions: antithesis-centered ones, thesis-centered ones, synthesis-centered ones, and dialogue-centered ones. Consider bringing up a few dialogue excerpts, perhaps from Plato, to prime students to think about parts of dialogues.

2. Try using think, pair, share to have students discuss the following question: How are we made responsible—as in, able to respond? Are we called to authentic responsibility or are we asked a question to which we respond (see the sections on Heidegger and Levinas)? Is there an underlying "I" who can choose to take responsibility, or is the "I" a function of already being responsible?

3. Consider using think, pair, share to have everyone think about the following question: How does oppression interfere with freedom? Are there ways of speaking with others that are oppressive? How so?

Conclusion: The End(s) of Questions

In addition to the "three things" protocol, I suggest just one activity related to chapter content.

Consider using think, pair, share to have students talk about why we ask questions at all. Is questioning (and dialogue) fun?

Glossary

A priori (Chapter 6) Something knowable independent of experience, or prior to experience.

Abductive argument (Chapter 5) Argument to support the best explanation or an explanation as the best.

Adversarial argumentation (Chapter 4) Treating argument as a fight or a debate between at least two sides, where there is a winner and a loser.

Alterity (Chapter 8) The essential otherness of other people, that which resists objectification and allows for respect for others.

Angst (Chapter 3) Existential anxiety.

Antecedent (Chapter 4) The first clause of an "if, then" statement.

Anticipatory projection (Chapter 9) Feeling about the future in trying to predict or bring about a certain event or meaning.

Antithesis (Chapter 7) A productively negative moment in dialogue by which it moves and goes further than merely a thesis statement.

Antithesis-centered question (Chapter 9) A question asking what reactive possibilities or possibilities

for negation are available from a thesis, bringing out larger possibilities for knowledge and understanding.

Aporia (Chapter 7) An unresolvable paradox or contradiction in a person's view.

Aretology (Chapter 9) A genre of biography in Ancient Greece where authors depict the hero of the biography as a role model for readers to try to emulate.

Argument (Chapter 4) An instance of reasoning, consisting of at least one premise and a conclusion, where both complete thoughts as well as the argument itself are understood as answers to specific and asked questions.

Ataraxia (Chapter 6) Literally, tranquility. The ideal state aimed at in Pyrrhonist philosophy.

Aufhebung (Chapter 7) Literally, sublimation. A determinate and productive negation.

Authoritarian (Chapter 8) The demand and enforcement of strict obedience and subordination to another, at the expense of personal autonomy.

Autonomy (Chapter 8) An individual's ability to self-govern and direct one's own thoughts and action, that which needs to be respected in dialogue.

Bad faith (Chapter 6) Where we deceive ourselves to deny something that is the case, such as claiming not to have freedom when you have it.

Begging the question (Chapter 5) An informal fallacy where the premise assumes the conclusion rather than supports it.

Closed question (Chapter 2) A question requiring a yes-or-no answer or the selection of one from two alternatives.

Cogent (Chapter 5) The highest compliment that can be paid to inductive arguments, where the support of premises for a conclusion is strong and the premises are true.

Collaborative argument (Chapter 6) The opposite of adversarial argument, where there are no sides but the dialogue partners work together and both benefit from the discovery of truth.

Complete thought (Chapter 1) The combination of a sentential subject and a predicate by means of an explicit or implicit copula, only grasped as an answer to a question that is asked. A sentence as it is understood. See sentence.

Conclusion (Chapter 4) A supported complete thought, inferentially related to a premise.

Conclusion-centered question (Chapter 6) A question where a premise is determined and open to a number of possible conclusions.

Consequent (Chapter 4) The second clause in an "if, then" statement.

Constitutive rules (Chapter 5) The necessary laws governing a field of activity such as a game, where if the laws were removed, the game would cease to exist.

Constructive criticism (Chapter 7) A rhetorical way people try to soften the negativity associated with criticism, implying that criticism is not intrinsically constructive when it is.

Conversation (Chapter 7) A set of expositions defined by turn-taking, that appears to be a dialogue. A conversation is a dialogue perceived, and a dialogue is a conversation understood. See also dialogue.

Conversion (Chapter 5) An immediate inference where the terms in a negative categorical statement are reversed, such as "No X are Y" is "No Y are X."

Copula-centered question (Chapter 3) A question with a defined subject and a defined predicate or complete thought, but where the truth of the complete thought is held in suspense, such as "Is this really the case?"

Critical thinking (Chapter 1) Use of different academic disciplines to be reflexive about particular thoughts.

Dasein (Chapter 9) Literally, being-there. Used in German philosophy for human existence.

Deductive argument (Chapter 5) Formally valid argument where if the premises are true, then the conclusion is true necessarily.

Dehiscence (Chapter 2) The separation of parts of one's body where it both feels and is felt, such as in holding one's own hands to cup water; the way bodies envelop experiences and meanings.

Dialectic-centered question (Chapter 9) A question about the dynamics within dialogue itself, not about the thesis or synthesis.

Dialectics (Chapter 7) The underlying dynamic of dialogue, that promotes ever further unfolding of topics.

Dialogue (Chapter 7) The ongoing cooperative coordination of multiple arguments into theses, antitheses, and syntheses in light of questions.

Ecstatic events (Chapter 9) Experiences where a person feels taken outside of or beyond themselves.

Ego (Chapters 1 and 3) Usually taken as oneself, but is actually the object of consciousness in reflection, where the ego is an objectification of oneself to oneself.

Epistemic imperative (Chapter 2) From epistemic, meaning knowledge, and imperative, meaning command. In the logical analysis of questions, used as the technical term for what questions are reducible to for logical analysis.

Epoche (Chapter 2) To bracket out; the phenomenological method of suspending beliefs or natural assumptions about how things work.

Equivocation (Chapter 5) Using two different meanings of the same word in two statements in an argument.

Erkenntnisverhalt (Chapter 3) Literally, state of affairs in the aspect of knowability or being known.

Erotetic logic (Introduction, Chapter 2) The propositional relations between questions and answers, based in treating questions as epistemic imperatives.

Eschatologically patient (Conclusion) A feeling about the final spiritual destiny of humankind, standing in contrast to apocalyptic impatience.

Essai (Introduction) to try; origin for the English word "essay."

Etymology (Chapters 1, 4, and 7) The study of the history of words.

Eudaimonia (Introduction) flourishing; happiness.

Exposition (Chapter 4) A potential argument that is not yet understood, a set of sentence perceived as an argument. See argument.

Fallacies (Chapter 5) Errors in argument and reasoning. Informal fallacies concern the content of the complete thoughts. Formal fallacies concern the argument pattern, where the form is invalid.

Field of intelligibility (Chapter 3) The broader network of predicative possibilities specific to a culture, such as egocentric directions and cardinal directions.

Freethinking industry (Chapter 5) The industry of publications and products advertised to help people "think" or to be a "free thinker."

Forms of life (Chapter 3) Ludwig Wittgenstein's phrase for a specific culture or meaningful community within a culture, such as the form of life of volleyball within US society. See also Lifeform and *Lebensform*.

Frageverhalt (Chapter 3) Literally, state of affairs in question, something in its aspect of questionability.

Fusion of horizons (Chapter 8) The aim of understanding in dialogue, where one's understanding grows through the application or creation of new predicates and predicative possibilities, where dialogue partners are at one on a subject matter.

Habitus (Chapter 9) The socially embedded skills and dispositions, shaping how individuals perceive the world and respond to it, shared with people within one's culture.

Hegemonic ethnocentrism (Chapter 8) A sense of one's own culture being superior in values and practices in comparison to other cultures, which turns hegemonic in that culture's attempt to take over and assimilate other cultures into it.

Hegemony of the sign (Chapter 3) An approach to language that centers on signs or names, one that dominates theories about language and philosophy of language today.

Hermeneutic priority (Chapter 3) Questions take precedence in understanding, where a complete thought is only understood if and only if it is an answer to a question someone actually asks.

Hermeneutics (Introduction) The science and art of interpretation in general, distinguished from exegesis, which is the attempt at developing a particular interpretation.

Horizon (Chapter 1) The wider field of predicative possibilities for a sentential subject, as well as the network of actual predicates putting subjects in context within a culture.

Ideology (Chapter 8) A misrecognized and unconscious hierarchical system of values, whereby one segment of humanity has and maintains power (economic and political) over others. Stands in contrast to worldviews, explicit perspectives and beliefs on the nature of reality and morality.

Imagination (Chapter 5) A cognitive faculty distinct from thinking, where images can be visualized mentally but cannot be as accurate or discrete as determinate concepts, such as in the difference between a triangle and a chiliagon.

Imperative (Chapter 2) Sentences in the mood of a command or demand.

Incessancy (Chapter 5) Reason's quest for the unconditioned, similar to the toddler continually asking, "But why?"

Incommensurability (Chapter 8) The lack of common ground or the possibility for translation between different languages and cultures.

Inductive argument (Chapter 5) Formally invalid argument, where, if the argument is strong, the conclusion is probable rather than certain.

Inference (Chapter 4) The relevant logical relations between premises and conclusions.

Inference-centered question (Chapter 6) A question with both a defined premise and a defined conclusion, radiating possibilities of inference, such as "Is this deductively valid or inductively strong?"

Instrumental reasoning (Chapter 6) The reduction of reason as information processing, such as in propositionalist ideology, coordinated by means and ends.

Intentionality (Chapter 3) The essential structure of consciousness exposed or made explicit by the phenomenological *epoche*, the suspension of our natural and naïve attitude. Consciousness always aims at something, where consciousness is always conscious *of* something. Can be shared in dialogue or other social practices like pushing a car.

Intersubjective (Chapter 8) Denoting the inherent sociality of human consciousness and experience.

Language game (Chapter 3) Specific languages in their use in a community or culture rather than in their reference to some mind-independent reality, always presuppose a form of life.

Law of noncontradiction (Chapter 5) A principal rule of logic where two mutually exclusive complete thoughts cannot both be true in the same sense at the same time.

Law of excluded middle (Chapter 5) A principal rule of logic where either a complete thought is true or its exact opposite is true, and both cannot be true at the same time in the same sense.

Lebensform (Chapter 3) See forms of life and lifeform.

Lifeform (Chapter 3) See forms of life.

Lifeworld (Chapter 3) The entire structure of interrelated relevance or significance of predicative possibilities, the broadest horizon for meaningful experience, distinct from a mere environment.

Loaded question (Chapter 2) A question where the questioner suggests or prompts a preference for a particular answer or corners the answerer with negative assumptions.

Logos (Chapter 4) Literally, word or discourse or reason or logic.

Modus Ponens (Chapter 5) A valid argument form where if a conditional statement ("if p then q") is posed and the antecedent (p) holds, then the consequent (q) logically follows.

Myth (Chapter 6) The coordination of symbols into narrative form, for the unconditioned or regulative ideals. See also symbols.

Myth of Babel (Chapter 8) An etiological explanation for the diversity of languages and cultures from the Hebrew Bible, on the surface suggesting that cultures are incommensurable.

Negativity (Chapter 9) Nihilating negativity is what stops a conversation, whereas productive negativity promotes further dialogue.

Neutrality (Chapter 2) For questions, where a questioner does not suggest or prompt a preference for a particular answer.

Nirvana (Chapter 1) From the Sanskrit word for blowing out a flame, the flames of desire by which people destructively cling to possessions or ideas.

Noema (Chapter 2) The end point or aim of consciousness and thinking, under the phenomenological reduction.

Noesis (Chapter 2) The origin point of consciousness and thinking, under the phenomenological reduction.

Objectification (Chapter 1) A process of taking something that is not a thing or object and treating it as if it is a thing or object.

Obversion (Chapter 5) An immediate inference, where an opposite inverse categorical statement can be derived from the original statement, such as "All people are human" from "No people are non-human."

Ontological priority (Chapter 3) Ontology is the study of being in all its aspects, and the priority concerns which aspects of being are more fundamental than others. For example, substance metaphysics grants ontological priority to entities over relations between those entities.

Open question (Chapter 2) Wh-questions, where the interrogative word (who, what, etc.) functions as an algebraic variable for which the answer has to solve.

Open-minded (Chapter 7) Often used as a compliment, but leads to a paradox: Are you so open-minded that you are willing to be closed-minded?

Parody (Chapter 5) Of thinking, where freethinking and the propositionalist ideology purport to be what thinking is but are not. An exaggerated mere imitation.

Performative force (Chapter 2) In Speech Act Theory, the quality of language and communication whereby people affect one another with words.

Phenomenology (Chapter 2) The study of phenomena, of what appears to consciousness as it appears to consciousness by bracketing out our natural or naïve attitude toward things.

Philosophical anthropology (Chapter 5) Theories of what it is and what it means to be human, where philosophical psychology focuses in particular on the nature of the mind or the thinking I.

Philosophical cosmology (Chapter 5) Theories about the nature of the universe.

Philosophical theology (Chapter 5) Theories about the nature of a fundamental generative principle of all things or gods, sometimes referred to as fundamental ontology.

Platonism (Chapter 1) A view, attributed to Plato and later followers, that there exist abstract, but specific, ideal entities, such as the Form of the Beautiful or the Form of Justice. These are taken to be more real than specific beautiful things or specific instances of justice.

Predicament-centered question (Chapter 3) A question with a specified sentential subject, radiating predicative possibilities in suspension, such as "Where are my car keys?"

Predicate (Chapter 1) The predicament or situation in which sentential subjects are placed, defined by a broader horizon of significance and relevance within a culture. These have an elucidatory function in that they bring particular things to light, the light of intelligibility or understanding. They are perpendicular rather than parallel to experience.

Prejudice (Chapters 2 and 3) Literally, prejudgment.

Premise (Chapter 4) A supportive complete thought, inferentially related to a conclusion.

Premise-centered question (Chapter 6) A question with a specified conclusion, radiating possibilities of premises held in suspension, such as in "What supports this claim?"

Presuppositions (Chapters 2 and 3) Complete thoughts assumed in making a particular question possible, such as how asking "What did you do today?" assumes a person must have done something.

Probability (Chapter 5) The likelihood of a conclusion following from a premise or set of premises in an inductive argument.

Problem of induction (Chapter 5) A question about the reliability of inductive arguments since they are technically invalid deductively.

Problem of reference (Chapter 1) The inability to explain, with language, how signs or words point to particular mind-independent (language independent) entities. This presupposes a representational view of language, as if complete thoughts are pictures that represent facts, running parallel to the world and experience.

Proof (Chapter 4) A formal track of inferences from premises to conclusion that preserves truth.

Proposition (Chapter 2) An abstract meaning or complete thought, supposedly existing independent of any particular languages and supposedly allows for exact translation from one language to another. See "propositionalist ideology."

Propositionalist ideology (Chapter 3) Michel Myer's critical notion for the dominant representational view of language as made of discrete propositions that match or do not match mind-independent states of affairs. Also called "propositionalism."

Question (Chapter 2) Suspension of suggestive combinations of subjects and predicates.

Questioning-centered question (Chapter 3) A question that is reflexive about the very act and activity of questioning, such as "Is this the way we want to go about investigating this?"

Rationality (Chapter 5) A theory of how thinking and reasoning work, the general structure of inferential relations between complete thoughts.

Rationality-centered question (Chapter 6) A question concerning the contested nature of rationality, such as "Is this theory of reason complicity with patriarchy?"

Reasoning (Chapter 4) The process of combining and separating complete thoughts in relevant relations of inference.

Reductio ad absurdum (Chapter 5) A valid argument form, where one assumes the opposite of the conclusion and shows that it leads to a contradiction.

Reference (Chapter 2) The assumption that words reach out to and point to mind-independent objects in the world.

Refutation (Chapter 4) Typically seen as a strategy to defeat an argument, but is really showing that what seems like an argument is just an exposition or not an argument.

Regulative ideals (Chapter 5) Projected priorities and values that go beyond what is ordinary and real, guiding our individual and collective actions.

Reification (Chapter 1) Treating something abstract or intangible as if it is concrete or tangible.

Relativism (Chapter 8) The purported belief that it is acceptable for individuals or cultures to hold beliefs that contradict those of other individuals and cultures, such as the phrase "What's true for you is true for you, and what's true for me is true for me."

Response tokens (Chapter 8) Speech used to indicate one is listening, such as "mmhmm."

Responsibility (Chapter 9) Our underlying ability to respond, preceding intentionality when it is originary responsibility.

Romanticist hermeneutics (Chapter 8) A theory of interpretation focused on empathetic experience the author or artist.

Sachverhalt (Chapter 3) Literally, facts, subject matters, or state of affairs.

Sapir-Whorf hypothesis (Chapter 3) The now-defunct theory that a community's language *determines* their perceptions and possibilities for experience, replaced by the theory that a language focuses what a community attends to or notices.

Semantics (Chapter 3) The science of sentences or complete thoughts.

Semiotics (Chapters 1 and 3) The science of signs and signifiers, as they function rhetorically in human and nonhuman communication.

Sense (Chapter 2) That characteristic of language where it is possible to understand complete thoughts rather than merely perceive written, spoken, or signed sentences.

Sentence (Chapter 2) A complete thought perceived, but not necessarily understood.

Sincere question (Chapter 2) Questions about particular things that aim at a specific answer, where no further dialogue ensues; typically deficit driven, where the questioner asks from a lack or need for something.

Skepticism (Chapter 6) The position that something is not knowable, either in principle or for the time being. Methodological skepticism, the principled use of skepticism in scientific experiments to show something is (probably) the case. Existential skepticism, doubt that creates uncertainty and takes courage to overcome. Pyrrhonist skepticism, the Ancient Greek school of philosophy that used skepticism and doubt as a religious practice.

Skole (Introduction) leisure; free time; origin of the English word "school."

Socratic method (Chapter 7) A teaching tactic that aims at exposing puzzling paradoxes implicit in people's perspectives.

Soundness (Chapter 5) The highest compliment that can be paid to a deductive argument, where the argument form is valid and the premises are true.

Speech Act Theory (Chapter 2) An approach to philosophizing about language focused on language use rather than what language represents or to what it refers.

Spoilsport (Chapter 7) Someone who refuses to play along but often tries to look like they are playing along.

Strong (Chapter 5) The quality of support of premises for a conclusion in an inductive argument.

Subject (Chapter 1) Sentential subject: selection of one particular thing against the backdrop of a broader horizon of experience, can be either abstract or concrete. Existential subject: the origin point of consciousness or the thinking I, subjectivity.

Subject-centered question (Chapter 3) A question where the predicate is determinate and specific, but radiates sentential subject possibilities held in suspense, such as "What is your name?"

Substance metaphysics (Chapter 3) The view that fundamental building blocks of reality are discrete self-subsisting entities.

Syllogism (Chapter 5) The form of argument using three categorical statements, with two premises and a conclusion.

Symbols (Chapter 5) The use of concepts or images to point to or disclose aspects of the unconditioned, where regulative ideals for individual and collective action are made concrete.

Synthesis (Chapter 7) A completion of dialogue, not in the sense of a final answer or solution, but in the sense of an overcoming, similar to a flight of stairs. See also fusion of horizons.

Synthesis-centered question (Chapter 9) A question asked to bring a dialogue to a closure or conclusion, resistant to absolute resolution.

Technocracy (Chapter 8) The organization and control of society by a technology, instrumental reasoning, and elites who profit from it.

Thesis (Chapter 7) The initiative or generative force for a dialogue, usually reconstructed as a hypothesis. A hypothesis is the assumed or projected likely topic returned to in the midst of dialogue tangents.

Thesis-centered question (Chapter 9) A question asked to try to get back to the thesis that seems to have set off a dialogue, where the effort is reconstructive and not an actual return to some purported origin.

Totalization (Chapter 7) The assumption that there can be a complete and final synthesis of all varying perspectives and arguments.

Tradition (Chapter 3) The historical dynamic of innovation and sedimentation in fields of intelligibility or network of predicative possibilities specific to a culture.

Transcendence (Chapter 1) The going beyond ordinary experience or the world, such as the ideal transcends the real or the supernatural transcends the natural.

Transcendental (Chapters 1 and 3) Conditions for the possibility of any particular process or thing; immanent within a system or world, not themselves transcendent. See transcendent.

Truth (Chapter 4) A quality solely of complete thoughts. Three approaches to truth: correspondence, the adequate representation of a proposition to a specific mind-independent fact; constancy, the consistency of a person or capacity over time; alethic, the standing out of a specific subject matter from an undifferentiated background or horizon.

Unconditioned (Chapter 4) Immanuel Kant's term for the fundamental principle underlying all other premises, a premise that is not itself supported by precedent premises. This is a transcendental condition of all other possible thoughts and conclusions, but cannot itself be adequately grasped in a category or concept.

Universality (Chapter 8) The expansive breadth of horizons of understanding, seeming to approximate something true for and in all situations and contexts.

Unwarranted question (Chapter 7) A question posed by someone who is in no position to expect an honest answer, where any response is taken as having negative implications, such as a student asking a teacher, "Where were you last night?"

Validity (Chapter 5) The formal relation of premises and conclusion where, if the premises are true, then the conclusion is true necessarily.

Virtue (Chapter 7) That which facilitates somethings reaching a state of flourishing or maximal exercise of its capacity, whereas vices inhibit this exercise of capacities.

Zazen (Chapter 7) Literally, seated meditation.

Bibliography

Adorno, Theodor. 2003. *The Culture Industry: Selected Essays on Mass Culture*, edited by J. Bernstein. New York: Routledge Classics.

Ahmed, Sara. 2006. *Queer Phenomenology: Orientations, Objects, Others.* Durham: Duke University Press.

Al-Saji, Alia. 2014. "A Phenomenology of Hesitation: Interrupting Racializing Habits of Seeing." In *Living Alterities: Phenomenology, Embodiment, and Race*, edited by Emily Lee, 133–73. Albany: SUNY Press.

Alderson-Day, Ben, and Charles Fernyhough. 2015. "Inner Speech: Development, Cognitive Functions, Phenomenology, and Neurobiology." *Psychological Bulletin* 141(5): 931–65.

Allison, Henry E. 1983. *Kant's Transcendental Idealism: An Interpretation and Defense.* New Haven: Yale University Press.

Alsaleh, Asaad. 2015. *Voices of the Arab Spring: Personal Stories from the Arab Revolutions.* New York: Columbia University Press.

Althusser, Louis. 1994. "Ideology and Ideological State Apparatuses." In *Mapping Ideology*, edited by S. Zizek, 100–40. London: Verso.

Anderson, Pamela Sue. 1998. *Feminist Philosophy of Religion: Rationality and Myths of Religious Belief.* Oxford: Wiley Blackwell.

Anderson, Pamela Sue. 2001. "Gender and the Infinite: On the Aspiration to Be All There Is." *International Journal for Philosophy of Religion* 50: 191–212.

Anselm. 2002. "'The Ontological Argument' from *Proslogian*." In *God*, 2nd ed. Timothy A. Robinson. Indianapolis: Hackett.

Aquinas, Thomas. 1993. *A Shorter Summa: The Essential Philosophical Passages*, edited by P. Kreeft. San Francisco: Ignatius Press.

Åqvist, Lennart 1965. *A New Approach to the Logical Theory of Interrogatives.* Uppsala: University of Uppsala.

Aristotle. 1983. *The Complete Works of Aristotle*, 2 vols., translated by Jonathan Barnes Princeton: Princeton University Press.

Aristotle. 1999. *Nicomachean Ethics*, 2nd ed., translated by. T. Irwin. Indianapolis: Hackett.

Aron, Arthur, Edward Melinat, Elaine N. Aron, Robert Darrin Vallone and Renee J. Bator. 1997. "The Experimental Generation of Interpersonal Closeness: A Procedure and Some Preliminary Findings." *Personality and Social Psychology Bulletin* 23(4): 363–77.

Asad, Talal. 2007/2008. "On Suicide Bombing." *The Arab Studies Journal* 15(2)/16(1): 123–30.

Ayer, A. J. 1952. *Language, Truth, and Logic*, 2nd ed. New York: Dover.

Baggini, Julian and Peter Fosl. 2010. *The Philosopher's Toolkit: A Compendium of Philosophical Concepts and Methods*, 2nd ed. Malden: Wiley-Blackwell.

Bakhtin, Mikhail. 1981. *The Dialogic Imagination: Four Essays*, translated by Caryl Emerson and Michael Holquist. Austin: University of Texas Press.

Bassham, Gregory, William Irwin, Henry Nardone, and James Wallace. 2019. *Critical Thinking: A Student's Introduction*, 6th ed. New York: McGraw-Hill Publications.

Baudrillard, Jean. 1983. *Simulations*, translated by Phil Beitchman, Paul Foss, and Paul Patton. Semiotext(e) series. New York: MIT Press.

Beatty, Joseph. 1999. "Good Listening." *Educational Theory* 49(3): 281–98.

Beauvoir, Simone de. 2015. *The Ethics of Ambiguity*, translated by B. Frechtman. New York: Open Road.

Bell, Catherine. 2009. *Ritual Theory, Ritual Practice*. New York: Oxford University Press.

Bell, Martin. 1975. "Questioning." *The Philosophical Quarterly* 25(100): 193–212.

Berlin, Isaiah. 1969. *Four Essays on Liberty*. London: Oxford University Press.

Blok, Vincent. 2015. "Heidegger and Derrida on the Nature of Questioning: Towards the Rehabilitation of Questioning in Contemporary Philosophy." *Journal of the British Society for Phenomenology* 46(4): 307–22.

Blum, Roland. 1983. "Emmanuel Levinas' Theory of Commitment." *Philosophy and Phenomenological Research* 44(2): 145–68.

Borge, Steffen. 2007. "Unwarranted Questions and Conversation." *Journal of Pragmatics* 39: 1689–701.

Bourdieu, Pierre. 2000. *Pascalian Meditations*. Stanford: Stanford University Press.

Browne, M. Neil, and Stuart M. Keeley. 2014. *Asking the Right Questions: A Guide to Critical Thinking*, Global Edition, 11e. Upper Saddle River: Pearson Publications.

Bruin, John. 2001. *Homo Interrogans: Questioning and the Intentional Structure of Cognition*. Ottawa: The University of Ottawa Press.

Buber, Martin. 1970. *I and Thou*, translated by W. Kaufmann. New York: Touchstone.

Bublitz, Wolfram. 1988. *Supportive Fellow-Speakers and Cooperative Conversation*. Philadelphia: John Benjamins.

Burrow, Sylvia. 2010. "Verbal Sparring and Apologetic Points." *Informal Logic* 30: 235–62.

Butler, Judith. 1997. *The Psychic Life of Power: Theories in Subjection*, 106–31. Stanford: Stanford University Press.

Butler, Judith. 2005. *Giving an Account of Oneself.* New York: Fordham
University Press.

Cage, John. 1973. *Silence.* Hanover: Wesleyan University Press.

Campbell, Joseph. 1991. *Joseph Campbell and the Power of Myth*, with Bill
Moyers. New York: Anchor Books.

Collins, Patricia Hill. 1990. *Black Feminist Thought.* Boston: Unwin Hyman.

Coltman, Rod. 1998. *The Language of Hermeneutics: Gadamer and Heidegger in
Dialogue.* Albany: SUNY Press.

Comay, Rebecca. 1991. "Questioning the question: a response to Charles Scott."
Research in Phenomenology 21: 149–58.

Conway, David and Ronald Munson. 2000. *The Elements of Reasoning*, 3rd ed.
Belmont: Wadsworth Publishing.

Coogan, Michael D. 2003. *The Illustrated Guide to World Religions.* Oxford:
Oxford University Press.

Courtright, Paul B. 1989. *Ganesa: Lord of Obstacles, Lord of Beginnings.* Oxford:
Oxford University Press.

Crystal, David and Derek Davy. 1975. *Advanced Conversational English.*
New York: Longman.

Curd, Patricia (ed.). 2011. *A Presocratics Reader: Selected Fragments and
Testimonia*, 2nd ed. Indianapolis: Hackett Publishing Company.

Daly, Mary. 1990. *Gyn/Ecology: The Metaethics of Radical Feminism.* Boston:
Beacon Press.

Danesi, Marcel. 2016. *The Semiotics of Emoji: The Rise of Visual Language
in Age of the Internet.* London, Oxford, New York, New Delhi, Sydney:
Bloomsbury Academic.

Descartes, Rene. 1998. *Discourse on Method and Meditations on First
Philosophy*, 4th ed., translated by D. Cress. Indianapolis: Hackett.

Deutscher, Guy. 2010. "Does Your Language Shape How You Think?" *The New
York Times.* August 16.

DiAngelo, Robin. 2011. "White Fragility." *International Journal of Critical
Pedagogy* 3(3): 54–70.

DiCarlo, Christopher W. 2011. *How to Become a Really Good Pain in the Ass: A
Critical Thinker's Guide to Asking the Right Questions.* Amherst: Prometheus
Publications.

Dickman, Nathan Eric. 2009. "The Challenge of Asking Engaging Questions."
Currents in Teaching and Learning 2(1): 3–16.

Dickman, Nathan Eric. 2014. "Between Gadamer and Ricoeur: Preserving
Dialogue in the Hermeneutic Arc for the Sake of a God Who Speaks and
Listens." *Sophia* 53: 553–73.

Dickman, Nathan Eric. 2016. "Linguistically Mediated Liberation: Freedom
and limits of understanding in Thich Nhat Hanh and Hans-Georg
Gadamer." *The Humanistic Psychologist* 44(3): 256–79.

Dickman, Nathan Eric. 2017. "Transcendence Un-extra-ordinaire: Bringing the Atheistic I Down to Earth." *Religions* 8: 4.

Dickman, Nathan Eric. 2018a. "Hermeneutic Priority and Phenomenological Indeterminacy of Questioning." In *The Significance of Indeterminacy: Perspectives from Asian and Continental Philosophy*, edited by Robert H. Scott and Gregory S. Moss. New York: Routledge.

Dickman, Nathan Eric. 2018b. "Call or Question: Toward a Rehabilitation of Conscience as Dialogical." *Sophia: International Journal of Philosophy and Traditions* 57: 275–94.

Dickman, Nathan Eric. 2018c. "Feminisms and Challenges to Institutionalized Philosophy of Religion." *Religions* 9: 113.

Dolcos, Sandra and Dolores Albarracin. 2014. "The Inner Speech of Behavioral Regulation: Intentions and Task Performance Strengthen When You Talk to Yourself as a You." *European Journal of Social Psychology* 44(6): 636–42.

Dostoyevsky, Fyodor. 1950. *The Brothers Karamazov*, translated by Constance Garnett. New York: Random House.

Dunne, John. 2004. *Foundations of Dharmakirti's Philosophy*. Boston: Wisdom.

Durkheim, Emile. 2008. *Elementary forms of Religious Life*, edited by Mark S. Cladis and translated by Carol Cosman. Oxford: Oxford World Classics.

Ellul, Jacques. 1964. *The Technological Society*, translated by John Wilkinson. New York: Vintage Books.

Fichte, Johann Gottlieb. 1982. *The Science of Knowledge*, translated and edited by Peter Heath and John Lachs. Cambridge: Cambridge University Press.

Fish, Stanley. 1973. "How Ordinary Is Ordinary Language?" *New Literary History* 5: 41–54.

Fiumara, Gemma Corradi. 1990. *The Other Side of Language: A Philosophy of Listening*, translated by C. Lambert. New York: Routledge.

Fiumara, Gemma Corradi. 2003. "The Development of Hermeneutical Prospects." In *Feminist Interpretations of Hans-Georg Gadamer*, edited by Lorraine Code. University Park: Pennsylvania State University Press.

Fogler, Joseph P. 1980. "The Effects of Vocal Participation and Questioning Behavior on Perceptions of Dominance." *Social Behavior and Personality* 8: 203–8.

Frankfurt, Harry G. 2005. *On Bullshit*. Princeton: Princeton University Press.

Freire, Paulo. 2001. *Pedagogy of Freedom: Ethics, Democracy, and Civic Courage*, translated by Patrick Clarke. Lanham: Rowan and Littlefield Publishers.

Gadamer, Hans-Georg. 1976. *Hegel's Dialectic: Five Hermeneutical Studies*, translated by P. Christopher Smith. New Haven: Yale University Press.

Gadamer, Hans-Georg. 1977. *Philosophical Hermeneutics*, translated and edited by David E. Linge. Berkeley: University of California Press.

Gadamer, Hans-Georg. 1986. *The Idea of the Good in Platonic-Aristotelian Philosophy*, translated by P. Smith. New Haven: Yale University Press.

Gadamer, Hans-Georg. 1989. "Text and Interpretation." In *Dialogue and Deconstruction: The Gadamer-Derrida Encounter*, edited by D. Michelfelder and R. Palmer, 21–51. Albany: SUNY Press.

Gadamer, Hans-Georg. 1996. "Anxiety and Anxieties." In *The Enigma of Health: The Art of Healing in a Scientific Age*, translated by J. Gaiger and N. Walker. Stanford: Stanford University Press.

Gadamer, Hans-Georg. 2007. *The Gadamer Reader: A Bouquet of Later Writings*, translated by Richard E. Palmer. Evanston: Northwestern University Press.

Gadamer, Hans-Georg. 2013. *Truth and Method*, 2nd revised ed., translated by Joel Weinsheimer and Donald G. Marshall. London and New York: Bloomsbury Academic, Reprint Edition.

Gardner, Rod. 2001. *When Listeners Talk: Response Tokens and Listener Stance*. Philadelphia: John Benjamins.

Giannoulis, Elena and Lukas R. A. Wilde (eds). 2019. *Emoticons, Kaomoji, and Emoji: The Transformation of Communication in the Digital Age*. New York and London: Routledge.

Gonzales, Richard. 2018. "Sessions Cites The Bible to Justify Immigrant Family Separation." *National Public Radio*. June 14.

Habermas, Jurgen. 2002. *Religion and Rationality: Essays on Reason, God, and Modernity*, edited by Eduardo Mendieta. Cambridge, MA: The MIT Press.

Hamby, Benjamin. 2013. "*Libri as Nauseam*: The Critical Thinking Textbook Glut." *Paideusis* 21(1): 39–48.

Harrah, David. 1961. "A Logic of Questions and Answers." *Philosophy of Science* 28(1): 40–6.

Harrah, David. 1982. "What Should We Teach about Questions?" *Synthese* 51: 21–38.

Harrison, Victoria. 2019. *Eastern Philosophy: The Basics*, second ed. New York: Routledge.

Hayes, Richard P. 1988. *Dignaga on the Interpretation of Signs*. Dordrecht: Kluwer Academic.

Hayes, Richard P. and Brendan S. Gillon. 1991. "Introduction to Dharmakirti's Theory of Inference as Presented in the *Pramana-varttika svopajñavrtti* 1–10." *Journal of Indian Philosophy* 19: 1–73.

Hegel, Georg Wilhelm Friedrich. 1977. *The Phenomenology of Spirit*, translated by A. V. Miller. Oxford: Oxford University Press.

Hegel, Georg Wilhelm Friedrich. 1988. *Lectures on the Philosophy of Religion: The Lectures of 1827*, translated by R. F. Brown, P. C. Hodgson, and J. M. Stewart. Berkeley: University of California Press.

Hegel, Georg Wilhelm Friedrich. 1997. *On Art, Religion, and the History of Philosophy: Introductory Lectures*, edited by J. Glenn Gray. Indianapolis: Hackett Publishing.

Heidegger, Martin. 1977. "The Question Concerning Technology." In *The Question Concerning Technology and Other Essays*, translated by William Lovitt, 3–35. New York: Garland Publishing.

Heidegger, Martin. 1982. "The Nature of Language." In *On the Way to Language*, translated by Peter D. Hertz, 57–110. New York: Harper & Row.

Heidegger, Martin. 1996. *Being and Time: A Translation of Sein und Zeit*, translated by J. Stambaugh. New York: SUNY Press.

Herbjørnsrud, Dag. "The African Enlightenment." *Aeon*. December 13, 2017. https://aeon.co/essays/yacob-and-amo-africas-precursors-to-locke-hume-and-kant

Heritage, John. 2002. "The Limits of Questioning: Negative Interrogatives and Hostile Question Content." *Journal of Pragmatics* 34: 1427–46.

Hintikka, Jakko. 2000. "Gadamer: Squaring the Hermeneutical Circle." *Revue Internationale de Philosophie* 54: 487–97.

Husserl, Edmund. 1975. *Experience and Judgment*, translated by J. Churchill and K. Ameriks. Evanston: Northwestern University Press.

Ibn Sina. 2005. "On the Soul." In *Medieval Islamic Philosophical Writings*, edited by Ali Khalidi, 27–58. Cambridge: Cambridge University Press, 2005.

Idhe, Don. 2007. *Listening and Voice: Phenomenologies of Sound*, 2nd ed. Albany: SUNY Press.

Irigaray, Luce. 2002. *The Way of Love*, translated by H. Bostic and S. Pluhacek. New York: Continuum.

Irigaray, Luce. 2007. *Je, Tu, Nous: Toward a Culture of Difference*, translated by Alison Martin. London: Routledge Classics.

Jameson, Fredric. 2009. *Valences of the Dialectic*. Brooklyn: Verso Books.

Kafer, Alison. 2013. *Feminist, Queer, Crip*. Bloomington: Indiana University Press.

Kant, Immanuel. 1993. *Grounding for the Metaphysics of Morals*, translated by James W. Ellington. Indianapolis: Hackett.

Kant, Immanuel. 2007. *Critique of Pure Reason*, translated by Marcus Weigelt. London: Penguin Classics.

Keller, Catherine. 2003. *Face of the Deep: A Theology of Becoming*. New York: Routledge.

Kendi, Ibram X. 2019. *How to Be an Antiracist*. New York: Oneworld.

Kierkegaard, Soren. 1982. *The Sickness Unto Death*, translated by Howard and Edna Hong. Princeton: Princeton University Press.

Kierkegaard, Soren. 1983. *Fear and Trembling/Repetition*, translated by Howard and Edna Hong. Princeton: Princeton University Press.

Kierkegaard, Soren. 1995. *Works of Love*, translated by E. and H. Hong. Princeton: Princeton University Press.

Klemm, David E. 1987. "Toward a Rhetoric of Postmodern Theology: Through Barth and Heidegger." *Journal of the American Academy of Religion* 55: 443–69.

Knitter, Paul F. 2013. "Death or Dialogue? Clash or Collaboration?" address for the *Calvin W. Didier Annual Seminar on Religion and Contemporary Thought*. March 1.

Kondracke, Morton. 1983. "Debategate." *The New Republic*. July 18. https://newrepublic.com/article/89585/debategate-carter-reagan-debate-scandal

Korn, Melissa. 2014. "Bosses Seek 'Critical Thinking,' but What Is That?" *The Wall Street Journal*. October 21.

Kraft, Jessica Carew. 2014. "Hacking Traditional College Debate's White-Privilege Problem." *The Atlantic*. April 16. https://www.theatlantic.com/education/archive/2014/04/traditional-college-debate-white-privilege/360746/

Kuhn, Thomas. 2012. *The Structure of Scientific Revolutions*, 4th ed. Chicago: The University of Chicago Press.

Kundera, Milan. 2005. *The Unbearable Lightness of Being*, translated by M. Heim. New York: Harper.

Lafrance, Adrienne. 2015. "An Unusual Way of Speaking, Yoda Has." *The Atlantic*. December 18.

Lakoff, George and Mark Johnson. 2003. *Metaphors We Live By*, 2nd ed. Chicago: The University of Chicago Press.

Lakoff, Robin. 2004. *Language and Women's Place: Text and Commentaries*, revised and expanded edition, edited by Mary Bucholtz. New York: Oxford University Press.

Lee, Emily. 2015. *Living Alterities: Phenomenology, Embodiment, and Race.* Albany: State University of New York Press.

Leech, Geoffrey and Jan Svartvik. 1975. *A Communicative Grammar of English.* London: Longman.

Levinas, Emmanuel. 1969. *Totality and Infinity: An Essay on Exteriority*, translated by A. Lingis. Pittsburgh: Duquesne University Press.

Levinas, Emmanuel. 1998a. "Hermeneutics and Beyond." In *Entre Nous: On Thinking-of-the-Other*, translated by M. Smith and B. Harshav, 65–76. New York: Columbia University Press.

Levinas, Emmanuel. 1998b. "Nonintentional Consciousness." In *Entre Nous: On Thinking-of-the-Other*, translated by M. Smith and B. Harshav, 123–32. New York: Columbia University Press.

Levinas, Emmanual. 1998c. *Otherwise than Being or Beyond Essence*, translated by Alphonso Lingis. Pittsburgh: Duquesne University Press.

Levinson, Stephen C. 1983. *Pragmatics*. Cambridge: Cambridge University Press.

Lincoln, Bruce. 1996. "Gendered Discourses: The Early History of 'Mythos' and 'Logos.'" *History of Religions* 36: 1–12.

Linker, Maureen. 2014. *Intellectual Empathy: Critical Thinking for Social Justice*. Ann Arbor: University of Michigan Press.

Lipari, Lisbeth. 2004. "Listening for the Other: Ethical Implications of the Buber-Levinas Encounter." *Communication Theory* 14: 122–41.

Lugones, Maria and Elizabeth Spelman. 1983. "Have We Got a Theory for You! Feminist Theory, Cultural Imperialism, and the Demand for 'The Woman's Voice'?" *Women's Studies International Forum* 6: 573–81.

MacIntyre, Alasdair. 1981. *After Virtue*. Notre Dame: University of Notre Dame Press.

MacIntyre, Alasdair. 1988. *Whose Justice? Which Rationality?* Notre Dame: University of Notre Dame Press.

Marx, Karl. 1970. *Critique of Hegel's Philosophy of Right*, translated by Annette Jolin and Joseph O'Malley. Cambridge: Cambridge University Press.

Mathewes, Charles T. 2002. "The Liberation of Questioning in Augustine's *Confessions*." *Journal of the American Academy of Religion* 70(3): 539–60.

Matsumoto, Kazuko. 1999. "*And*-prefaced Questions in Institutional Discourse." *Linguistics* 37: 251–74.

McFague, Sallie. 1982. *Metaphorical Theology*. Philadelphia: Fortress Press.

Merleau-Ponty, Maurice. 1968. *The Visible and the Invisible*, translated by A. Lingis. Evanston: Northwestern University Press.

Meyer, Michel. 1995. *Of Problematology: Philosophy, Science, and Language*, translated by D. Jamison. Chicago: The University of Chicago Press.

Mitchell, Kristina M. W. and Jonathan Martin. 2018. "Gender Bias in Student Evaluations." *PS: Political Science and Politics* 51(3): 648–52.

Moors, Kent F. 1978. "Plato's Use of Dialogue." *The Classical World* 72(2): 77–93.

Morgan, Norah and Juliana Saxton. 2006. *Asking Better Questions*, 2nd ed. Markham. Ontario: Pembroke.

Moyaert, Marianne. 2010. "Absorption or Hospitality: Two Approaches to the Tension between Identity and Alterity." In *Interreligious Hermeneutics*, edited by C. Cornille and C. Conway, 61–88. Eugene: Cascade Books.

Nagarjuna. 1995. *The Fundamental Wisdom of the Middle Way*, translated by Jay L. Garfield. Oxford: Oxford University Press.

National School Reform Faculty. 2014. "Text Rendering Protocol." *Protocols*. https://nsrfharmony.org/ (Accessed April 28, 2020).

Nhat Hanh, Thich. 2009. *The Heart of Understanding: Commentaries on the Prajnaparamita Heart Sutra*. Berkeley: Parallax Press.

Nhat Hanh, Thich. 2010. *Beyond the Self: Teachings of the Middle Way*. Berkeley: Parallax Press.

Nietzsche, Friedrich. 2008. *On the Genealogy of Morals*, translated by Douglas Smith. Oxford: Oxford University Press.

Nussbaum, Martha. 1995. "Objectification." *Philosophy and Public Affairs* 24: 249–91.

Nye, Andrea (ed.). 1998. *Philosophy of Language: The Big Questions*. Malden: Blackwell.

Paley, William. 2002. "'The Teleological Argument' from *Natural Theology*." In *God*, 2nd ed., edited by Timothy A. Robinson. Indianapolis: Hackett.

Perloff, Marjorie. 1994. "From Theory to Grammar: Wittgenstein and the Aesthetic of the Ordinary." *New Literary History* 25: 899–923.

Peters, John Durham. 1999. *Speaking Into the Air: A History of the Idea of Communication*. Chicago: The University of Chicago Press.

Piazza, Roberta. 2002. "The Pragmatics of Conducive Questions in Academic Discourse." *The Journal of Pragmatics* 34: 509–27.

Plantinga, Alvin and Nicholas Wolterstorff (eds). 1991. *Faith and Rationality: Reason and Belief in God*. Notre Dame: University of Notre Dame Press.

Plato. 1991. *The Republic*, 2nd ed., translated by Alan Bloom. New York: Basic Books.

Plato. 1997. *Theaetetus*. In *Plato: Complete Works*, edited by J. Cooper and D. Hutchinson, 157–234. Indianapolis: Hackett Publishing.

Plato. 2002. *Five Dialogues: Euthyphro, Apology, Crito, Meno, Phaedo*, 2nd ed., translated by G. M. A. Grube. Indianapolis: Hackett.

Plotka, Witold. 2012. "Husserlian Phenomenology as Questioning: An Essay on the Transcendental Theory of the Question." *Studia Phenomenologica* 12: 311–29.

Poole, Roger. 1993. *Kierkegaard: The Indirect Communication*. Charlottesville: University Press of Virginia.

Popper, Karl. 2002. *Conjectures and Refutations: The Growth of Scientific Knowledge*. London and New York: Routledge Classics.

Quirk, Randolph and Sidney Greenbaum. 1973. *A Concise Grammar of Contemporary English*. New York: Harcourt Brace Jovanovich.

Raphael, Taffy. 1986. "Teaching Question Answer Relationships, revisited." *The Reading Teacher* 39(6): 516–22.

Raphael, Taffy and Kathryn H. Au. 2005. "QAR: Enhancing Comprehension and Test Taking Across Grades and Content Areas." *The Reading Teacher* 59(3): 206–21.

Richards, Jack C. 1980. "Conversation." *TESOL Quarterly* 14: 413–32.

Ricoeur, Paul. 1974. "Religion, Atheism, Faith." In *The Conflict of Interpretations: Essays in Hermeneutics*, edited by Don Idhe, 440–67. Evanston: Northwestern University Press.

Ricoeur, Paul. 1975. "Phenomenology and Hermeneutics." *Nous* 9(1): 85–102.

Ricoeur, Paul. 1976. *Interpretation Theory: Discourse and the Surplus of Meaning*. Fort Worth: Texas Christian University Press.

Ricoeur, Paul. 1979. "The Function of Fiction in Shaping Reality." *Man and World*. 12(2): 123–41.

Ricoeur, Paul. 1984–1988. *Time and Narrative*, Vols. I–III, translated by K. Blamey and D. Pellauer. Chicago: University of Chicago Press.

Ricoeur, Paul. 1986. "Life: A Story in Search of a Narrator." In *Facts and Values: Philosophical Reflections from Western and Non-Western Perspectives*, edited by Marinus C. Doeser and John N. Kraay and translated by John N. Kraay and A. J. Scholten, 121–32. Dordrecht: Martinus Nijhoff Publishers.

Ricoeur, Paul. 1991. "The Model of the Text: Meaningful Action Considered as a Text." In *From Text to Action: Essays in Hermeneutics*, translated by K. Blamey and J. Thompson, Vol. II, 144–67. Evanston: Northwestern University Press.

Ricoeur, Paul. 1995a. *Oneself as Another*, translated by K. Blamey. Chicago: University of Chicago Press.

Ricoeur, Paul. 1995b. *Figuring the Sacred: Religion, Narrative, and Imagination*, translated by David Pellauer. Minneapolis: Fortress Press.

Ricoeur, Paul. 1998. "Violence and Language." *Journal of French and Francophone Philosophy* 10(2): 32–41.

Ricoeur, Paul. 2003. *The Rule of Metaphor*, translated by Robert Czerny. London: Routledge Classics.

Ricoeur, Paul. 2010. "Religious Belief." In *A Passion for the Possible*, edited by B. Treanor and H. Venema, 27–40. New York: Fordham University Press.

Ritchhart, Ron, Mark Church, and Karin Morrison. 2011. *Making Thinking Visible: How to Promote Engagement, Understanding, and Independence for All Learners*. San Francisco: Jossey-Bass.

Ronkin, Noah. 2009. "Theravada Metaphysics and Ontology." In *Buddhist Philosophy: Essential Readings*, edited by W. Edelglass and J. Garfield, 13–26. New York: Oxford University Press.

Ryle, Gilbert. 1953. "Ordinary Language." *The Philosophical Review* 62: 167–86.

Sacks, Harvey, Emmanuel Schegloff, and Gail Jefferson. 1974. "A Simplest Systematics of Turn-Taking for Conversation." *Language* 50: 696–735.

Samerhoff, Arnold. 2010. "A Unified Theory of Development: A Dialectic Integration of Nature and Nurture." *Child Development* 81: 6–22.

Sartre, Jean-Paul. 1960. *The Transcendence of the Ego: An Existentialist Theory of Consciousness*, translated by Forrest Williams and Robert Kirkpatrick. New York: Hill and Wang.

Sartre, Jean-Paul. 1984. *Being and Nothingness*. New York: Washington Square Press.

Saxton, Juliana, Carole Miller, Linda Laidlaw, and Joanne O'Mara. 2018. *Asking Better Questions: Teaching and Learning for a Changing World*, 3rd ed. Markham: Pembroke Publications.

Scharlemann, Robert P. 1981. *The Being of God: Theology and the Experience of Truth*. New York: Seabury Press.

Schumann, Karl and Barry Smith. 1987. "Questions: An Essay in Daubertian Phenomenology." *Philosophy and Phenomenological Research* 47(3): 353–84.

Seargent, Philip. 2019. *The Emoji Revolution: How Technology is Shaping the Future of Communication*. Cambridge: Cambridge University Press.

Searle, John. 1969. *Speech Acts*. Cambridge: Cambridge University Press.

Searle, John. 1992. "Conversation." In *(On) Searle On Conversation*, edited by Herman Parret and Jef Verschueren, 7–30. Philadelphia: John Benjamins.

Sells, Michael. 2007. *Approaching the Qur'an: The Early Revelations*, 2nd ed. Ashland: White Cloud Press.

Solomon, Robert and Kathleen M. Higgins. 2010. *The Big Questions: A Short Introduction to Philosophy*. Belmont: Wadsworth Publishing.

Sousa, Paulo, Richardo Pinheiro, and Ricardo Silva. 2003. "Questions about Questions: New Views on an Old Prejudice." *International Journal of Psychoanalysis* 84: 865–78.

Spaemann, Robert. 2007. *Persons: The Difference between "Someone" and "Something,"* translated by Oliver O'Donovan. Oxford: Oxford University Press.

Spinoza, Baruch. 1992. *Ethics, Treatise on the Emendation of the Intellect and Letters*, translated by R. Shirley. Indianapolis: Hackett.

Stenström, Anna-Brita. 1984. *Questions and Responses in English Conversation*. Malmö: CWK Gleerup.

Suzuki, Shunryu. 1995. *Zen Mind, Beginner's Mind*, edited by Trudy Dixon. New York: Weatherhill.

Swidler, Leonard J. 1990. *Death or Dialogue? From the Age of Monologue to the Age of Dialogue*. London: SCM Press.

Taylor, Charles. 1989. *Sources of the Self*. Cambridge, MA: Harvard University Press.

Thorsrud, Harald. 2009. *Ancient Skepticism*. Berkeley: University of California Press.

Tidman, Paul and Howard Kahane. 1999. *Logic and Philosophy: A Modern Introduction*, 8th ed. Belmont: Wadsworth.

Tillich, Paul. 1964. "Communicating the Christian Message: A Question to Christian Ministers and Teachers." In *Theology of Culture*, edited by Robert C. Kimball, 201–15. Oxford: Oxford University Press.

Tillich, Paul. 2001. *Dynamics of Faith*. New York: HarperCollins.

United Methodist Church (U.S.). 2012. *The Book of Discipline of the United Methodist Church*. Nashville: United Methodist Publishing House.

Vilhauer, Monica. 2016. "Verbal and Nonverbal Forms of Play: Words and Bodies in the Process of Understanding." In *Inheriting Gadamer: New Directions in Philosophical Hermeneutics*, edited by Georgia Warnke, 161–80. Edinburgh: Edinburgh University Press.

Walton, Douglas. 1998. *The New Dialectic: Conversational Contexts of Argument*. Toronto: University of Toronto Press.

Wang, Jinjun. 2006. "Questions and the Exercise of Power." *Discourse & Society* 17: 529–48.

Warnke, Georgia. 1987. *Gadamer: Hermeneutics, Tradition and Reason*. Stanford: Stanford University Press.

Warnke, Georgia. 2016. *Inheriting Gadamer: New Directions in Philosophical Hermeneutics*. Edinburgh: Edinburgh University Press.

Warren, Karen. 1988. "Critical Thinking and Feminism." *Informal Logic* 10: 31–44.

Weiss, Gail. 2008. *Refiguring the Ordinary*. Bloomington: Indiana University Press.

Welton, Don. 1999. *The Essential Husserl: Basic Writings in Transcendental Phenomenology*. Bloomington: Indiana University Press.

West, Cornell. 2008. *Examined Life*, directed by Astra Taylor and produced by Ron Mann and Silva Basmajian. Zeitgeist Films.

Weston, Anthony. 2009. *A Rulebook for Arguments*, 4th ed. Indianapolis: Hackett.

Wittgenstein, Ludwig. 1922. *Tractatus Logico-Philosophicus*, translated by C. K. Ogden. New York: Harcourt, Brace & Company.

Wittgenstein, Ludwig. 1965. "I: A Lecture on Ethics." *The Philosophical Review* 74: 3–12.

Wittgenstein, Ludwig. 2009. *Philosophical Investigations*, rev. 4th ed., translated by G. E. M. Amscombe, P. M. S. Hacker, and Joachim Schulte. Oxford: Wiley-Blackwell.

X, Malcolm. 1987. *The Autobiography of Malcolm X: As Told to Alex Haley*. New York: Ballantine Books.

Yancy, George. 2015. "White Gazes: What It Feels Like to Be an Essence." In *Living Alterities: Phenomenology, Embodiment, and Race*, edited by Emily Lee, 43–64. Albany: State University of New York Press.

Žižek, Slavoj. 1989. *The Sublime Object of Ideology*. New York: Verso.

Index